Lecture Notes in
Computer Science

Lecture Notes in Computer Science

Lecture Notes in Computer Science

Edited by G. Goos and J. Hartmanis

44

ECI Conference 1976

Proceedings of the 1st Conference of the
European Cooperation in Informatics
Amsterdam, August 9–12, 1976

Edited by K. Samelson

Springer-Verlag
Berlin · Heidelberg · New York 1976

AMS Subject Classifications (1970): 68-02, 68A50
CR Subject Classifications (1974): 4.33, 4.34, 5.24, 6.2

ISBN 3-540-07804-5 Springer-Verlag Berlin · Heidelberg · New York
ISBN 0-387-07804-5 Springer-Verlag New York · Heidelberg · Berlin

FOREWORD

The publication of the proceedings of the first ECI Conference (ECI 76)
is a notable event, because a number of national computer societies have
agreed to work together as partners to develop cooperation in informatics.
The name ECI stands for European Cooperation in Informatics.

ECI's main aim is to foster the advancement of informatics throughout
Europe and to be of the widest possible assistance to the members of
the partner bodies in their professional development. The partners agree
to help each other in the furtherance of their individual aims and objectives and "to do their best, working together, to promote the free
interchange of people, ideas and experience to the benefit of informatics
in Europe".

There is a need for the coordination of activities in Europe and for a
network of European relations through which the members of the partner
bodies can be kept in touch with European computing activities and developments. ECI intends to meet this need and to provide a means for professionals in Europe to contact one another for the mutual exchange of information.

With these aims in mind ECI has organised its first conference in Amsterdam, held from August 9 - 12, 1976.

Members of ECI are: AFCET (France), AICA (Italy), BCS (United Kingdom),
GI (Germany), NTG (Germany) and NRMG (The Netherlands).

The intention of this conference was to touch more specialized subjects
than usually is done in general conferences. On the other hand we did not
strive for a very specialized congress. Therefore three subjects were
chosen:
> Computer Architecture and Computer Systems Structure.
> Concepts and Techniques of Data Base Management.
> Program Development and Verification in Practice
> and Theory.

A Programme Committee that was headed by Prof. Paul carefully selected the papers in order to guarantee a high scientific standard. ECI is very grateful to the Programme Committee for the amount of work they have done.

I hope that this conference may be the beginning of a fruitful cooperation of the national computer organisations on a European basis.

May ECI become a prosperous organisation.

A. J. W. Duijvestijn

P R E F A C E

ECI, the European Cooperation in Informatics, with this volume presents
the proceedings of its first conference, and thus, in a way, presents
itself to the members of its own partners, and to the computing community in general.

The initiators of the event, the ECI partner's representatives, when
asking the Dutch partner to organize it in Amsterdam in the summer of
1976, had proposed to steer a middle course between general congress,
and one subject technical conference. Thus, a triad of separate but related subjects was chosen to be the lead theme of the conference. For
each subject, the Programme Committee invited two prominent speakers to
deliver lectures on general aspects of wide interest whereas submitted
papers by their nature treat more specialized topics. Consequently, contributions in this volume are arranged by main subjects, with the two
invited papers in front, followed by the submitted papers, thus deviating
from the sessions arrangement of the conference.

The noteworthy fact that all authors chose to write their contributions
in one and the same language, although no mention of publication, or
presentation languages was made in the call for papers, imparts a certain
outward uniformity to the proceedings, and may, or may not, have eased the
load on members of the Programme Committee who very carefully selected,
and attended to, the individual contributions to the conference, thus
alleviating to a considerable degree the editor's task who with great
pleasure takes this opportunity to express his sincere gratitude.

Thanks are also due to the publisher, Springer Verlag, Heidelberg, for
accepting the task of getting this volume into print in the very brief
interval of time left until the beginning of the conference at which time
the proceedings should be distributed to participants.

K. Samelson

CONTENTS

Program Development and Program Verification

NAMES AND OBJECTS

IN HETEROGENEOUS COMPUTER NETWORKS

Louis POUZIN
Institut de Recherche en Informatique et Automatique
78150 - ROCQUENCOURT (France)

ABSTRACT

Heterogeneous computers do not use compatible conventions for accessing resources. The problem faced by networks of that type is to introduce a level of commonality without disrupting existing operating systems and services. To that effect, several naming schemes may be considered. The most appropriate is a mapping of local system names into a global C-names space. This provides for a user tailored visibility of network resources.

Basic objects involved in network communication are liaisons, i.e. bridging mechanisms between objects in heterogeneous systems. Virtual terminals are more sophisticated tools for handling terminal oriented data structures. Several techniques may be used to name these objects. A simple and general one uses a pair of C-names.

Other aspects of name management include the use of short names within areas, and the decoupling of names from physical resources. It is shown how reliability and resource management are directly affected by the choice of a proper naming scheme. The CYCLADES name structure is summarized as an application of the concepts presented.

HETEROGENEOUS COMPUTER NETWORK

Networks belong to distinct classes :

a - network of terminals accessing a single computer

b - communication network, connecting pieces of equipment

c - network of computers.

E.g. TYMNET would fall in category b, while ARPANET and CYCLADES fall in category c . Topological diagrams are similar. Each of them appears as a collection of computers and terminal controllers interconnected through a store-and-forward communication network. Differences lie in the kind of associations made possible for exchanging information. Only terminal-computer associations are possible in TYMNET. Hence, the complete set of computing resources connected to the network is partitioned into disjoint sub-sets. Each sub-set is attached to a particular computer, and only one sub-set at a time is visible to each user.

Networks of computers make the complete set of resources visible to each user. If computer systems are homogeneous, it is possible to consider all resources as distinct elements of a single set, because access mechanisms are identical on all computers. Therefore, the partitioning of resources among computers is a matter of physical allocation without logical implications. This is similar to the partitioning of files among several disk units within a single computer system.

Networks of heterogeneous computers raise new problems, because there is no common access mechanism to resources, nor any consistent scheme for naming them. They are not even necessarily similar.

The problem

Given a set of heterogeneous resources, without any common exchange conventions, one must define mechanisms providing for mutual access. These are usually called proto-cols. Ideally, they should be added to existing computer systems, without requiring modifications. Practically, some adaptations may be necessary, but a complete over-haul of operating systems is to be ruled out.[1]

The first problem encountered in designing common access protocols is the naming of resources. This is the subject of this paper.

BASIC NEEDS

In order to be acceptable from an implementation point of view, common access proto-cols should leave maximum flexibility. They should be independent from the nature of resources, and leave entire freedom as to specific control procedures that might be required for accounting, security, etc.

Accessing all network resources as a single set requires a network-wide name space. Furthermore, associations are to be set-up between resources. The simplest kind of association is a pairing. More complicated kinds may be constructed out of pairs.

NAMING SCHEMES

Individual computer systems make use of various naming schemes, which may be specific for different types of resources. E.g. files, processes, peripherals. Names may have a fixed or variable length, and follow specific conventions : alphabetic, numeric, special characters, etc. It would be impractical to change naming conventions in existing systems, because they are usually so ingrained in the design that any change is a major upheaval.

From now on we shall term local names existing names in each computer system. Network-wide names shall be termed C-names. There may be several ways to construct C-names.

Hierarchy : each set of local names $\{Lj\}$ is given a C-name C_i. The network name space is $\{ \langle c_i \rangle \langle L_j \rangle \}$. In other words, a network name is obtained by concatenation of a local name and a header designating uniquely a local set.

Allocation : Only a few resources are given permanent C-names, e.g. loggers. Each one is associated with a set of local resources. Accessing a local resource requires the following steps :
. access a C-named resource
. request access to a local resource by its local name
. get a C-name for the local resource
. access local resource by C-name
. after usage, release C-name.

Mapping : each accessible local resource is given a C-name. A mapping between C-names and local names is performed within individual computer systems.

One might argue that the allocation technique is actually a combination of hierarchy and mapping. Other combinations are possible, introducing more complexity. In practice, network designers tend to cook up schemes that suit their implementation problems, rather than general use.

The hierarchy method is apparently the simplest one because a C-name may be parsed instantly into a network name and a local name. But it is only practical when local names are rather homogeneous. Otherwise, C-names take so many different formats that protocols become unwieldly and inefficient. In particular, the introduction of a new set of local names may require modifications in a number of network access protocols, when the characteristics of the new set have not been anticipated.

The allocation method is favored by a number of operating system-minded people. It has the advantage of fitting within conventional single computer structures. Most operating systems of the past ten years were designed as geocentric objects centralizing all critical functions. Accessing resources is usually a multi-step process starting from a well-known tree top, such a login procedure. This vision of a rigidly partitioned universe is taken for granted by a number of computer professionals.

Advantages of the allocation method is that users access computers in their own familiar way, as if there were no network. It is also contended that using a small number of C-names, for active resources only, saves overhead in network access machinery.

The deficiencies of this method may be derived from its advantages. Keeping network resources rigidly partitioned into computer systems is putting a straitjacket on the user, who would prefer a homogeneous visibility of all resources, with computer boundaries fading out. In other words, the proper vision is a network of resources, rather than a network of computers.

In addition, the allocation method is somewhat cumbersome in implementation, as it requires the management of changing associations between C-names and local resources. Due to transit delays and fuzzy states associated with any distributed system, there appear transient conditions which require specific safeguards to prevent errors.

The mapping method provides for a homogeneous name space in accessing any network resource. It is similar to a telephone numbering plan. Mapping C-names onto local names is a matter of local implementation. This allows permanent or temporary associations, or both. It is therefore more general than the allocation method. Any desirable access control procedure can be triggered as part of the mapping process, not just the login procedure. Such a facility makes it possible to offer homogeneous network-wide access protocols for specific services, which may be available on different computers, e.g. compilers, editors, mail, help, distributed data base.[2]

A criticism of the mapping method is that it takes overhead in scanning large tables of C-names, when they are permanently associated with local names. This is not well substantiated. Indeed, a search is always necessary, whether the key is a C-name or a local name, and there is no reason why searching by C-names should be less efficient.

Space occupied by the C-name table is not critical, as it can be on secondary storage, like any file directory.

Another criticism is that users prefer "symbolic names" rather than C-names. This objection is a typical misunderstanding of the method. Indeed, users (assumed human beings) always access a network through a local machinery (a terminal controller, or an intelligent terminal). Therefore they only have to use their own local names. Whether they prefer distant local names, C-names, or their specific lingo is their choice. Whichever name they use is translated into a C-name to be sent to the appropriate computer system. Therefore, the mapping method is the most flexible from a user standpoint as it does not impose any specific local name set for accessing resources.

A few examples of the flexibility inherent to the mapping method are following :

. A resource may be moved to a different computer without its users knowing it.
. Users may choose local names according to their own symbolism, e.g. in their native tongue.
. Aliases are possible : short or long local names.
. Homonyms may be avoided, since homonyms would appear when distant local names are used.

OBJECTS

It has become customary within operating systems to use specific objects for handling communications between resources. This is justified by a number of needs, e.g. :

. asynchronism between processes
. control of access rights
. dynamic binding
. Buffering, formatting

Communications between resources are constrained to use specific tools : queues, mailboxes, etc. When resources are scattered over a network, the same needs hold, with additional problems, such as :

. objects are managed by different systems
. communication conventions are not compatible
. there are new error conditions and recovery procedures.

In a single computer system resources may communicate through a single object, like a queue. In a network, there are a minimum of two objects, one at each end. The interface between a resource and its local communication object is a given characteristic which may not be altered. Therefore, the problem in a network is to establish communications between objects which interface resources. Of course, objects are also a variety of resource.

Matching object characteristics would require a specific conversion for any pair of different objects. Therefore, a desirable objective is to devise a common object-to-object set of conventions applicable at network level, and make local conversions, when necessary.

L I A I S O N S

A basic building block for communications is a mechanism capable of transferring blocks of information from one object to another, as if the two objects would share a common buffer. Carrying out this function with all the necessary safeguards and error procedures is the purpose of a transport protocol. Part of this protocol is devoted to the setting up of a logical association or liaison, which is a bridge between the two objects. Buffers and state variables make up a liaison context. Thus, a liaison is a network object interfacing with local objects at each end.

Designating a liaison at network level is not useful. What is necessary is that two objects be able to set up a liaison, and then use it for exchanging blocks of information.

Setting up a liaison requires that both objects know each other by a C-name of some sort. Thereafter, several cases may occur :

. Objects are limited to a single liaison

They only need to dicriminate between valid liaison messages and others. Received messages may carry a unique identifier, e.g. a password, which has to be predefined. It can be exchanged between objects when the liaison is set up.

. Objects may set up multiple liaisons

Messages must carry some identifier per liaison, which is a pointer to one of the contexts associated with each object. An index value is exchanged at set up time. Each end may use a different index. It does not matter whether an object uses its own or the other index when it sends messages, as long as this convention is known.

Index values may be assigned in monotonically increasing sequences. If the numbering cycle is big enough as compared to the lifetime of a liaison, there should not be any ambiguity. On the other hand, index values may be assigned, released, and reused dynamically. Since they are shared by two objects, there appear risks of transient conditions in which errors may occur. This is similar to the dynamic allocation of C-names.

A way to eliminate all problems associated with liaison index management is to use a pair of C-names as an index. As long as C-names are assigned in a stable or safe way, liaisons may be identified without ambiguity. The only restriction is that only one liaison at a time may be set up between any pair of objects ; but a single object may set up multiple liaisons with other distinct objects.[3]

Liaisons do not make any data or format conversion ; they are just a basic layer which is always necessary for transferring data in a transparent mode.

VIRTUAL TERMINAL

The concept of virtual terminal has been brought about by the need to use a variety of physical input-output devices in conjunction with a variety of computer systems. Problems associated with the physical characteristics of the devices are non-trivial, and will not be covered here. Rather, the virtual terminal concept will only be introduced as a network object.

Decoupling I-O devices from user programs is a typical feature of any operating system. User languages address logical I-O objects, which are mapped at execution time onto physical devices. The mapping device is what is often called an access method.

In a network context, user programs and I-O devices are normally attached to heterogeneous systems. Thus there is a need for a bridge between logical I-O devices as they are seen from both ends. No general solution has yet been invented. However, typical cases are usually tractable.

Data produced or processed by a program are somehow handled as pieces of a data structure. The mapping of this structure onto a physical device is sometimes elusive because what is really aimed at is a mapping onto a mental image of the structure as seen by a human user from the physical presentation on his terminal. When there is no human user, e.g. for program-to-program communication, only mechanized data structures are involved. Assuming that these structures can be mapped into one another, this mapping would be the task of the virtual terminal protocol. Thus, a virtual terminal may be considered as a network object making a data structure accessible from two heterogeneous domains.

Naming problems are the same as for liaisons, because a virtual terminal is only a sophisticated logical association between two local objects. Since it uses normally one liaison, the same designation can apply to both.

REGIONAL NAMES

When the total space of network names becomes very large, C-names become very long,
and may generate overhead or inconvenience. A counter-measure is to partition the
name-space into a hierarchy of subsets designated by area names. If the partitioning
is clever enough, most liaisons fall within a single area boundary. This is typical
of telephone numbers. Thus, there are two or more C-name formats, depending on the
number of partition levels crossed by a liaison.

There are cases where an area boundary must cross a large number of liaisons. E.g.
it must follow an administrative boundary, or some areas are too dense. A solution
is a partitioning in which each area owns a subset of names disjoint from its neighbors.
This means less names per area, thus more areas. But the advantage is that short names
may be used to communicate not only within an area, but also with every neighbor area,
(fig. 1) .

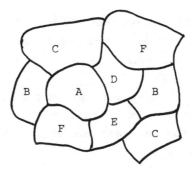

Fig. 1 - NEIGHBOR AREAS

E.g. short names may be used for liaisons between objects located in area A on one end
and objects located in any adjacent area B,C,D,E,F on the other end. Also area D may
use short names towards adjacent areas A,B,C,E,F.

This method is equivalent to a partitioning of the name space into large areas overlapping each other. The topological representation given here is just a logical model,
without geographical connotation. The distance between objects on a diagram may be
interpreted as a measure in inverse proportion to their density of intercommunication.
If this can be mapped onto a bidimensional representation, areas may be delineated
according to their topological properties. E.g. areas with 3 adjacent neighbors (trian-
gles) require 4 disjoint sets of short names. Areas with 6 adjacent neighbors (hexagons)
require 8 disjoint sets of short names.

Such methods are typical of telephone or telex numbering plans. They are intended to reduce the burden of using long names tailored to a world-wide space.

PHYSICAL VS. LOGICAL NAMES

It became long ago standard practice in operating systems to designate objects by names
(e.g. files or I-O devices). In some cases names are pointers or indexes in a table.
But it is extrelemy unusual that names be tightly associated with pieces of hardware.

On the contrary, names in telephone systems designate exchanges and physical subscriber ports. As a result, telephone numbers change whenever a subscriber moves, or when
the telephone company redistribute its subscribers among new exchanges. This is particularly awkward, as telephone numbers are becoming the most frequent names used to
access businesses or individuals. This constraint was understandable when telephone
plant was entirely electromechanical. Since the introduction of computers for circuit
switching, there is no technical justification for maintaining such an obsolete limi-
tation.

An essential by-product of logical naming is reliability. Indeed, designating an object
by means of a physical equipment leading to it creates a dependency on the availability
of that equipment. Failure, maintenance, reconfiguration are bound to disrupt accessi-
bility and continuity of service. E.g. a telephone subcriber is cut off when his local
loop is disabled, because there cannot be any alternate access, due to the physical
connotation of telephone numbers.

When logical naming is used, it is possible to organize the access to objects through
alternate paths, depending on the availibility of physical resources. This allows for
higher reliability. E.g. a data processing center offering services to a large population of users, through a public transmission network, may be composed of a duplex
computer system connected by two separate circuits to two different exchanges. As long
as the circuits do not follow the same physical path, there is complete redundancy in
access gear, with a single name.

Another benefit of logical naming is a higher degree of flexibility in physical resource management, since there is no predefined allocation. Reconfigurations may be performed without service disruption. It is also possible to introduce classes of service,
for which specific resource management strategies can be devised, e.g. bulk, interactive,
real time.

THE CYCLADES NAME STRUCTURE

An application of the concepts presented in this paper is the CYCLADES[4] computer network,
of which CIGALE[5] is the packet switching sub-net.

The C-name structure follows :

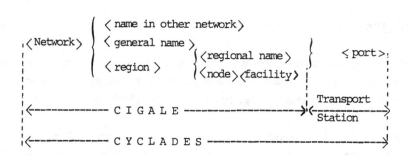

The distinctive characteristics are :

- The name space includes all name spaces of other networks.

- The name space includes specific addressable facilities within CIGALE nodes.

- All other names are hardware independent.

- At the CYCLADES level, C-names designate ports.

- At the CIGALE level, C-names designate transport stations.

- Transport stations names are usually regional, but they can also be known as general names at the whole CIGALE level.

- C-names are independent of local names and are mapped locally.

CONCLUSIONS

An observation of existing computer and communication networks shows that the naming problem is usually not well understood. In most designs, names are just ad hoc conventions tailored for limited implementation purposes, rather than being viewed as a critical tool for resource management at network level. This is all the more a concern that planned public data networks do not appear more advanced in that matter than antiquated telephone systems.

R E F E R E N C E S

1 - ZIMMERMANN H. - Insertion d'une station de transport dans un système d'exploitation
    (Jan. 75),   Réseau CYCLADES SCH 546. 8p.

2 - POUZIN L. - Access protocols in a network environment. (Mar. 1975)
    Réseau CYCLADES SCH 549. 2p.

3 - ZIMMERMANN H. - The CYCLADES end-to-end protocol, Fourth Data Communications
    Symposium, Québec city, (Oct. 75) 6p.

4 - POUZIN L. - Presentation and major design aspects of the CYCLADES computer network,
    3rd Data Comm. Symp. IEEE Tampa, Florida (Nov. 73) 80-87.

5 - POUZIN L. - CIGALE, the packet switching machine of the CYCLADES computer network,
    IFIP Congress, Stockholm, (Aug. 74) 155-159.

<u>TRENDS IN COMPUTER SYSTEM STRUCTURE AND ARCHITECTURE</u>

W.G. Spruth

IBM Entwicklung und Forschung
7030 Boeblingen, Germany

1. INTRODUCTION

An information processing machine of the most general type is characterized by its
ability to generate information for a predefined purpose. This information is the
result of a processing operation for which both input data and internally stored data
have been utilized. There are many types of information processing machines. Examples
are the Touring Machine, the Analog Computer and the Digital Differential Analyzer.
The digital computer, or as we nowadays call it, the data processing system, is another
special case. It is characterized by the sequential processing of individual instructions of a prestored program and the fact that program and data occupy a common "Main
Store". Data Processing Systems can be classified by their major application as Information Systems, Problem Solving Systems, and Object Systems. As to mode of operation, they can be classified as batch systems and interactive systems:

	BATCH	INTERACTIVE
INFORMATION SYSTEM	DATA BASE	RESERVATION SYSTEM, DATA BASE/DATA COMMUNICATION SYSTEM
PROBLEM SOLVING SYSTEM	STANDARD BATCH	TIME SHARING
OBJECT SYSTEM	DATA COLLECTION	AUTOMATION & CONTROL

There are three major elements which make a data processing system into an information
processing machine: hardware, system software and application programs. Hardware and
system software are supplied by the manufacturer of a data processing system. There
is no clear distinction between those two functions, and there are some types of
systems which perform functions in hardware which other types of systems perform
through system programs.

The application program contains the algorithm which defines how to generate output information using both input and internally stored data. In addition it contains features which adapt it to the executing system. A data processing system is thus a machine which is capable to execute many, independently produced application programs. Its architecture and structure can be described independently of its application programs.

The *architecture* of a data processing system can be defined as the functional appearance of the system to a user, its phenomenology. The structure of a system is characterized by the manner in which the individual building blocks are interconnected to implement the architecture. A modern system architecture has three major components (Fig. 1):

Processing
Storage
Input/Output

A possible implementation is shown in Fig. 2.

2. UNDERLYING DRIVING FORCES

Features and characteristics of a computer system architecture and structure are driven by three underlying forces. The first of these has to do with the *concept* of the digital computer. Characteristics are indicated in Fig. 3.

The second underlying driving force is controlled by consideration of the *technology* used for implementation *and* the resulting *operational efficiency*. During the last 30 years technology developments have to a significant extent, been one of the underlying driving forces in the development of computer structures. Fig. 4 indicates some of these developments. It has been popular to indicate technological progress on an exponential curve, but it is unusual to see exponential development curves continue for periods as long as 30 years. Usually, a technological development curve is S-shaped with a period of slow evolution, rapid growth and final maturity. The extended progress in data processing technology has been sustained by the repeated superposition of several of those curves, as indicated in Fig. 5. The replacement of the Williams tube by the core memory and later by the monolithic memory are an example in point.

Because of technological deficiencies, emphasis has been placed on improving the operational characteristics of a data processing system. Features are implemented to achieve optimum results from given technological capabilities. Examples are:

> Multiprogramming
> Multiprocessing
> Job and Task Management
> Allocation and Resource Management

The third underlying driving force has to do with the *"Management of Complexity"*. Data processing systems are among the most complex structures ever invented and built by man. Managing this complexity has been a problem of ever increasing importance. Problems associated with the Management of Complexity have to do with designability, useability and adaptability:

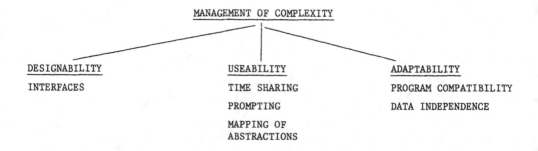

MANAGEMENT OF COMPLEXITY

DESIGNABILITY	USEABILITY	ADAPTABILITY
INTERFACES	TIME SHARING	PROGRAM COMPATIBILITY
	PROMPTING	DATA INDEPENDENCE
	MAPPING OF ABSTRACTIONS	

The problem of *designability* in particular is being attacked by creating interfaces within a system structure. Interfaces decrease performance and increase manufacturing cost. They do, however, reduce the development effort, and improve reliability, recovery, and repairability. They are not defined by physical science and strongly impacted by technological progress. Examples are:

> /370 channel interface
> 3830 DCI interface
> Machine-micro-nano-instructions
> Supervisor/Problem status, SVC interrupt
> Operating System control blocks, e.g. TCB, DCB, UCB
> Disk physical data organization (count, key, data fields)
> Disk access methods, e.g. VSAM
> Data Base schema and subschemata, DL/1
> Branch and Link
> Structured Programming

There are probably many cases of "natural interfaces" which impact performance and cost only to a moderate degree. Finding such natural interfaces appears to be anything but an exact science.

In many cases there are strong pressures for architectural standardization of existing interfaces. It should be emphasized that only well understood functions lend themselves to standardization. Our understanding of data processing functions is much more limited than we frequently believe. For example, a function like the EDIT instruction in the /360 architecture found poor utilization because it is not properly defined. Every system in the /370 product line succeeded in implementing a different address translation buffer scheme. The VS1 and VS2 operating systems have different page replacement algorithms, with only limited understanding as to the advantages and disadvantages of the different algorithms being utilized.

The three underlying driving forces mentioned so far, have had different levels of importance over the years. This is indicated in Fig. 6.

3. MANAGEMENT OF COMPLEXITY

Next to designability, improvements in *useability* are a major issue in the management
of complexity. Prompting, checkout and debugging aids fall into this category. Interactive use, especially time sharing in problem solving applications is another case.
The most important contribution to improvements in useability have been achieved
through the use of abstractions. The user works with *logical abstractions* of a data
processing system which are simpler and easier to understand than the actual physical
features of the system. To this purpose, simplified logical structures are *mapped* onto
the more complex physical structures. A modern system contains several levels or layers
of abstractions which in turn apply to programs, data, and system commands. Mapping
is performed in 4 major system areas: language translators, system programs, CPU hardware, and channel and control unit hardware. An overview over this multilayered mapping
of abstractions is given in Fig. 7.

The most important abstraction level is the layer of machine architecture, characterized by machine instructions, I/O instructions, and data addressing facilities for
both main store and external data. Most application programs are written for a higher
abstraction level in a "Higher Level Language" like Cobol, RPG, Fortran or PL/1. A
given system usually has a single architecture interface but multiple higher level
languages, thus the duality of these two layers.

Mapping of one level of abstraction onto the layer below is usually done interpreta-
tively; higher level language compilation being one major exception. CPUs very often
execute machine instructions through an interpretation hierarchy. Early computers had
relatively limited instruction sets. As time evolved, the instruction sets of intermediate and large size systems became more comprehensive both in the size of the
repertoire and the complexity of system control functions implemented in individual
instructions.*

The system /360 architecture, introduced in 1964, utilized therefore in most implementations the microprogramming concept originally proposed by Wilkes [1]. The first
/360 machines had microinstructions of the horizontal type characterized by the fact
that they usually could be executed within one machine cycle. Lateron microinstructions

---

*It is interesting to note that the increase in instruction set complexity applied most
 to logical and system control functions. Early computers, e.g. the Harvard Mark II,
 had special instructions to perform complex mathematical functions (e.g. sin). Modern
 machines use mostly subroutines for this purpose.

themselves became more complex, in particular with the introduction of the writable control store in intermediate size systems [2]. Because of their complexity, intermediate systems started to use an interpretation approach for the microinstructions themselves, which leads to nano- or picoinstructions, as indicated in Fig. 8. The 2-level instruction interpretation implies some inefficiency in instruction execution. Large systems therefore do not use microinstructions or at least not a dual interpretation hierarchy. Because they perform instruction execution mostly in parallel, the utilization of a complex instruction repertoire is an advantage. With the use of these two parallel implementation approaches we see a trend to utilize the same architecture for both intermediate and large systems. Mini systems (e.g. S/32, PDP 11, Eclipse) feature a functionally more limited architecture to achieve lower cost (Fig. 9).

Data structures are mapped into several layers of abstractions in a similar way as programs. Particular examples are the virtual store concept and the data models and data submodels used in data base systems.

In actuality, the storage part of a system architecture gives to the user the external appearance of 3 independent stores, two of them implemented by a storage hierarchy. This is indicated in Fig. 10. Of particular importance is the fact that data sets are stored in a different type of logical store than program instructions and working buffers. The READ-, WRITE-, GET-, PUT-operations logically map a single record of an external data set logical store into a corresponding work buffer area of the virtual store (Fig. 11). The MULTICS system has tried to merge both types of logical storages into a single storage [3]. However, the industry so far has not been able to find ways and means to implement this concept in today's systems.

Adaptability is the third major element to manage complexity. Emulators, virtual systems, link edit and data independence functions are its major components. In particular data base system structures are to a large extent impacted by the requirement for easy adaption to an ever changing set of external influences.

4. ARCHITECTURAL CLASSIFICATION

System complexity results in a stratification of abstraction levels within a given
system architecture. System size leads to a classification of different system architectures. It is interesting to compare subsequent generations of machines of the same
architecture. Fig. 12 shows the CPU cycle time vs. the CPU speed for two subsequent
generations of machines of the /360 and /370 architecture. Faster machines get their
speed, compared to slower machines, partially through faster CPU cycles, and partially
by using fewer CPU cycles for each machine instruction execution (and a corresponding
increase in CPU hardware). It is also interesting to see that the more powerful, but
also more complex /370 architecture requires a noticeably shorter CPU cycle time than
the /360 architecture for each average machine instruction execution. A similar trend
can be observed if we plot the CPU circuit count against CPU speed, as indicated in
Fig. 13. Main store access time seems to have very little relationship to CPU speed
(Fig. 14), while the main store transfer rate grows more than linear with CPU speed
(Fig. 15). Large systems compensate for slow memory access time through techniques
like parallel memory access, cache, etc.

CPU speed is only one of several factors which determine system performance. The
industry presently manufactures and uses a wide spectrum of different system sizes.
A classification of these system sizes into microcomputers, mini systems, intermediate
systems, and large systems is given in Fig. 16. Important classification factors are
addressing and I/O architecture, operating system characteristics, main store and disk
store size. A significant break can be observed between a microcomputer, which has
programmed I/O, and the minicomputer which works with interrupt I/O. The next significant architectural differentiation is between the mini system which advantageously
utilizes a 16 bit addressing scheme in a non-virtual memory operation, and the intermediate system which eliminates both these limitations. As indicated before, intermediate and large systems often have fewer architectural differences. Microprocessors
and minicomputers have a less complex and less powerful architecture than larger
systems; they feature many characteristics which were typical for larger systems 15 to
25 years ago.

The last few years have seen a very significant proliferation of mini computer systems.
This has been partially due to the first time availability of fairly inexpensive hardware (especially LSI). Another reason is the "sponsor problem". It becomes increasingly difficult in large organizations to reach agreement between various departments
as to optimum computer operation and utilization. This particular "Management of
Complexity" problem often gets resolved by a single department taking the responsibility for buying, installing, operating and maintaining its own system. Additional

motivation is given by "organizational reliability". This addresses the fact that a particular department can maintain access to its *own* computer more easily, than to a central computer, when another higher priority area in an organization gets into difficulties.

The "Departmental" approach offers another attractive possibility. A single, well understood application of moderate complexity can be shaped such that it fits on a system not only of moderate size but also of moderate functional capability. The machine gets programmed at what is essentially the microprogramming level of an intermediate system. Programming is more complicated than if done in a Higher Level Language on a full function system. On the other hand, the lower functional capability of the mini system tends to decrease programming complexity.

Assuming the application is small, well understood, and needs to be done only "once and for all", this approach is often very attractive. Large organizations therefore now often maintain multiple small "Departmental Systems" in addition to their large computer center system(s). As it turns out, however, applications of these departmental systems are often not as isolated as originally assumed. We therefore observe a recent trend to interconnect these independent and usually architecturally incompatible machines into loosely or tightly coupled computer networks, possibly with interaction by a large central computer. This is sometimes done to share workload, functional capabilities, or I/O devices , more often, however, to share data. Network structures feature layers of abstractions just like individual computer systems: Link Control, Path Control, Session Control. Especially the last two require additional system architecture and system structure innovations which are still in the process of evolution.

A related trend has to do with the observation that many "once and for all" applications grow in time, both in terms of size and complexity. As a consequence, the departmental system grows: more main store, more disk storage, more complex system software. Very often the increased capabilities can only be obtained in a system with a different architecture, featuring more powerful hardware functions like extended addressing, protect mechanisms, supervisor-state functions, I/O channels, more powerful I/O devices (especially disk storage), and more powerful operating system functions like data management, resource control, overlay supervisor and virtual storage. The switch to a different architecture usually implies an expensive conversion process.

5. CONCLUSION

Management of Complexity is the overriding concern in the development of modern Data
Processing Systems. We observe a split into systems which are used in a computing
center, and systems which are used by an individual department. The first class of
systems is characterized by general purpose attributes of its structure and features
for adaption to a wide spectrum of individual users. The second class is characterized
by a tayloring of hardware and software features to individual applications.

Decentralized departmental systems can achieve significant efficiency improvements
through application tayloring, if and when their applications can be treated as isolated from each other. Where this is not possible we observe a development trend
towards computing networks with distributed intelligence, very often with a powerful
central host system. In this case, issues of architecture integrity, compatibility,
program and data portability are a major concern, and will impact future developments
to a significant extent.

LITERATURE

[1] M.V. Wilkes, "The best way to design an automatic calculating machine",
     presented at the Manchester University Comp. Inaugural Conference, Manchester,
     England, 1951, p. 16

[2] C. Schuenemann, "Micro- and Picoprogram Stores", Proceedings of the IBM Infor-
     matik Symposium on Rechnerstrukturen, R. Oldenbourg, 1974, p. 36-74

[3] E.I. Organick, "The Multics System", MIT Press, 1972

22

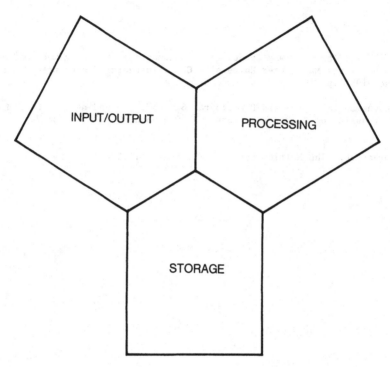

FIG. 1   SYSTEM ARCHITECTURE

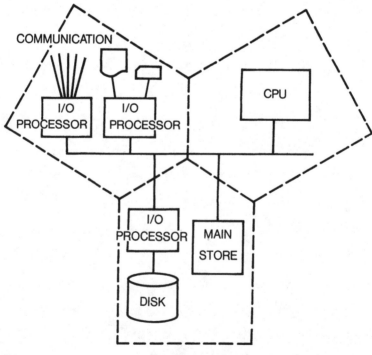

FIG. 2   SYSTEM STRUCTURE

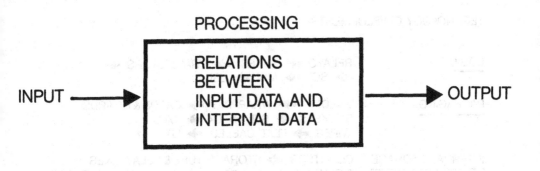

PROCESSING

RELATIONS
BETWEEN
INPUT DATA AND
INTERNAL DATA

INPUT

OUTPUT

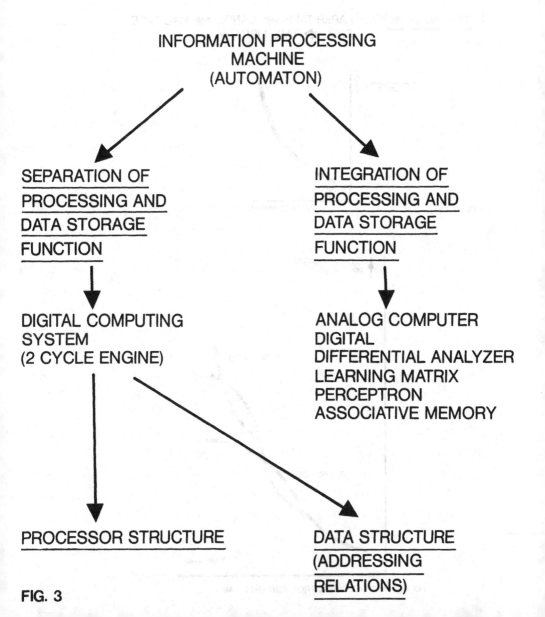

INFORMATION PROCESSING
MACHINE
(AUTOMATON)

SEPARATION OF
PROCESSING AND
DATA STORAGE
FUNCTION

INTEGRATION OF
PROCESSING AND
DATA STORAGE
FUNCTION

DIGITAL COMPUTING
SYSTEM
(2 CYCLE ENGINE)

ANALOG COMPUTER
DIGITAL
DIFFERENTIAL ANALYZER
LEARNING MATRIX
PERCEPTRON
ASSOCIATIVE MEMORY

PROCESSOR STRUCTURE

DATA STRUCTURE
(ADDRESSING
RELATIONS)

FIG. 3

TECHNOLOGY DEVELOPMENTS

LOGIC

RELAYS ➡ TUBES ➡ TRANSISTORS ➡
➡ SLT ➡ MSI ➡ LSI

PACKAGING

SOLDER ➡ WRAPPING ➡ CARDS & BOARDS
SOCKETS ➡ SLT ➡ C4 ➡ MLC
WIRES ➡ FLAT CABLES ➡ LIT

INTERNAL STORAGE

COUNTERS ➡ STORAGE TUBE & DELAY LINES
& REVOLVERS ➡ CORES ➡ MONOLITHIC MEMORIES

EXTERNAL STORAGE

PAPER TAPE ➡ CARDS ➡ MAG TAPE
DISK ➡ TAPE LIBRARY

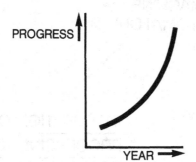

FIG. 4

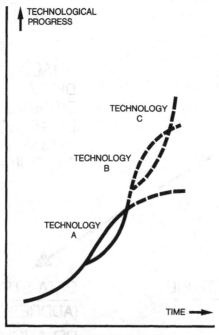

FIG. 5   TECHNOLOGICAL PROGRESS OVER TIME

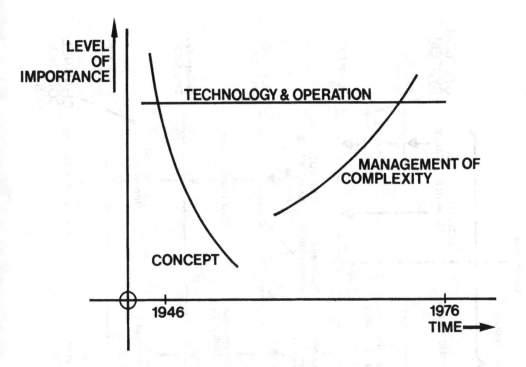

TRENDS IN THE LEVEL OF IMPORTANCE

FIG. 6

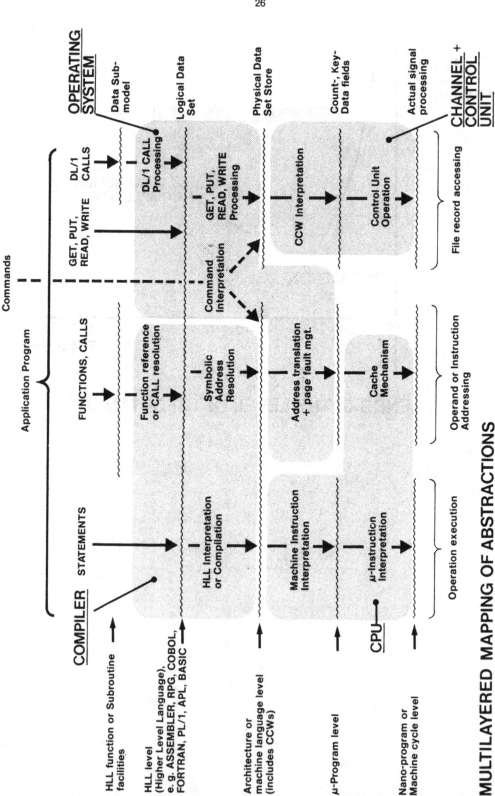

MULTILAYERED MAPPING OF ABSTRACTIONS

FIG. 7

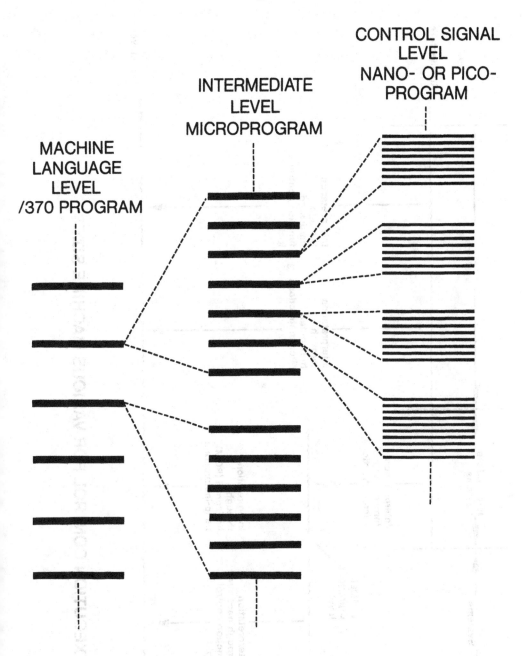

MACHINE LANGUAGE LEVEL /370 PROGRAM

INTERMEDIATE LEVEL MICROPROGRAM

CONTROL SIGNAL LEVEL NANO- OR PICO- PROGRAM

INSTRUCTION INTERPRETATION HIERARCHY

FIG. 8

28

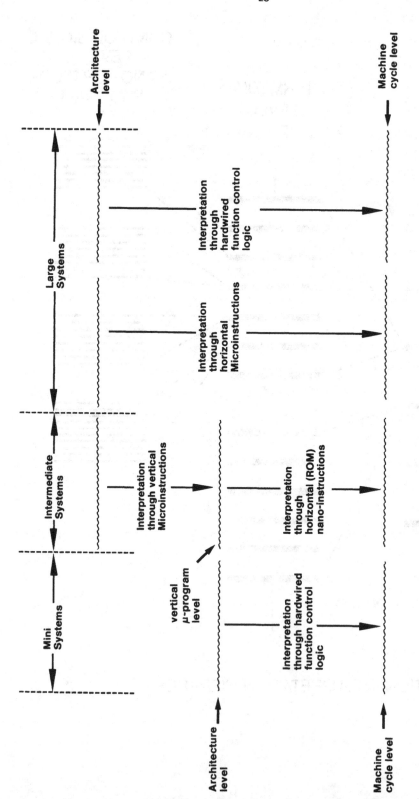

INSTRUCTION EXECUTION CONTROL FOR VARIOUS MACHINE SIZES

FIG. 9

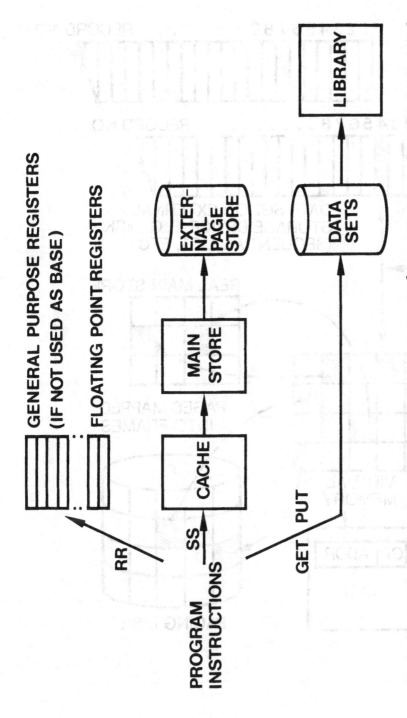

STORAGE ADDRESSING HIERARCHY (AT ASSEMBLER LEVEL)

FIG. 10

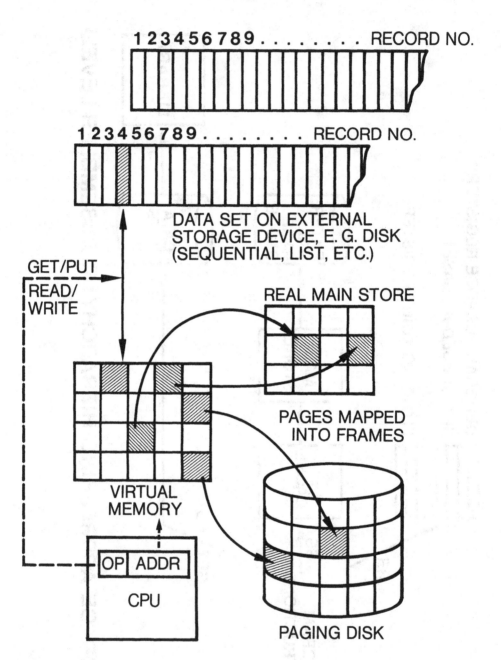

1 2 3 4 5 6 7 8 9 . . . . RECORD NO.

1 2 3 4 5 6 7 8 9 . . . . RECORD NO.

DATA SET ON EXTERNAL
STORAGE DEVICE, E. G. DISK
(SEQUENTIAL, LIST, ETC.)

GET/PUT
READ/
WRITE

REAL MAIN STORE

PAGES MAPPED
INTO FRAMES

VIRTUAL
MEMORY

OP ADDR

CPU

PAGING DISK

FIG. 11

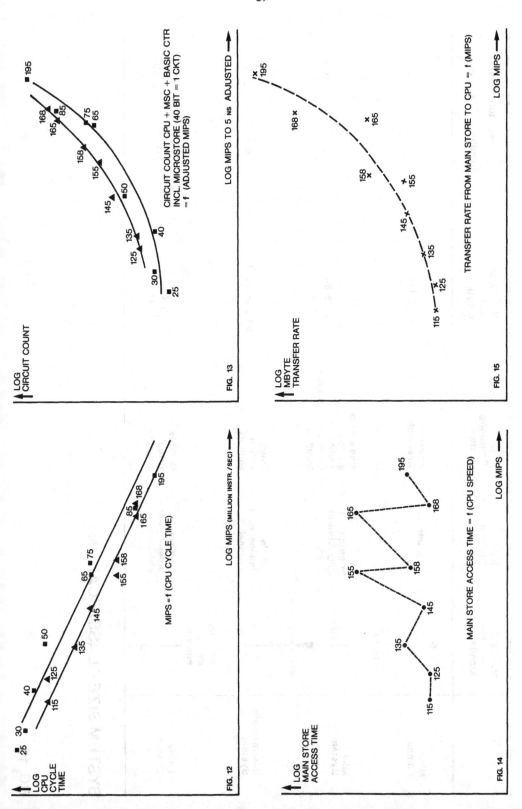

LOG
CPU
CYCLE
TIME

MIPS = f (CPU CYCLE TIME)

LOG MIPS (MILLION INSTR./SEC)

FIG. 12

LOG
CIRCUIT COUNT

CIRCUIT COUNT CPU + MSC + BASIC CTR
INCL. MICROSTORE (40 BIT = 1 CKT)
= f (ADJUSTED MIPS)

LOG MIPS TO 5 ns ADJUSTED

FIG. 13

LOG
MAIN STORE
ACCESS TIME

MAIN STORE ACCESS TIME = f (CPU SPEED)

LOG MIPS

FIG. 14

LOG
MBYTE
TRANSFER RATE

TRANSFER RATE FROM MAIN STORE TO CPU = f (MIPS)

LOG MIPS

FIG. 15

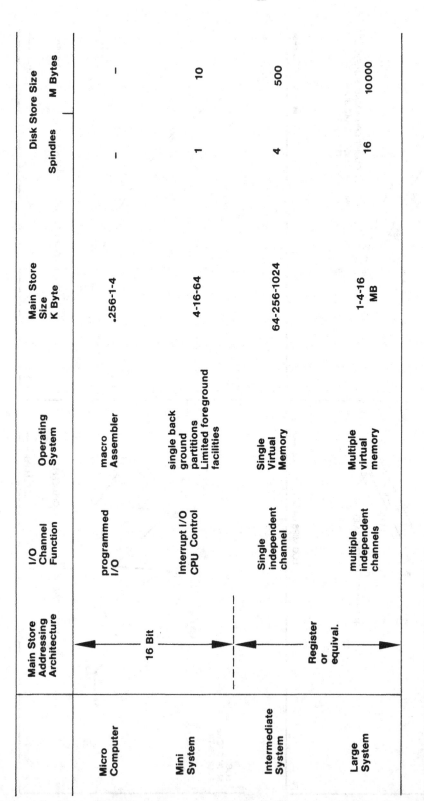

Main Store Addressing Architecture	I/O Channel Function	Operating System	Main Store Size K Byte	Disk Store Size	
				Spindles	M Bytes
Micro Computer	programmed I/O	macro Assembler	.256-1-4	–	–
16 Bit					
Mini System	Interrupt I/O CPU Control	single back ground partitions Limited foreground facilities	4-16-64	1	10
Intermediate System	Single independent channel	Single Virtual Memory	64-256-1024	4	500
Register or equival.					
Large System	multiple independent channels	Multiple virtual memory	1-4-16 MB	16	10 000

SYSTEM SIZE CLASSIFICATION

FIG. 16

ASPECTS OF THE COMMUNICATION WITHIN A
MULTISUPPLIERS COMPUTER NETWORK

F.J. van den Bosch and R.P. de Moel
National Aerospace Laboratory (NLR)
Amsterdam, The Netherlands

SUMMARY

This paper describes the existing NLR hierarchic computer network, especially the
communication aspects of the datatransmission between computers of the various levels.
From the user and network requirements a "most desirable" set of rules for communications is derived. The existing communication procedures are compared with the most
desirable set of rules. The major part of the discrepancies, originated by this comparison, can be solved by the implementation of a programmable front-end processor.

CONTENTS

1. INTRODUCTION

The National Aerospace Laboratory of the Netherlands (NLR) has two settlements, geographically separated about 100 km (Amsterdam and North Eastern Polder).

Fig. 1 Geographical location of both NLR settlements

The computer related activities of NLR can be divided into four classes:

a) acquisition and processing of data
   a.1) windtunnel tests
   a.2) flight tests

b) pure digital simulation
   b.1) flows
   b.2) structures and materials
   b.3) operational aspects of airplanes

c) simulations with systems that contain digital computers as well as other
   specific hardware
   c.1) flight simulator containing an airplane cockpit on a four degrees of
        freedom motion system

c.2) flight simulator containing a three axis servo driven flight table for space flight simulation

d) miscellaneous computer applications (including the management information system).

The above mentioned activities contain time critical elements. Due to the NLR philosophy to execute this type of tasks locally, three categories of computer systems have become necessary (ref. 1):

- dedicated computers for the airplane flight simulator and the space flight simulator (c)
- local or source computers to fulfil tasks in the areas of data acquisition, measurement equipment control, and real time processing: monitoring, data logging, data conversion, and quick-look mainly for windtunnel and flight tests (a, partly)
- large general purpose computer(s) for extensive data processing, pure digital simulation and miscellaneous computer applications (a, partly, b and d).

The first category (dedicated computers) is beyond the scope of this paper. For the other two categories (local computers and large general purpose computers) the historical development gives a better understanding of the motives leading to the architecture of the present network with the related problems.

In the following chapter this historical development is described; furthermore the definition of the partly solved, partly unsolved problems is given. From the problem definition and experience communication rules are derived, which may be useful to solve similar problems. The communication characteristics of the presently available network components are compared with the characteristics prescribed by these rules. Finally, the occurring discrepancies are considered as well as the measures to be taken. Moreover, NLR experience related to system responsibility, and to required computer communication characteristics will be considered in so far as they may benefit other network managers.

2. HISTORICAL DEVELOPMENT AND PROBLEM DEFINITION

The present NLR network, its development and justification is extensively described
in ref. 1.

2.1 Historical development

The development of the network has started in the years 1969-1970 as a long term plan
for the coming decade. In both settlements a stand-alone general purpose computer was
available, the system in the settlement Amsterdam being obsolete at that moment. It
was decided to realise a system with one large general purpose computer for both
settlements and adequate communication and remote entry facilities. As a first step
towards this objective, several measures were taken:
- the realisation of a simulation package, which enabled simulation of the obsolete
  computer in the Amsterdam settlement on the general purpose computer in the other
  settlement, communication between both settlements was achieved by a paper tape data
  link and by mail;
- the obsolete general purpose computer in the settlement Amsterdam was removed;
- for some activities - such as extensive data processing and large digital simulation
  packages - initiated in both settlements, a large general purpose computer of an
  external commercial data center was enlisted. In order to facilitate the use of that
  computer in the settlement North Eastern Polder a rented non-intelligent terminal
  was installed. In the settlement Amsterdam a rented process computer was installed;
  besides the terminal activities, this computer enabled NLR to acquire experience in
  the area of connecting windtunnel data acquisition equipment to a process computer;
- in September 1973 the stand-alone computer in the settlement North Eastern Polder
  was replaced by a larger general purpose computer provided with the most advanced
  communication equipment then available from the same manufacturer. Again this computer was installed in the settlement North Eastern Polder for reasons of long term
  planning. The connection of the rented process computer in the settlement Amsterdam
  was switched over from the external data center computer to the computer in the
  other settlement. Moreover, a local processor for flight test magnetic tape conversion activities - in the mean time installed in Amsterdam - was connected to this
  computer as well.

As will be seen in fig. 2, all computer elements in the network were obtained from one
manufacturer, to enable that manufacturer to carry the system responsibility for the
entire network.

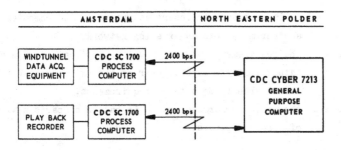

fig. 2   Network at the end of 1973

Summarizing, at the end of 1973 the first part of the system was realised: one large general purpose computer for both settlements provided with simple connections and remote entry facilities. For the next phase of the realisation of the network the following developments are important.

2.1.1. Changing attitude towards system responsibility

The windtunnel data acquisition hardware had to be replaced by local computers because of technical obsolescence and the introduction of more demanding measurement and control techniques. For cost reasons it was not attractive to select computers of the same make as the computers already installed in the network. The primary selection criterion was the fulfilment of the renovated data acquisition tasks, for the communication only the possibility of hardware connection to the available process computer was considered.

This development - connection of multi-supplier hardware - is based on a management decision. This implies that the system responsibility of the manufacturer from this moment on is limited to his components within the network. The heart of the matter is that the network manager takes at least the responsibility for the integration of the various components into a total system. NLR has accepted the system responsibility for this integration because of the in-house availability of knowledge and capabilities.

In general, there is a number of reasons, which may have a strong impact on multi-supplier's network considerations, for instance:
- historical reasons: several computers of different make are available and in use
                        before the idea to set up a network is born;

it is necessary to insert as yet dedicated computer systems of
another make into an existing network.

- technical reasons: the requirements of some specific applications are of such a
nature that the manufacturer of the existing network elements
is not able to meet these requirements.
- economical reasons: the price/performance ratio is bad in comparison with computers
of other suppliers.

2.1.2. Workload

The workload from both settlements for the central computer had been increased.

2.1.3. Communication facilities

The Dutch PTT was able to offer more extensive communication facilities, such as voice
lines up to 9600 BPS and special 48 KHz circuits for transmission speeds up to 50.000
BPS.

2.1.4. I/O facilities

More and better input/output facilities were required: terminal facilities in both
settlements as well as line-printer and plotter facilities in the control rooms.

2.2 Problem definition

The above mentioned developments made it easy to predict that the capacity and flexibility of the network would not be sufficient for a long period. The demanded capacity
and flexibility is expressed in the following rough user requirements:
- adequate turn around time
- data stream identification facilities
- independency of code.

Phase one having been completed (with emphasis on the implementation of one general
purpose computer for both settlements), phase two is characterized by the realisation
of more adequate communication and remote entry facilities. The problem definition
which is in principle the same for both phases, but with different emphasises in practice, may be formulated as follows:

Set up a network consisting of one large general purpose computer and of a
number of remote entry systems (intelligent or not) from which some systems
have, apart from the remote entry task, also specific local time critical

tasks, in such a way that the network will meet the user requirements.

2.2.1. Present situation

The in phase one realised communication facilities had insufficient capacity to process the total workload and to meet the demanded turn around time. To solve this problem a 48 KHz circuit (50.000 BPS) was ordered.

Also the capabilities of the in phase one rented process computer were insufficient to execute the modified and more demanding tasks within the network. The task extensions are in the areas of:

- large increase of data, offered by the local computers due to modified measurement techniques;
- increase of the number of connected processors;
- more demanding communication facilities (48 KHz circuit).

The distribution of tasks between the process computer and the local computers changed: the application oriented checking procedures are executed at the source. The above mentioned new policy concerning the system responsibility enabled an extensive market investigation. This resulted in the purchase of a computer having a good price/performance ratio suited to the communication tasks required by NLR.

To safeguard the continuity of the applications, the decision was taken to attain the solution of NLR's communication problem in three steps:

- implementation of the concentrator computer;
- implementation of the 48 KHz circuit;
- extension of the front-end communication facilities.

At this moment the first two steps have been taken.

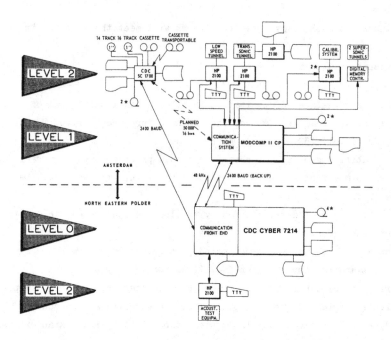

Fig. 3 Details of the present NLR computer network (April 1976)

2.2.2. Near future

In the present situation it is not possible to meet completely the user requirements, such as addressing facilities and code independency. A third step has to be taken: the implementation of a programmable front-end processor.

Making use of the experience acquired during phase one – implementation of one large general purpose computer for both settlements with simple communication and remote entry facilities – and acquired during the first part of phase two, a set of rules concerning communication aspects will be drawn up. These rules may serve as a guide for similar situations in other networks.

3. COMMUNICATION REQUIREMENTS

In this chapter the above mentioned user requirements are more fully described, the network requirements are derived, and based on the user and network requirements a set of rules concerning communication aspects of the NLR network is drawn up.

3.1 User requirements

The most determining user requirements for communication between computers are:
- adequate turn around time.

At this moment this requirement is covered in the network, because the capabilities of the central computer, the remote communication controller, and the transmission lines are selected on an average workload of all applications. It seldom occurs that peakloads of various applications run concurrently. Moreover, the basic philosophy of the network is that time critical data processing has to be executed by local computers.
- data stream identification facilities.

The network contains (remote) entry facilities of several types, such as batch terminals, TTY compatible terminals, and local computers in various control rooms of experimental facilities. Furthermore, it contains (remote) output facilities at several locations such as terminal sites and control rooms. Data, submitted by the entry facilities, must be processed by the central computer in the settlement North Eastern Polder, and the results must be presented at an output facility selected at wish. It is therefore necessary to have the capability to send information (via the central computer) from each input device in the network to any output device, on certain security conditions. This implies that every block of data to be transferred, has to be provided with sufficient identification.
- independency of the code.

For some applications it is not possible to execute code conversions with the available equipment. In some applications the large amount of data to be transferred requires the most efficient transmission code in order to limit transfer time and thus turn around time. This implies either the possibility to transmit arbitrary bit patterns or conversion capabilities.

3.2 Network philosophy and entailing requirements

The network philosophy, related to the communication aspects of the existing network, is:
- the suppliers of the various components of the network keep system responsibility for their own hardware and software. The network manager is responsible for the integration of the components into the network. This principle leads to the following requirements:

. the selection of communication hardware and software should be based on
general purpose I/O facilities such that interfacing with other components
can be done without complex modifications.

. arrangements should be embedded in the contractual matters concerning sup-
plier's approval of the possibly necessary modifications and adjustments.

. the network manager should have at his disposal equipment and procedures
which enable him to locate malfunctions within the network.

- the remote communication controller is regarded as a functional part of the central
facility, because both settlements should have equal access to the central computer
for off-line batch processing and on-line connection of data acquisition systems.
This implies that data streams, submitted to the communication computer, should have
the same characteristics as the data streams directly submitted to the central computer. This leads to the following network requirements:

. data, submitted by local computers to the remote communication controller,
must be complete jobs, as if submitted directly to the central computer. This
implies that, apart from the measurement data, job control information should
be provided as well. In general, this information (such as accounting info,
type of processing indications, device and/or file identification) is only
available at the source.

. preparation of data blocks to be transmitted has to be done uniformly for the
entire network according to the line protocol, selected for the communication
between the central computer and the remote communication controller. This
preparation includes addition of information about addressing, about type
of code, and for transmission error detection. This implies that only one
error detection method will be used for the entire network.

3.3 "Most desirable" set of rules

The user and network requirements result in the following "most desirable" set of rules
for communication in the NLR network:

A. The addressing facilities should be sufficient.

B. It should be possible to transmit arbitrary bit patterns.

C. Data, submitted by local computers, should be in the form of complete jobs.

D. Preparation of data blocks to be transmitted should be done uniformly for
the entire network, according to some selected line protocol.

E. Consequences of interfacing should be taken into account, when selecting
communication equipment.

F. System responsibility arrangements in the contract should include arrangements concerning modifications and adjustments related to interfacing.

G. Network test equipment and procedures should be developed.

4. COMMUNICATION EQUIPMENT: SURVEY AND COMPARISON WITH THE RULES

In this chapter the characteristics of the communication equipment within the network will be enumerated and compared with the "most desirable" set of rules. The last rule can not be considered, as this rule concerns the entire network. Attention to this rule will be paid in section 4.4.

4.1 Central computer communication equipment

The central computer — a CDC Cyber 72, 64 K words main memory and 460 M bytes background memory — is provided with two types of communication devices:
- Device that supports serial asynchronous communication lines (110–1200 bps) and synchronous lines (up to 4800 bps).

Rule	Available	According to rules
A. Addressing	108 data streams/line	yes
B. Arbitrary bit patterns	ASCII or BCD per line	no
C. Complete jobs	not applicable	-
D. Uniform blocks	yes, LPC error check	yes
E. Interfacing	not applicable	-
F. Contract	not applicable	-

Table 1: central computer low speed comm. device characteristics

- Device that supports serial synchronous lines (up to 50,000 bps).

Rule	Available	According to rules
A. Addressing	5 data streams/line	no
B. Arbitrary bit patterns	ASCII and free format	no
C. Complete jobs	not applicable	-
D. Uniform blocks	no, CRC 16 error check	no
E. Interfacing	not applicable	-
F. Contract	not applicable	-

Table 2: central computer high speed comm. device characteristics

4.2 The remote communication controller communication equipment

This computer – a MODCOMP II CP, 32 K words main memory and 20 M bytes background memory – is selected especially for communication purposes. Four types of communication devices are connected, supporting:

- serial synchronous lines (up to 250,000 bps)
- serial asynchronous lines (up to 19,200 bps)
- programmed I/O 16 bits parallel lines (up to 5,000 words/sec.)
- 16 bits parallel lines with direct memory access (up to 50,000 words/sec.).

In table 3 the characteristics of all types will be included.

Rule	Available	According to rules
A. Addressing	programmable	yes
B. Arbitrary bit patterns	yes	yes
C. Complete jobs	not applicable	–
D. Uniform blocks	programmable	yes
E. Interfacing	yes	yes
F. Contract	yes	yes

Table 3: remote concentrator comm. devices characteristics

4.3 Local computers communication equipment

Referring to the communication equipment and procedures the local computers may be divided into two categories.

4.3.1. Hewlett Packard 2100 program controlled 16 bits parallel I/O

This communication equipment is developed by NLR.

Rule	Available	According to rules
A. Addressing	implicit	no
B. Arbitrary bit patterns	ASCII	no
C. Complete jobs	no	no
D. Uniform blocks	no	no
E. Interfacing	yes	yes
F. Contract	no	no

Table 4: HP 2100 comm. device and procedure characteristics

4.3.2. Control Data SC 1700 16 bits parallel I/O with direct memory access

This communication equipment is developed by NLR.

Rule	Available	According to rules
A. Addressing	yes	yes
B. Arbitrary bit patterns	no	no
C. Complete jobs	yes	yes
D. Uniform blocks	yes, LPC error check	yes
E. Interfacing	no	no
F. Contract	yes	yes

Table 5: CDC SC 1700 comm. device and procedure characteristics

4.4 Network test equipment and procedures

The test facilities should enable the network manager to check separate components
(such as various computer parts, modems, communication lines) and interconnected components up to the entire network. Depending on the status of the network (in development or operational) test activities will generally begin with the separate components
in the case of development and with the entire network in the case of an operational
system. Although test procedures in these cases may be different, the test equipment
may be the same.
The test facilities under the responsibility of the NLR network manager may be divided
into two categories:
- tools locating malfunctioning components, such as:
   . wrap around facilities;
   . line test equipment;

  . network diagnostic software.

This type of tools is sufficient as long as it concerns manufacturer's equipment.

- tools locating malfunctions within components, build by NLR, such as:

  . static input simulation equipment;

  . dynamic input simulation equipment;

  . dump analyzer.

5. TECHNICAL SOLUTION

In the last chapter a number of discrepancies has been revealed between the communication device and procedure characteristics, and the requirements of the "most desirable" set of communication rules. These discrepancies are related to the communication devices of the central computer, and to the communication facilities and procedures of the local computers; because the remote concentrator has been selected in accordance with these rules, there are no discrepancies.

The discrepancies related to the communication devices of the central computer are due to the lack of flexibility of this equipment, because of which adjustments to increasing and more severe requirements can not be realised. The communication devices of the central computer consist of a hardware multiplexer and a firmware communication station; both devices are not programmable. The present problems - for the high speed device: insufficient addressing facilities, intransparency to the code, and context depending block formats; for the low speed device: intransparency to the code - can only be solved by implementing a programmable front-end processor, as the third step of the in section 2.2.1. described phase 2.

The discrepancies related to the communication facilities of the local computers, are mainly due to the procedures. These discrepancies may be eliminated by modifications of the procedures; however, this may bring on a too heavy workload for the local computers. A trade-off study is required. The most important question of this investigation concerns the selection of the transmission block error check method. Based on the experience with the 48 KHz circuit (until this moment) NLR prefers to implement the cyclic redundancy check (CRC 16) method (generating polynominal is $x^{16} + x^{15} + x^2 + 1$) for the entire network instead of the longitudinal parity check (LPC) method; communication oriented computers have the ability to accumulate such check characters in hardware. The presently connected local computers do not have this ability, therefore the accumulation of the check characters has to be done in software.

6. CONCLUDING REMARKS

It can only be recommended to carry the system responsibility for the integration and management of a multi-suppliers network, if sufficient knowledge is available in the areas of the relevant applications, the hardware and software features of the components, and hardware and software interfacing techniques. Attention should be paid to the contractual agreements with the suppliers.

The NLR network is realised in phases, because of budget and continuity reasons. This approach has proven to be attractive, as it enabled effective tuning of the network to the application package. In each phase advantage could be taken of the experiences acquired during preceding phases.

When selecting local computers, (possibly) to be inserted in a network, it is recommended to add the communication requirements to the selection criteria. The presently obtainable minicomputers enable such an approach.

The major part of NLR's communication problems can be solved by implementation of a programmable front-end processor. When selecting a programmable front-end processor, attention has to be paid to the critical elements of the interfacing. It is recommended to consider the front-end processor together with the coupler as one component as far as system responsibility is concerned.

7. REFERENCE

W. Loeve   An hierarchic multi-suppliers computer network of a research
laboratory with two settlements.

Paper presented at the combined American European CDC-users conference in Amsterdam, 1975
NLR MP 75012.

COMMUNICATION AND SYNCHRONIZATION TOOLS
IN A DISTRIBUTED ENVIRONMENT*

H. Le Goff, G. Le Lann

IRISA, Université de Rennes, BP 25A

35000 Rennes, France

Key words : computer networks, distributed systems, communication protocols, flow
control, resource utilization.

Characterization of a distributed environment

Most of computer systems are operated and controlled from a central unit which
is in charge of running an Operating System. This kind of architecture is not flaw-
less : it is not easily expandable, not very efficient because of the potential
bottleneck at the central unit level and is highly vulnerable.

Multiprocessors were first designed to speed up computation, by taking advantage
of the inherent parallelism of these machines and to increase their reliability. We
see now that they have the potentiality of being operated in a decentralized mode.
Nevertheless, in most cases, some kind of centralization can be found inside these
multiprocessors : one processor is monitoring the others, internal communications
are possible only through the common memory space, all the tasks to be run are queued
up in a unique location, and so on.

* This work was supported by the Direction des Recherches et Moyens d'Essais,
Ministère de la Défense, contrat n° 74/540.

Up to now, the best examples of real distributed systems are computer networks [1], [2], [3]. Computer networks behave according to some specific sets of rules called Protocols which relieve network processors from the need for a central "controller" in order to perform their own tasks. As will be shown later, processors having equal rights and equal responsabilities are said to belong to the same functional layer and this decomposition leads to a hierarchical architecture.

We think that centralized and distributed systems differ from each other on two important points :
- entities willing to communicate do so directly in a distributed system, instead of referring first to a unique monitoring process which is then responsible for establishing communications.
- it is meaningless to define the "state" of a distributed system.

The communication and synchronization tools to be described in this paper are intended for general purpose computer networks and are not tied to a specific system. These tools can thus be used in any distributed system, whatever its size.

Servers in a distributed system. The transparency concept

Locating a process in a distributed system like a computer network is a many solutions problem, each of these solutions having some drawbacks. For instance, processes can be accessed by the means of physical addresses ; in that case, users have to be aware of the existence of all processes (updating problems) and are bound to the naming convention of the hosts where these processes reside ; processes are not allowed to migrate on different hosts and their availability is thus directly dependant upon the host's failures ; furthermore, fair load sharing is very hard to achieve.

Another solution is to access processes by using logical names. One then must be able either to handle directly logical names or to map logical names into physical addresses ; the first solution has been chosen for the DCS network [4] where logical names are recorded into associative memories distributed over a ring topology allowing for natural broadcasting ; the second solution is used in the Cyclades subnetwork [5] in which a Transport Station name is translated into a physical node address by accessing a table.

In that latter case, the number of processes has to be kept rather small in order to avoid large search times. Consequently, this approach does not seem to be workable with private user processes because of their dynamically evolving nature. On the contrary, this solution is quite appropriate for standard processes like system Loggers, Compilers or library Subroutines which we call Servers.

Assuming now that many different Servers perform a specific service, for instance NLED$^{(*)}$ Compilation, we are faced with the problem of selecting one of the Servers when receiving a corresponding request. The user issuing the request has to be kept unaware of that situation for many reasons ; first of all, he is surely not interested in that problem because he is currently trying to solve another one ; second, if we want the user to be provided with a good service, we have to achieve automatic load sharing and the user is obviously not the best person to perform that internal balancing ; third, Servers failures should be ignored as far as the user is concerned and this is also directly related to load sharing.

This is what we call transparency and some methos are currently being investigated which allow for a decentralized allocation of resources [7], [8] and internal load sharing into distributed systems [6] ; a diffusion technique, similar to the Arpanet adaptive routing mechanism has been proposed for distributed network topologies ; another scheme, the circulating vector technique, is based on the virtual ring concept and is usable on any physical topology.

With these methods, automatic selection of one server among many is possible ; the current physical location of that server is then notified to the user and from this point, communication and synchronization between the user and the server proceed on a conventional point to point basis.

In what follows it will be shown how communication and synchronization are performed for a specific class of processes in a computer network. Evaluation of a very general flow control mechanism has been undertaken ; a conflicting optimization case is then reported which is very similar to some situations observed in hierarchical and centralized Systems.

(*)Nicest Language Ever Designed, precisely the Language you are in love with.

<u>ﬞication and synchronization in a computer network</u>

        ‚nal systems, processes willing to exchange data do so according to
      ‚es. Most of the time, implicit assumptions are made ; for instance,
     ‚ange is error free. In computer networks, stronger constraints have to
    ‚h : data may be corrupted during the transfer, time references are not
   for the sender and the receiver, a common physical space is not shared by
  ‚r and the receiver, data transmitted are not kept is sequence.

 ‚sequently, a good transmission tool is such that :
 no desynchronization may occur between the communicating processes
 transmission errors are rapidly detected and corrected
 flow control is performed efficiently.

s a result, for the processes, the transmission delay will be minimum and the
‚able throughput will be maximum [9].

‚ommunication networks handle standard data blocks called packets. Packets are
limited for many reasons and the maximum size value depends on the transmission
m characteristics.

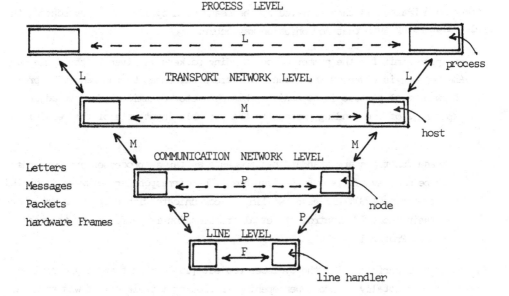

FIGURE 1

User processes exchange data records called Letters ; Letters which do not f
into one packet have to be fragmented before being transmitted and need to be rea
sembled before delivery ; a fragment of a Letter is called a Message (see figure

Processes are run on physical hosts and several processes may initiate simulta-
neous communications from one host ; moreover, any given process should be allowed
to handle many concurrent communications too. Then the need for a multiplexing/de-
multiplexing function and for an activation/termination function.

How can transmission errors be rapidly detected and corrected ? Each packet
carries some extra-information allowing for error detection (CRC, for instance). The
receiving process is then able to ask for a transmission if needed. But this does
not work if packets are lost ; another scheme has to be devised. Most of communication Protocols use a Timer + Positive Acknowledgment mechanism ; for each packet, if
a preset time interval has elapsed before receiving the corresponding acknowledgment
then a retransmission of this packet takes place. Obviously if timeout values are
too short or packet transmission delays are sometimes too large, duplicates of packets will be created. These duplicates must be detected. This is an easy task if
only one packet at a time is travelling between two processes ; an alternate numbering scheme may be used in that case. For the sake of efficiency, some "anticipation"
hould be allowed and many packets may be outstanding on the virtual path existing
etween two processes ; such a path is called a Liaison. Unique identification of
tters on a Liaison is then achieved by the means of a cyclic numbering scheme, the
le value being such that no confusion may occur.

One upper limit for the number of outstanding packets is given by the cycle va-
Another one is given by the amount of buffers allocated by the receiving pro-
Flow control purpose is to monitor this parameter dynamically and to adjust
tput rate of the sending process to the variable input rate of the receiving
`.

these functions are standard requirements as far as processes are concerned
ld be made available on any given host. The corresponding software is called
rt Station (TS). Processes willing to communicate with each other do so by
their local TS. Control of actual transmission is performed by the means
ort Protocol.

ons performed for the Cyclades project [10] showed that desynchroniza-
be totally avoided when opening or closing a Liaison ; it was shown al-
ute credit values should not be used in flow control ; credit values
ute when not refering to a specific location in the data flow. An
nchronisation is given on figure 2. This uncertainty requires a
h in which desynchronizations at a given level can be detected and

55

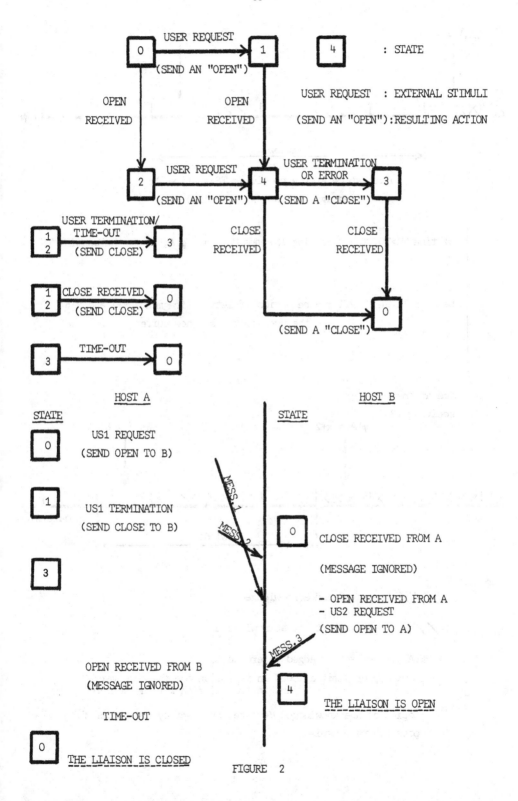

FIGURE 2

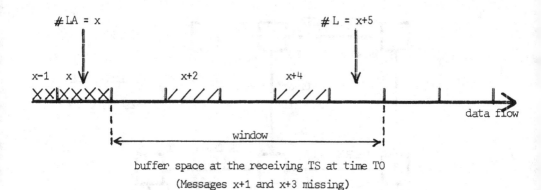

#LA = x   #L = x+5

x-1   x   x+2   x+4

data flow

window

buffer space at the receiving TS at time T0
(Messages x+1 and x+3 missing)

at time T1>T0, the receiving TS sends Message (#LA, 5) to the sending TS

between T1 and T2>T1 : - reception of letters/fragments x+1 and x+5
                            - the user provides a new buffer

time at the
receiving TS

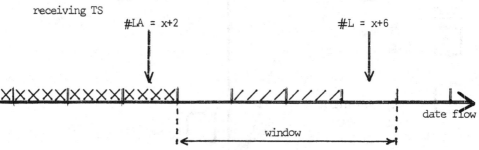

#LA = x+2   #L = x+6

data flow

window

Legend :

XXX   received and acknowledged

///   received but not acknowledged

#LA : last acknowledged reference

#L   : upper limit allowed in reception for the receiver
                          and in transmission for the sender

Copies of unacknowledged Messages are kept by the sender for a
possible retransmission.

FIGURE 3

corrected at higher levels.

One widely accepted flow control scheme is the Window mechanism, first introduced in Cyclades. With such a scheme, Messages sent on to a Liaison are given sequential references ; because of transmission failures or race conditions, resequen-
cing of Messages has to be performed by the receiving TS which acknowledges the data
flow up to the first missing Message (see figure 3) ; credits are indicated as incre-
mental values refering to the last acknowledged reference ; acknowledgments Messages
are periodically issued ; loss or duplication of these Messages do not lead to desynchronization.

In order to get a better insight into the problem of designing interprocess communication Protocols, description and evaluation of one INWG* proposal is now reported. This Protocol, the ZE Protocol [11] makes use of the Timer + Repetition, Positive Acknowledgment and Window technique :

- error control
When fragmentation is on (Letters not fitting into one packet), the ZE Protocol
requires one acknowledgment per whole Letter only. When a Letter is timed out,
the ZE Protocol provides for the retransmission of that Letter and all subsequent
Letters.
- flow control
The ZE Protocol requires an agreement to be reached by the processes at the Liaison set-up time, on a common Letter size ; then, the credit values are indicated in Letters.

Evaluation results (figure 4)

The user throughput versus credit is a step function. If n is the Letter length,
the same throughput is achieved for all credit values included in the interval
[Kn, (K + 1) n[, K integer. This is due to the flow control policy requiring an
allocation of a buffer of size n before a transmission of a Letter takes place. Thus,
to achieve a given throughput, more space is needed as Letter size increase ; for
two different sizes n and m with n < m, the ratio of the credit values required in
both cases to achieve the same throughput is smaller than m/n.

For small credit values, for instance 700 octets, it is more efficient to transmit short Letters (120 octets) instead of long Letters (480 octets). We felt necessary to investigate this phenomenon in more depth.

* International Network Working Group, IFIP WG 6.1

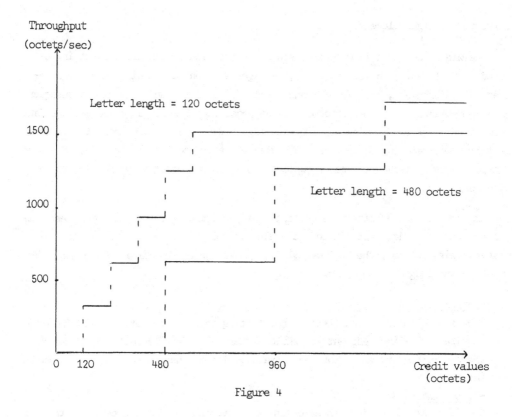

Figure 4

Optimal resource utilization

Both at the communication network level and at the line level, the important goal to achieve is a good utilization of the offered transmission facility. Most of Network designers have agreed on a basic packet size ranging around 2000 bits. The fixed overhead payed per packet transmission seems to be quite acceptable for such a size.

But what is the real overhead to be experienced when the full packet capacity is not used ? This happens for instance with interactive traffic. Most of interactive letters are short - a few characters - and obviously, a variable fraction of the potential throughput is wasted in that case. It is usually accepted that wasting the throughput is the price to pay in order to achieve fast transmission, which is precisely the important criteria in interactive applications. But what delay and what throughput ? If it is true to say that a short transmission time is important to the user then, the right question to ask is how much of the throughput is wasted at the user level too and not at the communication network level. Optimization of that latter level is another problem and global optimization of both the communication and the transport levels may turn out to be a tradeoff.

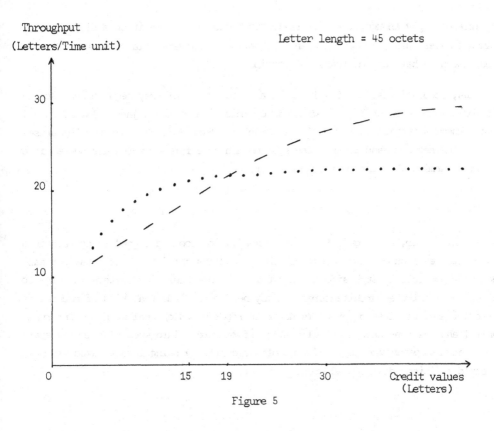

Figure 5

User Letters are handled by Transport Stations which are in charge of both error control and flow control. Then, the highest achievable throughput is the one allowed by the TS flow control mechanism.

Results of a simulation study are shown in figure 5 (several cases have been simulated). Multiplexing several short Letters into packets has been tried against the one Letter per packet case. These results indicate very clearly the existence of a threshold value, T. Multiplexing is efficient only when credit values larger than T are made available by the receiving TS ; for smaller credit values, optimal user delay and throughput are achieved by not multiplexing Letters into packets. This is due to the fact that multiplexing letters into packets leads to longer packets which are much slower than the one letter packets to travel across the various network layers ; for the same reason, acknowledgments being transmitted with the reverse traffic are slower to come back ; new credit values are carried with these acknow-ledgments ; it may happen then that the sending TS having spent all its credits has to wait for a future acknowledgment carrying a non-zero credit value before resuming the letter transmission. This leads to a non-optimal throughput.

Interestingly enough, the most realistic values for a credit on a Liaison are values smaller than T ; this is even more obvious as several Liaisons may be in use simultaneously between two Transport Stations.

Thus, good utilization of a layer in a computer network may require some specific tools which are conflicting with the optimization of the adjacent layer. This is a well known situation in conventional structured Systems ; the same problem arises in computer networks and distributed systems and some further works are needed in order to determine what the real tradeoffs are.

Conclusion

In this paper, synchronization and communication tools designed to operate in a distributed environment have been described. Good insight into their behaviour has been made possible through simulation studies. Future Operating Systems may have to be run on distributed architectures and may need to include that kind of mechanisms. Moreover, another class of problems has been reported which deal with the internal control and the non-centralized allocation of resources into such distributed systems. The transparency concept and some others currently being investigated may help to build efficient distributed architectures.

References

[1] BARBER D., _The European computer network project_, Washington, ICCC 1972, pp. 192-200.

[2] ROBERTS L., WESSLER B., _Computer network development to achieve resource sharing_, SJCC 1970, pp. 543-549.

[3] POUZIN L., _Presentation and major design aspects of the Cyclades computer network_, 3rd Data Communication Symposium, Tampa 1973, pp. 80-87.

[4] FARBER D. et al, _The Distributed Computing System_, 7th Annual IEEE Computer Society International Conference, 1973.

[5] POUZIN L., _Cigale, the packet-switching machine of the Cyclades computer network_, IFIP 1974, pp. 155-159.

[6] LE LANN G., _Une approche des futurs réseaux informatiques_, Congrès International sur les Mini-ordinateurs et la Transmission de Données, Liège 1975.

[7] LE LANN G., NEGARET R., _Operating principles for a distributed multimicroprocessor_, First Euromicro Symposium, Nice 1975, pp. 219-222.

[8] LEHON A., NEGARET R. and LE LANN G., _Distribution of access and data in Large Data Bases_, International Symposium on Technology for Selective Dissemination of Information, Rep. di San Marino, 1976.

[9] LE GOFF H., PEDRONO R., _Les Protocoles de Transport dans les réseaux à commutation par paquets : présentation et évaluation_, International Telecommunication Union, Genève 1975 Symposium, pp. 3.5.6.1.-3.5.6.9.

[10] LE LANN G., _La simulation et le projet Cyclades_, Congrès Afcet Informatique et Télécommunications, Rennes, 1973, pp. 297-304.

[11] ZIMMERMANN H., _The Cyclades end-to-end protocol_, 4th Data Communication Symposium, Québec City, 1975, pp. 7.21-7.26.

MULTIPROGRAMMED MEMORY MANAGEMENT FOR RANDOM-SIZED PROGRAMS*

Bernhard Walke

AEG-TELEFUNKEN, Research Institute

D-7900 Ulm, W-Germany

Abstract

We consider a probabilistic model of a computer system with multiprogramming and paging. The applied work-load is derived from measure-
ments in scientific computer applications and is characterized by a
great variance of compute time. Throughput of a cyclic model is computed approximately presuming program sizes with negative exponential distribution. After a review of previous results for a memory
allocation policy with prescribed number, n, of working sets at least
to be loaded, an adaptive memory allocation policy is introduced
which dynamically changes the number, n. Thereby, it is possible to
reach the goal of having always enough memory available to load the
parachor of each program. Simulation results establish our approximations as being very good. CPU scheduling is chosen to be throughput optimal. Our results are useful to demonstrate the benefits of
allocation policies with adaptive controlled degree of multiprogramming. Previous contributions to this problem are to that date only
by means of simulation [5].

1. Introduction

Throughput of a computer can be enhanced by increasing the degree
of multiprogramming, which results in better parallel work of central
resources (CPU, channels). But generally, this is only true if the
main memory is also enlarged adequately. Each of the multiprogrammed
jobs must be given enough space to keep its working set there, otherwise thrashing [2] would occur and throughput would vanish.

In this paper, we introduce a policy for controlling the degree of
multiprogramming in a paged memory with respect to maximum throughput. This policy, ACM-n (adaptive control of the multiprogramming
degree of a number, not greater n, of partly loaded programs) is a
working set policy in that it aims at keeping the parachor [3] of
each program in the main memory and dynamically changes the degree

---

*) This work was partly supported by the 2nd EDP-Program of the
Federal Republic of Germany.

of multiprogramming to reach that goal.

A queueing network model of a computer system is developed and through-put for a given workload is computed for the ACM-n algorithm. Program size is assumed to be negative exponentially distributed. From this assumption follows that for a memory of given size, the number of fully (or partly) loadable programs changes over time, e.g. sometimes only one working set could be loaded (when a program happens to be very large), at other times many working sets together could be kept there. We use a new technique (of the decomposition type [1]) to approximately compute the steady-state utilization of the CPU and from this the throughput.
A special case of the ACM-n policy which is called MPM-n policy (minimal prescribed multiprogramming degree, n, is fixed) was already dealt with in [7]. Under this policy a number, n, or more programs are multiprogrammed whenever they happen to fit completely together in the main memory, otherwise n uncompletely loaded programs must be multiprogrammed. The results are reviewed in chapter 4 of this paper.

The subject of this paper is the case of a dynamically changing, ACM-n controlled, multiprogramming degree of partly loaded programs. For reasons of simplification of computation we restrict our model to the case where this degree, n, is limited, $n \leq 2$. More than two programs are admitted whenever they happen to be small enough to be completely loaded into the main memory. Simulation results show that our computational results are acceptable.

2. Model of the workload

We assume all programs being of the same type, there are no different classes of programs. Program size is assumed to be given by an independent and identically distributed random variable, G, with probability distribution function (p.d.f.)

$$P(G \leq g) = 1 - \exp(-g/E_G) \qquad (2.1)$$

with mean E_G. (Big letters without index denote random variables throughout this paper, the corresponding small letter denotes an assumed value of such a variable). The work for a program loaded completely into the main memory consists exactly of two service intervals: one transport from the background to the main memory and one compute interval, which may be preempted but could be serviced uninterruptedly. The term 'program' in this context is chosen for such parts of service for jobs, for which the given description is appropriate (e.g. compilation, execution, etc.). The transport back from main memory to the secondary storage is not modeled explicitly. It should be thought of as included in the loading transport of the program.

If the main memory, available for a distinct program, is limited so that program size is greater than memory space, only a part of the program (which is usually called the working set) is loaded. In this situation a compute interval is limited by two I/O-demands, one of which in front of the compute interval the other at the end. For example page exception, segment call, or buffer overflow are reasons to limit a compute interval (provided they could not be serviced in parallel to CPU service for the same program). We call the sequence of I/O-demand and compute interval a service interval of a program. Fig. 1 illustrates this model for the execution of a program: An alternating sequence of I/O-demand, T (transport), and CPU service, C (compute).

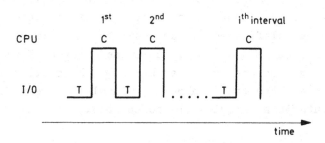

Fig. 1: Model of the progress of service for a not completely loaded program (no concurrent programs assumed).

For our queueing model we assume the variable, T, to be an independent random variable with p.d.f.

$$P(T \leq t) = 1 - \exp(-t/E_T) \tag{2.2}$$

and mean E_T.

Compute intervals, C, are defined by a degenerate exponential d.f.
[6], fig. 2,

$$P(C \leq t) = 1 - (1-p) \exp(-t/E_{C'}) \qquad (2.3)$$

with mean

$$E_C = (1-p) E_{C'} \qquad (2.4)$$

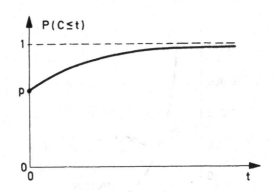

Fig. 2: Degenerate exponential distribution
function.

This distribution is a special case of the well-known two-phase
hyperexponential d.f. and is much more suitable to approximate
measured cumulative d.f.'s of compute intervals, C, than the exponential function (wich is a limiting case of eq. (2.3) for p = 0).
'Short' compute intervals are approximated by compute intervals of
the length zero, which appear in eq. (2.3) with probability p. Non-
zero compute intervals are approximated by a negative exponential
d.f. with mean $E_{C'}$. Together with the LCFS-P (last come first serve
preemptive) CPU-scheduling algorithm [4] this d.f. can be handled
computationally in the same way as a simple negative exponential
d.f. [6].

We have chosen these two simple d.f.'s (eqs. 2.2, 2.3) for reasons
of mathematical tractability. As will be seen later, refinements
at these points seem to be of subordinate influence on throughput
compared with the influence of the parachor curve of programs.

Next we assume that the probability for each service interval being
the last one of a program is constant. From this follows that the
number, I, of intervals per program is given from a geometric dis-

tribution. The mean, m, depends on the portion, x, of the whole program which is brought to the main memory. For fully loaded programs,
x = 1, there results exactly one service interval per program and
therefore m equals one. For very uncompletely loaded programs,
x ⟶ 0, the mean number of intervals approximates infinity, m ⟶ ∞ ,
fig. 3. The function m(x) has been approximated in the literature
in numerous ways, e.g. [2], and was sometimes called parachor curve.

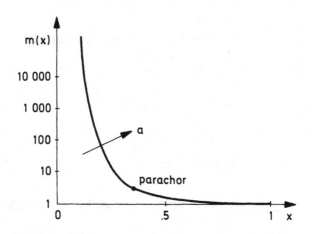

Fig. 3: Mean number of service intervals, m,
dependent on the portion, x, of a
program loaded to main memory (parachor
curve).

For a demand paging system, for instance, the expression (m(x)-1)
may be the number of page faults during program execution. We choose
a simple function to describe the dependency of m(x) on x

$$m(x) = x^{-a} \qquad (2.5)$$

where the variable, a, is a parameter. Measured parachor curves can
be approximated [7] by eq. (2.5) with parameter values a ≥ 2. The
reciprocal, 1/m(x), is sometimes called life-time function.

Next we assume that the CPU-time to execute a program is subdivided
in compute intervals whenever the program is loaded uncompletely,
but the whole mean compute time per program, E_{Cp}, remains unchanged
(no CPU-overhead is involved). For I/O-time, however, the analogue
must not be true.

Instead of this we introduce for our computations a function

$$E_T = g(E_{Tp}, x) \qquad (2.6)$$

where E_{Tp} is the mean transport time of completely loaded programs. Remember that by our definitions the expected values of compute intervals, E_C, and I/O-demands, E_T, are functions of x. Our workload description is chosen so that

$$E_{Cp} = m(x) \; E_C(x) \qquad (2.7)$$

3. Model of the computer systems

The computer is modeled by a cyclic queueing network with two servers in tandem and n circulating programs, fig. 4. The queue discipline is FCFS for the channel-queue (on the secondary storage) and LCFS-P for the CPU-queue (in main memory).

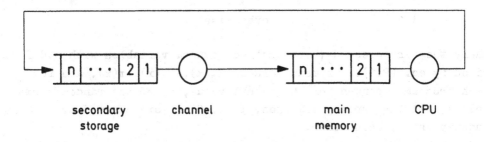

Fig. 4: Cyclic queueing network model of a computer system.

If the number, n, of programs is constant, which is equivalent to a fixed degree of multiprogramming and a fixed program size, CPU-utilization, U, is known from [6] to be

$$U = D \cdot E_{Cp} = \frac{\rho^n - 1}{\rho^{n+1} - 1}, \qquad \rho = \begin{cases} g(E_{Tp}, x) \cdot m(x)/E_{Cp} & (x<1) \\ \\ E_{Tp}/E_{Cp} & (x=1) \end{cases} \qquad (3.1)$$

where the variable, D, is the program throughput. Mean turn-around time, E_B, is computed from throughput, D, by

$$E_B = 1/D \qquad (3.2)$$

When program size follows the p.d.f. given by eq. (2.1) and the memory size, s, is limited, the number of completely loadable programs becomes a random variable. The probability, p_n, for "n[and not (n+1)] independent programs completely fit in the main memory" is computable [7] to be Poisson distributed

$$p_n = \frac{\gamma^n}{n!} \exp(-\gamma), \qquad \gamma = s/E_G \qquad (3.3)$$

Independent of memory size there is a certain probability, p_0, that no complete program can be loaded. If we demand a given degree, $n > 1$, of multiprogramming being upheld, the probability for "n complete programs are not loadable" increases over p_0. In what follows we decide to load programs only in such a manner that all of them have the same portion, x, of their full size loaded. Then the portion, X, which is now a random variable can be computed from

$$X = \begin{cases} s/\sum_{i=1}^{n} G_i & \text{for} \quad s < \left(\sum_{i=1}^{n} G_i\right) = G_n \\ 1 & \text{otherwise} \end{cases} \qquad (3.4)$$

where the variables, G_i, are distinct random variables with p.d.f. given by eq. (2.1). Our mean values, $E_C(x)$, $E_T(x)$, $m(x)$, are for each program dependent on the actual value, x, of the random variable X. All the random variables, T, C, G, I, are assumed to be independent of each other.

Now we are interested in the p.d.f. of the size of a number, n, of programs which fit together each with a portion, x, in a memory of given size, s. This can be computed to be (cf. [7])

$$P(xG_n < s \mid G_n \geq s) = 1 - \sum_{j=0}^{n-1} \frac{(\gamma/x^2)^j}{j!} \left(\sum_{j=0}^{n-1} \frac{\gamma^j}{j!}\right)^{-1} \exp(-\gamma(1/x-1)) \qquad (3.5)$$

$$(x \leq 1)$$

x, G_n are defined from eq. (3.4). If we now prescribe the degree of multiprogramming, n, which must be upheld, then we have from eq. (3.3) the probability, $p_k(k \geq n)$, of multiprogramming a number, k, of completely loaded programs and from eq. (3.5) the p.d.f. of the portion X, of partly loaded programs under a multiprogramming degree, n.

4. Approximate throughput computation by decomposition methods

Decomposition methods are used to compute steady-state values of complex systems with a large number of state variables from subsystems with small groups of variables. From [1] we know that this technique still yields good approximations when interactions among subsystems do exist but are weak compared to the interactions within subsystems. Such systems are called nearly completely decomposable and have the property that short run dynamics can be distinguished from long run dynamics.

In our simple queueing network, fig. 4, a great complexity in time is involved by the assumption that program size is a random variable and from this the degree of multiprogramming, n, becomes a random variable, N. This causes the portion, x, of uncompletely loaded programs (which appear whenever less than a prescribed number, n, of programs are loadable) also to be a random variable, X, eq. (3.4).

We interpret a time interval in which a number, n, of programs is allocatable to main memory (fully, or each with a portion, x) as a subsystem with short run dynamics and describe it by a network given by fig. 4. Whenever a program has completed all its service intervals, the next randomly chosen program with random size, G, is generated and the portion, x, or the degree, n, of multiprogramming is altered, if programs had not been or had completely been loaded, respectively. Such changes can be interpreted as long run dynamics.

Steady-state CPU utilization of the (in time) complex network, fig. 4, is aggregated from the steady-state solutions for the subsystems weighted with the probabilities of appearance of these subsystems. Subsystems each are not time dependent but differ in the portion, x, or the degree, n, of partly or completely loaded programs, respectively. The whole system utilization is only approximately computable because it is not completely decomposable. The decomposition technique for our problem, which is a decomposition in time, has been developed independently of the work reported on in [1] and, by simulation, has proven to yield good results.

Now shortly we review the results for the policy MPM-n from [7]. From eq. (3.1, 3.2) we have the mean turn-around time, E_B, for n completely, (i.e. x = 1) and also for n not completely (x < 1) loaded programs assuming constant program size. In the case of a

random program size and a number, n, or more completely loaded programs, one fraction of the whole turn-around time, E_{Bw}, is computed
by the weighted composition of subsystems with exactly n programs,
the weighting factor being the probability p_n, (eq. 3.3). The other
fraction of E_{Bw} results from all subsystems with exactly n partly
loaded programs, each subsystem with another portion, x. The probability density function for a number, n, of programs being partly
loaded with exactly the portion, x, can be computed from eq. (3.5)
to be

$$p(x) = \gamma^n / \left\{ x^{n+1} [n-1]! \sum_{j=0}^{n-1} \gamma^j / j! \right\} \cdot \exp(-\gamma(1/x-1)); \quad (x \leq 1) \qquad (4.1)$$

The whole mean turn-around time of a program, E_{Bw}, is composed from

$$E_{Bw} = \sum_{m=n}^{\infty} p_m \, E_B(x=1) + \sum_{j=0}^{n-1} \gamma^j / j! \, \exp(-\gamma) \cdot \int_{x=0}^{1} p(x) . E_B(x<1) dx \qquad (4.2)$$

with $E_B(x=1)$ and $E_B(x<1)$ from eq.(3.1, 3.2) with x=1 and x < 1, respectively, and the multiplicative factor of the integral relating
to the probability of the event "n programs do not fit completely
in the main memory".

For reasons of discussion of this result, we use approximations for
the parachor curve, eq.(2.5), and the dependency of the mean I/O-
service time, E_T, per demand of partly loaded programs on the portion, x, and on the mean, E_{Tp}, (cf. eq. 2.6)

$$E_T = [e + (1-e) \, x^b] \, E_{Tp}$$

$$(4.3)$$

with e = 0.2, b=2

It has been found that the parameter values, e, b, have nearly no
influence on the decision which fixed number, n, for the MPM-n policy should be chosen to minimize the mean turn-around time. The main
influence comes from the parameter, a, in eq. (2.5).

From fig. 5 we learn that for small values, a = 2, there is a dependency of the optimum number, n, of the MPM-n policy on the memory
size. Programs with a good locality are represented by such a -
values [7]. For greater values, e.g. a = 5, the policy with n = 1

gains the greatest CPU utilization of all MPM-n policies independent of main memory size. These qualitative results are independent of the parameter, ρ.

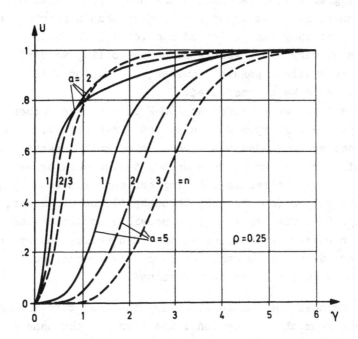

Fig. 5: CPU-utilization, U, over normalized memory
size, γ, for the MPM-n policy and two parameter values, a, eq. (2.5). The parameter ρ
is given from eq. (3.1).

Under the MPM-n policy with n > 1 sometimes the situation appears that n very large programs must be loaded into a memory of given size which results in a very small portion, x, for each. Then the resulting mean number m(x) of service intervals is very large. It could be argued that in such situations it would be better to temporarily lower the prescribed degree of multiprogramming, n, thereby reducing the number, m(x), substantially. This is the basic idea of the ACM-n policy.

5. Throughput under adaptive control of the multiprogramming degree

Instead of prescribing a fixed numer, n, of programs at least to be multiprogrammed, as is done by the MPM-n policy, we now interpret the number, n, as an upper limit. More than n programs are permitted only if they can be loaded completely. Theoretically the number, n, is arbitrary. For reasons of computability we decide to limit it to the smallest possible number, n = 2, for which an adaptive control could be demonstrated.

This means we consider an ACM-2 policy. The number, n, in the ACM-n policy corresponds to n in the MPM-n policy. In addition we introduce an estimated value, of a program's parachor, x_2, the portion of a program which corresponds to the working set size to be loaded to avoid thrashing. During our approximate computation of the CPU utilization (and thereby throughput) the parameter, x_2, is arbitrary. From the results it is possible to decide whether or not an ACM-n policy is superior to an MPM-n policy and by how much. Moreover, depending on the parachor curve parameter, a, the optimal parachor value, x_2, can be determined.

We now compose for the ACM-2 policy the mean turn-around time of programs from three fractions. The first is the same as for the MPM-n policy (cf.eq.4.2) and relates to a number, n, or more fully loaded programs. The second fraction comes from subsystems (in time) where exactly two programs, each with a portion $x_2 \leq x \leq 1$, are multiprogrammed. This fraction is closely related to the second term of the sum in eq. (4.2), the only difference being that the integral is only computed for values $x_2 \leq x \leq 1$. The third fraction is characterized by only one program being loaded completely or partly, because sometimes two programs together happen to be too large, so that they do not fit together with the prescribed portion, x_2, in the main memory. The related probability, P_1, is (cf.eq.(4.2) with n = 2))

$$P_1 = \sum_{j=0}^{1} \gamma^j/j!\exp(-\gamma) \cdot \int_{x=0}^{x_2} p(x)dx = (1+\frac{\gamma}{x_2}) \exp(-\gamma/x_2) \qquad (5.1)$$

The computation of the third fraction of the mean turn-around time, E_{Bw}, is separated into two parts. One of them results from the situation that exactly one program fits completely which appears with probability, P_1^*, the other part results from "one program fits only with a portion x, $(0 \leq x < 1)$, in the memory" which has the probability, P_0^*. We assume now that programs that are too large to be allocated together and therefore must be monoprogrammed, have the same size d.f. (eq. 2.1) as all other programs. From the appendix (eq. A7, A8) we have

$$P_1^* = \gamma \exp(-\gamma/x_2) \tag{5.2}$$

$$\text{and} \quad P_0^* = [1 + \gamma (1/x_2 - 1)] \exp(-\gamma/x_2) \tag{5.3}$$

The first term of the third fraction of E_{Bw} is computed from $P_1^* \cdot E_B(x=1)$, cf. eq. (4.2), the second term from

$$P_0^* \cdot \int_{x=0}^{1} p(x)\bigg|_{n=1} \cdot E_B(x < 1)\, dx$$

cf.eqs. (4.1, 4.2).
So we have the composed mean turn-around time, E_{Bw}, from

$$E_{Bw} = \sum_{k=2}^{\infty} p_k E_B(x=1) + (1+\gamma)\exp(-\gamma) \int_{x=x_2}^{1} p(x) E_B(x<1)\, dx + P_1^* E_B(x=1) +$$

$$P_0^* \int_{x=0}^{1} \gamma/x^2 \cdot \exp(-\gamma(1/x-1)) \cdot E_B(x<1)\, dx \tag{5.4}$$

To discuss our results we again insert our assumptions, eqs.(2.5, 4.3), and compute the mean turn-around time, E_{Bw}, and from that the throughput, D, which we normalize on E_{Cp} (cp.eq. 3.1). We do this for different assumed parachor curves represented by the parameter, a, and for distinct assumed parachor values, x_2. For two limiting values, $x_2 = 1$ and $x_2 = 0$, we obtain the same results as for the MPM-1 and MPM-2 policies, respectively. This is quite clear from the definition of the ACM-2 policy.

From fig. 6 it becomes evident that the ACM-2 policy is superior in respect to CPU utilization to both policies, MPM-1 ($x_2 = 1$), and MPM-2 ($x_2 = 0$), whenever the parachor value, x_2, is chosen appropriately. The utilization gain for small memories, $0.4 \leq \gamma \leq 2$, is sometimes 10 % and more.

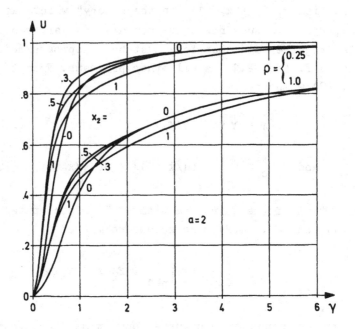

Fig. 6: CPU-utilization, U, over normalized
memory size, for the ACM-2 policy and
two parameter values, $\rho = 0.25,1$. The
assumed parachor values are chosen to
be $x_2 = 0.3, 0.5$. $a = 2$.

Remember that the CPU utilization of the ACM-2 policy does not depend critically on the estimate of the parachor, x_2. A wrong estimate,
for example, does not result in thrashing. Our results correspond
in some sense to the work, published in [3], where also the degree
of multiprogramming, n, may change dynamically, but we have used an
analytic model while simulation methods are used in [5].

From the graph, fig. 5, we obtain for an assumed parachor curve,
described by a value, a = 5, that under the MPM-n policy it would
be optimum to allocate only one program to main memory whenever more
than one program does not fit completely into it. Under the ACM-2
policy it results from eq. (5.4) that for a value, a = 5, it is also
superior to the best MPM-n policy, namely the MPM-1 policy. Our
findings establish the adaptive control of the degree of multiprogramming being much better than a fixed degree of multiprogramming
for partly loaded programs whenever the parachor value could be
estimated approximately in advance. The well-known rule of thumb

is verified that multiprogramming is only advantageous if the programs each have their parachor loaded into the main memory.

From the graphs, fig. 5,6, we find that for large memory sizes, ($\gamma > 1.4$), the MPM-3 policy is advantageous over the ACM-2 policy, independent of the parameter value, x_2. This indicates that an ACM-n policy, with $n > 2$, would be better than the ACM-2 policy. Analytical computations to verify this suspicion have not been carried out.

One important advantage of the ACM-n policy is that its CPU utilization is never less than the smallest possible utilization, under any MPM-n policy. A second advantage results from the chance to reach a substantially better CPU utilization by an appropriately chosen parachor value, x_2, for the ACM-n policy than under any MPM-n policy. Further work on this subject may be successful for the general ACM-n policy with different assumed parachor values, x_n, for the dynamic change of the degree of multiprogramming from n to n-1 programs.

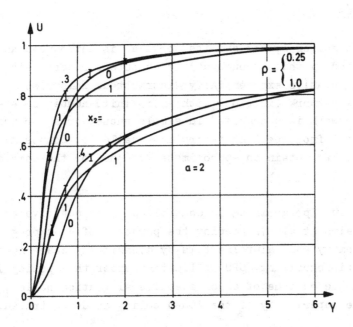

Fig. 7: Computational and simulation results for the CPU-utilization. The marks are the confidence intervals for a 95%-level of confidence. Parameters of the model are as given by fig. 6.

A simulation study made has had two objectives: firstly to verify
our computational results and secondly to test whether or not the
optimal value x_2, could be determined by experiments. From the graph,
fig. 7, we learn that the CPU utilization of our simulation model
is in-satisfactory agreement with the computed results. The
optimal parachor values, $x_2 = 0.3, 0.4$ for parameters $\rho = 0.25, 1$,
respectively, for which the marks are defined were automatically
found by our simulation model. The automatism was obtained by rerunning the same workload, characterized by the parameter, a, on
the same system, characterized by the parameters, ρ, γ, changing for
each run the assumed parachor value, x_2, as, long as a nearly maximum CPU utilization was reached. From the graph, fig. 6, we know
that the utilization depends uncritically on the chosen value, x_2,
as long as it is near the optimum value of x_2. This was also confirmed by the simulation results. From eq. (5.4) it could be shown
that the optimum value, x_2, depends on the memory size but this dependency is non-essential and can be neglected in most applications.

6. Conclusions

A model of a computer system and its workload is introduced and CPU
utilization (and by this throughput) is computed. Program size is
assumed to be negative exponentially distributed. This results in
a very complex network (in time) with an infinite number of states.
The complex network is decomposed in simple subnetworks for which
closed solutions from queueing theory are available. Composing
these solutions we obtain an approximate outcome for the complex
network.

The degree of multiprogramming is controlled by an adaptive policy,
ACM-n, which aims at always keeping the parachor of each program
in the main memory and maintains this by dynamically changing the
degree of multiprogramming. CPU utilization under this policy is
compared with the outcome of a non adaptive allocation policy,
MPM-n, and the superiority of the ACM-n policy is demonstrated.

Acknowledgments

The author is indebted to Prof. Dr. J. Swoboda for valuable dis-
cussionsand the computations added as an appendix.

References

[1]   P.J. Courtois, Decomposability, instabilities and saturation in multiprogramming systems, Comm. ACM, Vol. 18, No. 7 (1975) pp. 371-77.

[2]   P.J. Denning, G.S. Graham, Multiprogrammed memory management, Proc. IEEE, Vol. 63, No. 6, June 1975, pp. 924-39.

[3]   C.J. Kuehner, B. Randell, Demand paging in perspective, Am. Fed. Inform. Proc. FJCC, 1968, pp. 1011-1018.

[4]   R.R. Muntz, Analytic models for computer systems analysis, Lecture Notes Comp. Science, 8, 1974, Springer Berlin/ Heidelberg/New York, pp. 246-65.

[5]   H. Opderbeck, W.W. Chu, Performance of the page fault frequency replacement algorithm in a multiprogramming, environment, IFIP congress 1974, Stockholm, Inf.Process. 74, North Holland Publishing Company (1974), pp. 235-41.

[6]   B. Walke, Queueing networks with degenerate exponential servers, Wiss. Ber. AEG-TELEFUNKEN 48, 1975, H.4, S.153-57.

[7]   B. Walke, Durchsatzberechnung für Rechenanlagen bei wählbarer Aufteilung des Arbeitsspeichers unter mehrere Programme unterschiedlichen Platzbedarfs, PhD-Thesis, University of Stuttgart, 1975 (in German).

Appendix

Assume the random variables, $G1$, $G1'$, having the p.d.f. given by eq. (2.1). We are interested in the p.d.f. of $G1$ conditioned on the sum, $(G1+G1')$, being greater than a given value $g2$. The abbreviations $G1+G1'=G2$, $B = \{G1 > g1\}$, $F = \{G2 > g2\}$ are introduced with $G1$, $G2$, being independent variables. Then for $g1 = s$ and $g2 = s/x_2$ the p.d.f. $P(B|F)$ means that one program out of two randomly chosen programs fits not completely in the main memory, conditioned on the event "two programs together do not fit each with the portion, x_2, $(0 \leq x_2 \leq 1)$" (i.e. $x_2 \cdot G2 > s$ and $G1 > s$). From eq. (2.1) we have

$$P(B) = \exp(-g1/E_G) \qquad (A1)$$

The p.d.f., $P(F)$, can be computed from the density eq. (4.1) inserting parameter values, $n = 2$, $s = 0$, by integration $\int_0^1 p(x)dx$ to be an Erlang -2-d.f.

$$P(F) = (1+g2/E_G) \exp(-g2/E_G) \qquad (A2)$$

The probability, $P(F|B)$, is computable and from this the computation of the probability, $P(B|F)$, is possible using the well-known relationship

$$P(B \cap F) = P(B|F) \cdot P(F) = P(F|B) \cdot P(B) \qquad (A3)$$

The condition, B, means that a program of size, G1, has a minimum size, g1, but if it is larger than g1 then the variable G1 is negative exponentially distributed with mean E_G. The other program with the size G1' follows the d.f., eq. (2.1). From these considerations we derive

$$P(F|B) = P(\{g1+G2\} > g2) = P(G2 > \{g2-g1\}) \qquad (A4)$$

without a condition in the expression on the right hand side.

Eq. (A4) is related to eq. (A2) in that it also is an Erlang -2-d.f.

$$P(F|B) = \begin{cases} (1 + \dfrac{g2-g1}{E_G}) \cdot \exp\left(-\dfrac{g2-g1}{E_G}\right) & \text{for } g2 \geq g1 \qquad (A5) \\ 1 & \text{otherwise} \end{cases}$$

We are only interested in the solution for $g2 \geq g1$. From eqs. (A1, A2, A3) we then have, with $g2 = s/x_2$ and $g1 = s$,

$$P(B|F) = \frac{1 + \gamma(1/x_2 - 1)}{1 + \gamma} \qquad (A6)$$

To compute the unconditional probability, P_0^*, i.e.

$$P_0^* = P(\{G1 > s\} \cap \{G2 > s/x_2\})$$

we use the relationship of eq. (A3)

$$P_0^* = P(B \cap F) = P(B|F) \cdot P(F) = [1 + \gamma(1/x_2 - 1)] \cdot \exp(-\gamma/x_2) \qquad (A7)$$

From the complementary probability, $1-P(B|F)$, we have the probability, P_1^*, for monoprogramming with a completly loaded program

$$P_1^* = [1-P(B|F)] \cdot P(F) = \gamma \exp(-\gamma/x_2) \qquad (A8).$$

INTEGRITY, CONCURRENCY, AND RECOVERY
IN DATABASES

Rudolf Bayer[*]
Institut für Informatik
Technische Universität München
8 München 2, Germany

1. INTEGRITY

In this paper we will discuss some aspects of obtaining correctness of
databases. Several conditions must be met to achieve correctness:

1) proper operation of the hardware,

2) proper construction of the software,

3) proper use of the system.

1) will be of interest only to the extent that the recovery scheme described in
section 10 can also be used to recover from hardware failures, see also [Wil 72].
This paper deals mainly with 2). 3) is concerned with techniques to prevent
mischievous or accidental misuse of a computer system, i.e., with its security.
This will not be discussed here.

Correctness is of particular concern in database systems for several reasons:

1) Longevity: Even rare errors will in the long run lead to contamination and
    degradation of a database. Purging erroneous data and their consequences from
    a database is difficult.

2) Limited repeatability: Even if errors are discovered, it may be impossible or
    useless to rectify them due to time constraints, unavailability of the correct
    source data, unavailability of a correct system state preceding the fault.

3) The need for immediate and permanent availability: This prevents a practice
    often used elsewhere, namely running a program and checking the results
    repeatedly until correctness is obtained.

4) Multiaccess: Databases are manipulated by many users with different quality
    standards. It is infeasible to completely entrust the quality control to these
    users and difficult to track the source and the proliferation of errors.

[*]During the Academic Year 1975/76 visiting at IBM Research Laboratory, San Jose, CA
95193, USA

It seems hopeless to give a precise and complete description of what we mean intuitively by a "correct database." Still from our knowledge about the meaning of the data, a set of necessary (but not sufficient) conditions can be derived which must be satisfied by a correct database. We call much conditions integrity-constraints and we say that a database is in a state of integrity, if all integrity-countraints are satisfied.

Integrity might be enforced by allowing on certain data only a limited set of precisely specified meaningful, and therefore integrity preserving operations [Bay 74], [LiZ 74] by adopting a set of strict programming and interaction conventions, by dynamically checking the results of updates, or by proving for each program manipulating the database, that the integrity-constraints will be satisfied. Much work still needs to be done on how to describe, to enforce, and to implement such integrity-constraints.

2. TRANSACTIONS AND CONSISTENCY

In multiaccess database systems certain activities of users must, for several reasons, be considered as atomic operaTions, called transactions [CBT 74]. Thus, performing a set of transations $\{t_1, t_2, \ldots, t_n\}$ on a database must have the same effect as performing some sequence (precisely which is irrelevant) $(t_{i_1}, t_{i_2}, \ldots, t_{i_n})$ of transactions where $(i_1, i_2, \ldots, i_n)$ is some permutation of $(1, 2, \ldots, n)$.

The execution of a transaction requires in reality a sequence of actions. We write $t_j = (a_{j_1}, a_{j_2}, \ldots, a_{j_k})$ for a transaction t_j composed of the actions $a_{j_1}, a_{j_2}, \ldots, a_{j_k}$. Performing transactions serially may be too costly (because of too low a utilization of hardware resources) or too slow (since other transactions must wait for people to react). Therefore transactions should run concurrently, subject to the constraint, that concurrency produces the same net effect on the database as some serial execution.

We call this last constraint consistency [EGLT 74]. It can be considered as a special integrity constraint establishing the conditions under which transactions can run concurrently. To achieve consistency, one could run transactions serially after all, or one might prove that running two transactions, t_1, t_2, concurrently is consistent.

More formally, we write $\{t_1, t_2\}$ for parallel execution, (t_1, t_2) for serial execution of t_1 followed by t_2, and $\equiv$ for equivalence of two executions in the sense of yielding the same result for the database. Showing that $\{t_1, t_2\}$ is consistent amounts to establishing the truth of

$$\{t_1, t_2\} \equiv (t_1, t_2) \vee \{t_1, t_2\} \equiv (t_2, t_1). \tag{1}$$

The generalization of (1) to an arbitrary set of transactions is obvious.

A third technique is generally followed in database systems to guarantee consistency. Before a transaction is allowed to execute, it must acquire all the resources it might possibly need. Here resources are the data objects in the database. Resources are acquired by locking them in the proper mode. We will see later that more complicated lock-modes than the read-locks and write-locks (or shared and exclusive locks) commonly found in operating systems are needed for database locking.

Most work to date concerned with integrity has been limited to consistency, i.e., to those integrity problems arising from the activity of the operating system:
1) the effort to schedule transactions to be processed in parallel as far as possible [EGLT 74], [Eve 74], [KiC 73], [CBT 74],
2) the need to acquire resources, in particular sets of data objects or individual data objects (also called "records" in [CBT 74] and "entities" in [EGLT 74]), for exclusive or shared use by a transaction and to lock those resources accordingly,
3) the induced problems of deadlock among locking transactions, of deadlock discovery, of deadlock prevention, and of preemption of resources from transactions to resolve deadlocks.

Locking techniques and the associated problems have been investigated extensively for operating systems. These techniques are of limited applicability in database locking and require considerable modifications to become useful here.

3. LOCKING IN OPERATING SYSTEMS

We will briefly survey locking techniques developed for operating systems and indicate, why they are not satisfactory for database applications. As usual in this field we use "process" as the analogon for "transaction." The list of techniques is adopted from [Eve 74] and [CES 71]. Our main interest is in the treatment of the deadlock problem.

Presequence Processes: Processes potentially competing for resources must be presequenced and must execute one after the other. For database transactions it is often not known a priori, which data resources will be needed. This means that any two transactions will be potentially competing and must be sequenced. Therefore, no parallelism is possible. Still presequencing transactions, e.g., through time-stamping, may be useful for other purposes, like preventing indefinite delay of transactions.

Preempt Processes: This technique relies on discovering deadlocks after they have occurred. It then terminates (or backs up to an earlier state) one of the processes involved in the deadlock, the resources locked by that process are freed. As we shall see, this technique plays an important role in database locking, too, but its application is difficult due to the large number of transactions and resources involved. Deadlock discovery, preemption of resources, and transaction backup to recover a state of integrity of the database become complicated and expensive. Suitable algorithms to solve these problems are challenging.

Preorder all System Resources: The processes are required to claim their resources according to a total order defined on the set of all resources. In databases the resources are data objects, which often do not have such a natural order.

Furthermore a process might not be able to claim resources according to such an order, since his needed resources might be data dependent [EGLT 74], [CBT 74].

Preclaim needed Resources: Before starting to execute, a process must claim all the resources it will ever need. Typically they are specified on the control cards preceding a job or job-step, and the process is not started until the operating system has granted to it all the requested resources.

In databases this technique requires considerable modifications to become feasible. Claiming resources may itself be a complicated and lengthy task requiring searching through large areas of a database. These searches themselves should run concurrently if possible.

Deadlock Prevention Algorithms: They often rely on too special properties of resources - like Habermann's banker's algorithm [Hab 69] - or on too special models of computation - like Schroff's algorithm [Sch 74] - to be generally applicable here.

4. A PROPOSAL FOR DATABASE LOCKING

In [CBT 74] a technique is proposed to provide consistency for database locking. The technique can be considered as a modification and combination of several methods described in section 3. Since transactions are to be considered atomic, integrity of the database must be guaranteed at the beginning and again at the end of a transaction, it may be - and generally must be violated by the single actions. Due to the potential interference of two or more transactions executing in parallel, transactions must lock certain parts of the database for exclusive or shared use. The scheme proposed in [CBT 74] therefore requires each transaction to lock all its resources (parts of a database, e.g., individual records or fields of records) during a so-called "seize phase" before starting the "execution phase." During the seize phase the database must not be modified by the seizing transaction. For such a transaction preemption of locked resources and backup to wait for the preempted resource are easy.

Once a transaction has started its execution phase, it is not allowed to claim more resources, thus no backup will be necessary due to deadlock. At the end of an execution phase a transaction must free all its resources before starting a new seize phase.

The seize phase may be a rather complicated task and seize phases of transactions should be run in parallel. This raises the deadlock problem again as usual: Let t_1, t_2 be two transactions. t_2 trying to seize resource r_1 already locked by t_1 must wait until r_1 is freed by t_1. But since resources are not locked in any particular order, t_1 may wish to lock first r_1, then r_2. If t_1 successfully seizes r_1 and t_2 successfully seizes r_2, then a deadlock has occurred. Such deadlocks must be discovered and a resource must be preempted from a transaction involved in the deadlock, say r_2 from t_2, causing t_2 to wait for t_1 on r_2.

In [CBT 74] an aging mechanism is attached to transactions to avoid indefinite delay. It is then shown in [CBT 74] that in the scheme described each transaction will eventually be processed. This requires, of course, suitable algorithms for discovery of deadlocks between transactions in their seize phases, for preemption of resources, and for backing up transactions to certain points within their seize phases.

It is now clear, that the scheme proposed in [CBT 74] is a shrewd modification and combination of the following:

1) Try to preclaim needed resources.

2) If 1) would lead to deadlock, preempt resources.

3) Superimpose a presequencing scheme for transactions - e.g., through timestamping - to enforce an aging mechanism and to avoid deadlock due to indefinite delay of transactions.

5. ON-LINE TRANSITIVE CLOSURE ALGORITHMS FOR DEADLOCK DISCOVERY

The deadlock discovery algorithm [KiC 73] mentioned as useful in [CBT 74] is not really applicable, since it requires that a transaction t may wait for at most one other transaction. In general, however, t may be waiting for several transactions.

To clarify this, let us assume that a lock request for a resource r is a pair (t,μ) where t is a transaction and μ is a lock mode, meaning that t requests a lock of mode μ. Associated with each resource r there is a FIFO waiting queue $Q(r)$ of lock requests and a set $G(r)$ of granted lock requests, also called the granted group [GLP 75]. The next request in $Q(r)$ can be granted if the mode of the request is compatible with the modes of all requests in $G(r)$.

To grant the request (t,μ) perform:

$G(r) := G(r) \quad \cup \setminus \{(t,\mu)\};$

$Q(r) := Q(r)$ remove $\{(t,\mu)\}$

We also say that t now has a μ-lock on r.

To release the granted request (t,μ) perform:

$G(r) := G(r) \setminus \{(t,\mu)\}$

To issue a request (t,μ) for r perform:

$Q(r) := Q(r)$ append $\{(t,\mu)\}$

When t_i issues a request (t_i,μ) for r, t_i will enter a wait state until the request is granted. Thus, t_i will be waiting in at most one queue for a resource r. Before the request (t_i,μ) can be granted all transactions with lock-request-modes incompatible with μ which are in $G(r)$ or ahead of t_i in $Q(r)$ must finish their execution phase and release their locks. We denote this set by $B_i = \{t_{i_1}, t_{i_2}, \ldots, t_{i_{k_i}}\}$ and say that t_i is (directly) waiting for t_j if $t_j \in B_i$. Therefore, any transaction t_k, for which $B_k \neq \phi$ is in a wait state. We may then formally define the wait relation $w \subseteq T \times T$ where T is the set of transactions, such that $(t_i, t_j) \in w$ iff $t_j \in B_i$.

The wait graph G_w is the directed graph

$$G_w = (T, w).$$

Deadlock discovery amounts to finding cycles in G_w or, equivalently, to finding pairs (t, t) in the transitive (but not reflexive) closure w^+ of w. Thus deadlock exists iff $t \in T : (t,t) \varepsilon w^+$.

Maintaining w is trivial. Calculating w^+ from w is, on the other hand, quite expensive, the best known algorithms requiring $O(n^3)$ [War 62] or $O(n \cdot m)$ [Bay 74] [Pur 70] steps, where n is the number of nodes in G_w and m the number of arcs, i.e., $n = |T|$, $m = |w|$. It would be sufficient, however, to have a good "on-line" transitive closure algorithm since w^+ need only be partly modified as arcs are added to and deleted from w.

More precisely, "on-line" transitive closure algorithm means an algorithm solving the following problem:

$$\text{Given } w, w^+, \qquad \text{calculate}$$
$$w', w'^+ \qquad \text{where}$$
$$w' = w \cup \{(t_i, t_j)\} \qquad \text{or}$$
$$w' = w \setminus \{(t_i, t_j)\}.$$

Although it is simple to add an arbitrary arc and calculate w'^+ from w^+, it seems in the general case notoriously difficult to delete an arbitrary arc and to calculate w'^+ from w^+. No better alternative seems to be known than calculating w'^+ from scratch, i.e., starting with w' and ignoring the fact that we already have w^+.

Fortunately, we have a very special case yielding a simple on-line transitive closure algorithm. Since we remove deadlocks immediately the wait graph G_w is acyclic. Therefore, we can represent w^+ as an integer matrix M with the interpretation: $M[t,u] :=$ number of different paths in G_w from t to u. Then tw^+u iff $M[t,u] > 0$.

To insert or delete an arc from t to u in G_w update M as follows:

$$M[s,v] := M[s,v] \pm M[s,t].\ M[u,v]\ ;\ s \neq t;\ u \neq v$$
$$M[s,u] := M[s,u] \pm M[s,t]\ \qquad ;\ s \neq t$$
$$M[t,v] := M[t,v] \pm M[u,v]\ \qquad ;\ u \neq v$$
$$M[t,u] := M[t,u] \pm 1$$

It is clear that the worst case complexity of this on-line update of w^+ for inserting or deleting a single arc in G_w is $O(n^2)$. This algorithm can easily be modified to have an average complexity of $O((\frac{|w^+|}{n})^2)$.

To discover deadlock, tentatively update M when inserting an arc. Then check the diagonal of M for the existence of a t such that $M[t,t] > 0$. If such a t exists, the insertion of the arc caused a deadlock. The action to be taken to break the deadlock is described in section 6. The tentative update of M is cancelled. If a deadlock does not exist make the tentative update of M definite.

Another highly special case arises when w^+ and therefore M must be updated at the end of a transaction t when t releases all its locks. Since t was executing, it was not waiting for other resources, and therefore it is a sink of G_w. t and all arcs leading into t can be removed from G_w. w^+ is now simply updated by removing a row and a column from M if necessary, a very simple operation. A similarly simple update of M is performed when granting a lock request to t. For further details on on-line transitive closure algorithms see also [Bay 75].

6. BREAKING A DEADLOCK

Assume that adding t to the end of $Q(r)$ and updating w and w^+ accordingly would cause a deadlock. Then one of the following actions can be taken to break the deadlock.

6.1: <u>Move t forward in Q(r)</u>: Since t issued a lock-request before causing the deadlock, t was not waiting. Therefore moving t forward in Q(r) reduces the number of transactions t is waiting for, hereby the deadlock may be broken. The deadlock will definitely be broken, if t can be added to the granted group G(r). Note that this strategy overrides the FIFO rule for servicing lock-requests for the purpose of breaking deadlocks only. Note also that the available w^+ can be used to find out very easily, how far t should be moved forward in Q(r) in order to break the deadlock.

6.2: <u>Backup t</u>: Note that all cycles in G_w after tentatively appending t to Q(r) and updating w^+ pass through t. Thus backing up t towards the beginning of its seize phase, taking away resources previously granted to t in the opposite order, in which they were granted, will eventually break all cycles in G_w.

6.3: <u>Minimal-cost node cut set</u>: Find a cheapest node cut set breaking all cycles in G_w and back up all transactions in this cut set to the beginning of their seize phases, thus taking away all their resources. This technique may be attractive, if the cost of backing up and rerunning the seize phase of a transaction is available and is very high.

7. <u>PREVENTING INDEFINITE DELAY</u>

The methods just described can cope with the deadlock problem, but they do not guarantee that a transaction t will eventually reach its execution phase and complete. t might be prevented from execution by being backed up again and again.

The relation w^+ can be used advantageously to cope with indefinite delay. Let us assume that all transactions in the system are time-sttamped. We can then use w^+ to partition the set T into priority classes $P_1, P_2, \ldots, P_k$ for some integer k. Let $\bar{t}_1$ be the oldest transaction in T, the set of transactions in the system. Define the highest priority class P_1 as follows: $P_1 := \{\bar{t}_1\} \cup \{t : \bar{t}_1 \, w^+ \, t\}$. In general, define the classes, $P_1, P_2, \ldots, P_k$ by:

$$U_o := \phi$$
$$\bar{t}_i := \text{oldest transaction in } T \setminus U_{i-1}$$
$$P_i := \{\bar{t}_i\} \cup \{t : \bar{t}_i \; w^+ \; t\} \setminus U_{i-1}$$
$$U_i := U_{i-1} \cup P_i$$
$$\text{for } i = 1,2,\ldots,k \text{ where } U_k = T$$

We now propose four increasingly effective, but also increasingly radical strategies for preventing indefinite delay. It seems quite feasible to employ several strategies within one system successively in order to force transactions which have passed a certain age threshold into their execution phase and out of the system.

Strategy 1: Use the priority classes for scheduling, starting with the highest priority class P_1. This strategy will tend to move older transactions through the system faster.

Strategy 2: Stop all transactions in seize phases, except those in P_1.

Strategy 3: Let $\bar{t}_1$ preempt r from $t \in P_1$ if $\bar{t}_1$ is directly waiting for t unless t is executing, i.e., move $\bar{t}_1$ ahead of t in $Q(r)$ or replace t in $G(r)$ by $\bar{t}_1$.

Strategy 4: Stop all t which are not in their execution phases, apply strategy 3.

Strategy 5: When breaking a deadlock do not allow t to pass $\bar{t}_1$ in 6.1, do not backup $\bar{t}_1$ in 6.2 or 6.3, but backup some cutset of transactions (not necessarily the cheapest) not containing $\bar{t}_1$.

It is clear that all five strategies will tend to bring $\bar{t}_1$ closer to its execution phase. Strategies 1 and 3 might still allow indefinite delay in very special circumstances, but it is easy to construct plausibility arguments that strategies 2, 4, and 5 do prevent indefinite delay.

8. PHANTOMS AND PREDICATE LOCKING

In [EGLT 74] a technique is described to use predicate locks ("predicate locking") for locking logical, i.e., existing as well as potential subsets of a data base instead of locking individual data objects ("individual object locking"). This technique also solves the "phantom problem." To explain briefly, what phantoms are, let us assume that there is a universe $\mathcal{D}$ of data objects (called "entities" in [EGLT 74] and "records" in [CBT 74] which are the potential data objects in the data base B. Thus $B \subseteq \mathcal{D}$. Two transactions t_1, t_2 may have successfully locked all their needed resources, and they may be executing. t_1 may add a new object $r_1 \in \mathcal{D}$ to B and t_2 may add a new object $r_2 \in \mathcal{D}$ to B, such that t_1 would have locked r_2 and t_2 would have locked r_1, if t_1 or t_2 would have seen r_2 or r_1 resp. during their seize phases. r_1 and r_2 are called "phantoms," since they might, but not necessarily will appear in B (materialize) while t_1 or t_2 are in their execution phases. It is clear that individual object locking as described so far does not solve the phantom problem.

The appearance of a single phantom, say r_1, does not cause any difficulty. The parallel schedule $\{t_1, t_2\}$ has the same effect as running the transactions t_1, t_2 serially, namely in the order t_2 followed by t_1, therefore, $\{t_1, t_2\}$ is consistent. It is the goal of predicate locking to schedule transactions in parallel as far as possible under the restriction, that consistency is preserved.

To enforce consistent schedules each transaction t is required to lock (for read or write access) all data objects $E(t) \subseteq \mathcal{D}$ - irrespective of whether they are in B or are just phantoms - which might in any way influence or be influenced by the effect of t on B. $E(t)$ shall be locked by specifying a predicate P defined on $\mathcal{D}$ (or on a part of $\mathcal{D}$, e.g., on a relation [Cod 70]) such that $E(t) \subseteq S(P)$ where $S(P)$ is the subset of elements of $\mathcal{D}$ satisfying P.

Two transactions t_1, t_2 are then said to be in conflict, if for their predicates P_1, P_2 it is true that $\exists r \in S(P_1) \cap S(P_2)$ and t_1 or t_2 performs a write action on r. Thus conflict can arise even if r is a phantom. In this case t_1, t_2 must be run serially. The order in which they are run is irrelevant for consistency. This order might be important for other reasons which are not of interest here. The main difficulties in using such a locking and scheduling method are the following:

1) Find a suitable predicate P_t for t. Ideally $E(t) = S(P_t)$ should hold, but then P_t might be too complicated. If P_t is chosen in a very simple way, then $S(P_t)$ might be intolerably large, increasing the danger of phantoms, which are really artificial phantoms.

2) The problem "$S(P_1) \cap S(P_2) = \phi$" may be very hard. For first order predicates this problem is undecidable. Thus for practical applications and a given $\mathcal{D}$ it is necessary to find a suitable class of locking predicates, for which the problem "$S(P_1) \cap S(P_2) \neq \phi$" is not only decidable, but for which a very efficient decision procedure is known. For more details and a candidate class for suitable locking predicates see [EGLT 74].

Phantoms might turn out to be a very serious but mostly artificial obstacle to parallel processing in the following sense: phantoms in $S(P_1) \cap S(P_2)$ prohibit t_1 and t_2 from being run in parallel. But if these phantoms do not materialize, and if furthermore $S(P_1) \cap S(P_2) \cap B = \phi$, then, of course, t_1 and t_2 could have been run in parallel. How much of an artificial obstacle phantoms are to parallel processing seems to be unknown and can probably be answered only for concrete instances of databases.

9. LOCK MODES AND PROTOCOLS FOR A PARTITIONED DATABASE

Let us start with an important observation which will lead to the simple strategy 1 for handling phantoms: "Transactions, which are readers, do not need to lock phantoms." A transaction is a _reader_, if it does not contain any write actions, it is a _writer_ otherwise. Obviously for many database applications the readers are a very important class of transactions.

To understand our observation, consider two readers t_1, t_2 first. Since there are no write actions, there is no possibility for phantoms to materialize, and they need not be locked. Now let t_3 be a writer. Consider the interaction between t_1

and t_3. Assume there is a phantom $r \varepsilon S(P_1) \cap S(P_3)$ such that t_3 might perform a write on r. Then t_1 and t_3 could not run concurrently, if t_1 would use predicate locking. If, however, t_1 uses individual object locking and successfully terminates its seize phase, then t_1 can run in parallel with t_3 provided that

$$\widehat{S(P_1)} \cap S(P_3) = \phi$$

where $\widehat{S(P_1)} = S(P_1) \cap B$, i.e., the set of real data objects (without phantoms) in B which t_1 needs to lock in order to see a consistent view of B. But now $\widehat{S(P_1)}$ can be locked by t_1 using conventional "individual object locking" as, e.g., described in [CBT 74] instead of predicate locking. If t_3 should materialize phantoms, then obviously $\{t_1, t_3\} \equiv (t_1, t_3)$.

The following observation should also be clear now: To control the interaction between the writer t_3 and the reader t_1 if suffices, that t_3 use individual object locking according to [CBT 74]. t_3 need not lock its phantoms except as they are materializing since t_1 is not interested in phantoms anyway. We can conclude that the problem of phantoms - and therefore of predicate locking - arises only between writers. The preceding observations suggest several alternative approaches for handling the phantom problem:

Strategy 1: Serialize Writers:

Since, as we just observed, phantoms cause difficulties only between writers, the simplest solution is, not to schedule any writers to run concurrently. Concurrency is possible between arbitrarily many readers and at most one writer. Consistency is guaranteed by individual object locking and by handling deadlocks and preemptions as described in the earlier part of this paper. The problem of phantoms does not arise.

As mentioned before, in many applications most transactions are readers. Serializing writers in those cases should not cause a significant loss of concurrency and has the advantage that predicate locking with its associated difficulties is not needed. Several more involved strategies are described in [Bay 75].

Strategy 2: Partition Database:

The following approach can be thought of as a highly specialized and simplified predicate locking technique, although predicates are no longer used explicitely. The technique allows a high degree of concurrency between transactions, and avoids the phantom problem, if all transactions use the proper locking protocols. A similar technique is described in [GLP 75], [GLPT 75] and has been implemented in System R, an experimental relational database system [ABC 76]. For explanatory purposes we first describe a simplified case, a sketch of the general case should then be easy to understand.

Assume that our database B is partitioned into a finite number of blocks $B_1, B_2, \ldots, B_k$. Each object of B belongs to a unique block. When inserting, deleting or modifying an object in B, we assume that the block or blocks affected by such an update are known. Partitioning of databases, e.g., into files or relations, is a widely used technique. In terms of predicate locking, the sets $B_1, B_2, \ldots, B_k$ can be thought of as:

$$B_1 = B \cap S(P_1)$$
$$B_2 = B \cap S(P_2)$$
$$\vdots$$
$$B_k = B \cap S(P_k)$$

for a fixed set of predicates $P_1, P_2, \ldots, P_k$ having the special property that for all possible database contents B and blocks B_i, B_j, $i \neq j$ it is true that

$$B_i \cap B_j = (B \cap S(P_i)) \cap (B \cap S(P_j)) = B \cap S(P_i) \cap S(P_j) = \phi.$$

Now assume that we can lock the blocks $B_1, \ldots, B_k$ and also individual objects of B in various lock modes as we shall see suitable shortly.

Partition Locking: Obviously a transaction t could then guard itself against phantoms which might materialize in B_i by simply locking B_i in exclusive mode X. It suffices, however, that t lock B_i in a mode preventing other updaters from modifying B_i in any way while still allowing objects of B_i to be read by t and by other transactions. A shared lockmode S allowing read access to all objects in a partition block serves that purpose as long as locks used for update purposes on B_i are not compatible with this lock.

In addition to allowing X- and S-locks on blocks, we also introduce an analysis-lock, called an A-lock. This A-lock can be used by a transaction t while analyzing a block with the intent to update it. Also a new version of the block can already be prepared while still maintaining the old version available for read access to other transactions.

During this analysis phase no phantoms may be created by t or other transactions. Thus read accesses, but no update accesses by other transactions are allowed. Furthermore, no analysis accesses by other transactions can be allowed since the intended update of B_i by t would invalidate such analyses.

To finally perform the update, or to finalize (commit) an already prepared update for B_i, first convert the A-lock into an X-lock. Thus the update cannot be committed, until all S-locks which might coexist with the A-lock on a block have been released. From the intended use of the locks it is now clear that the compatibility matrix for the three lock-modes S,A,X should be defined as follows:

	S	A	X	
S	+	+	-	+ means compatible
A	+	-	-	- means incompatible
X	-	-	-	

Fig. 1: Compatibility Matrix for Lock Modes S,A,X.

Data Object Locking: Locking at such a coarse level as the partition blocks may cause an inacceptable decrease of concurrency since much larger parts of the database than really necessary might have to be locked. Although it requires more overhead in setting locks it is, therefore, desirable to be able to lock at a finer level, namely individual data objects, in order to increase potential concurrency of transactions. This is expecially true for transactions, e.g., readers as we saw before, which are not concerned about phantoms and which can run consistently, as long as they are able to lock all objects in the database, in which they are interested, in the proper mode.

In addition to readers there are many writers which have additional knowledge about the semantics of the database and need not be concerned with guarding themselves against phantoms in order to obtain consistency. Therefore, they do not need to lock out other transactions at the block level.

In order to make partition locking still work it must be known what sort of object locking is going on within a block. This can be achieved by leaving certain traces at the block level [Ram 74] or equivalently by introducing additional lock modes at the block level [GLP 75], [GLPT 75]. These lock-modes are:

IS: (intention share) to indicate that a transaction intends to set S-locks on objects within the block locked with IS.
IX: (intention exclusive) to indicate the intention for setting S-locks or X-locks.
SIX: (shared, intention exclusive) to guard against phantoms within the block and thereby getting (without further object locking) read access to all objects in

the block, and to indicate the intention to set X-locks on objects in the block locked with SIX.

Note: It is not necessary to set S-locks on objects in a block already SIX-locked. Also there is no need for an SIS-lock (with the obvious meaning) since SIX would imply read access to all elements within the block already without setting further object locks. Thus, using S instead of SIS serves the same purpose.

These considerations then lead to the following system of locks which is similar to the one arrived at in [GLP 75] with a somewhat different motivation than the one given here. This lock system with appropriate protocols serves to solve the phantom problem, allows locking at the proper granularity – to allow a trade-off between overhead work for setting locks and the degree of concurrency achievable – and still allows highly concurrent access to a partitioned database using a relatively simple locking protocol.

Locks for Objects: The objects in a block can be locked in one of the following modes:

a) S-mode for concurrent read access

b) X-mode for exclusive access for read or write purposes.

c) although the A-mode could be allowed, it seems hardly worthwhile and is omitted here.

Locks for Partition Blocks: The partition blocks can be locked in any of the modes S,A,X,IS,IX,SIX. Locking at the block level really serves two rather different purposes:

1) to guard against phantoms

2) to avoid the overhead of setting many locks on objects, thereby potentially accepting a decrease in concurrency.

To perform the actual update of a block after an analysis, t can follow two courses:

1)   Convert A to X as described before, then update.

2)   Convert A to SIX and individually X-lock those objects in the block which

      must be updated.

We can now expand the compatibility matrix of Fig. 1 by adding the lock modes

IS, IX, and SIX. From the meaning of those modes described before it should be

clear that IS must be incompatible with X only, but can be compatible with S, A,

IS. An IX-lock is used to indicate that X-locks are set at the object level to

perform updates and possibly to create phantoms. Therefore IX must be incompatible

with S, A, X, it can be compatible with IS and IX only. An SIX lock is used to

guard against phantoms and to set X-locks on objects for updates. Thus SIX must

be incompatible with S, A, X, IX, and SIX, it is only compatible with IS. Since

compatibility is symmetric, we obtain the complete compatibility matrix of Fig. 2.

	S	X	A	IS	IX	SIX
S	+	−	+	+	−	−
X	−	−	−	−	−	−
A	+	−	−	+	−	−
IS	+	−	+	+	+	+
IX	−	−	−	+	+	−
SIX	−	−	−	+	−	−

Fig. 2:   The Compatibility Matrix for the Modes

S, X, A, IS, IX, SIX.

The following combinations of locks are then obviously meaningful and constitute

allowed lock protocols:

lock held on partition block:	meaningful locks for objects:
S	-
X	-
A	-
IS	S
IX	S,X
SIX	X

Generalization to Hierarchy: In a next step one can now iterate the scheme and use a sequence of partitions $\Pi_1, \Pi_2, \ldots, \Pi_\ell$ such that Π_{i+1} is a refinement of Π_i, i.e., Π_{i+1} splits the blocks of Π_i into smaller blocks. This leads to a database, which for locking purposes is hierarchically organized. The hierarchy describes which blocks are subsets of other blocks. To prevent phantoms and gain read access within a partition block one of the locks S, A, X, and SIX can be used. SIX, IX, and IS are used to indicate what locks may be set at the next level of refinement. It is now prudent to also add the additional lock modes IA and SIA with the following extensions of the compatiblity matrix:

	S	X	A	IS	IX	SIX	IA	SIA
IA	+	-	-	+	+	-	+	-
SIA	+	-	-	+	-	-	-	-

Fig. 3: The Compatibility of the Modes IA and SIA

Before t converts an A-lock on a block B_i to an X-lock it must convert all IA-locks and SIA-locks it holds on ancestors of B_i to IX- or SIX-locks, respectively. To avoid potential deadlocks due to conversions this conversion should be performed top-down in the hierarchy, obviously the conversions of A to X, of IA to IX, and of SIA to SIX cannot be granted until any coexisting S-locks have been released.

Note: The two lock-modes A and SIA have the same compatibilities, but they differ in the way they should be converted. Thus SIA could be omitted allowing the conversion of A to both SIX or X after finding out which conversion is preferable.

The following table describes the generalized lock protocols, assuming locks are set top-down in the hierarchy:

locks for partition blocks	allowable on next level	allowable on object level
S	-	
X	-	
A	-	
IS	S, IS	S
IX	all modes	S,X,A
SIX	X,A,IX,IA	X,A
IA	S,A,IS,IA,SIA	S,A
SIA	A,IA	A

Note: There would be no difficulty to allow S, IS, SIX, SIA locks on sons of a block with an SIX-lock, or to allow S, IS, SIA locks on the sons of a block with an SIA-lock.

The locking techniques described in this section offer a means to handle the phantom problem. The issue has been investigated in more detail, but without using the A, IA, and SIA modes in [GLP 75] and [GLPT 75]. In a partitioned database transactions can choose to lock at a coarse or a fine level depending on the desired tradeoff between low locking overhead and high concurrency.

The issue of potential deadlock still prevails, unless additional restrictions on locking protocols are imposed [Ram 74]. The techniques described in sections 5, 6, 7 can be used to handle the deadlock issue.

10. RECOVERY

Backup of a database to an earlier state of integrity should be planned for and may become necessary for many reasons: hardware failure, system failure due to program errors, deadlock and deadlock resolution, prevention of indefinite delay, violation of integrity constraints discovered during or at the end of a transaction, attempt to perform unauthorized operations.

We will present the basic design principles, ignoring many technical details, for a revocery scheme. It is assumed that a safe pseudo-random-access store, e.g., a disk containing the database is available and that recovery of a previous state of integrity must be possible from the contents of the backup store alone, if one of the above failures including failure of the central processor or main memory occurs.

We assume that such a failure has precisely the same effect as halting the operation of the whole system at an arbitrary moment resulting in an undefined state of the central processor and main memory. Any read or write operations in progress on the backup store shall also halt, without having any destructive side effects on the state of the backup-store. Only the contents of the backup-store shall be useable to determine, how far such operations might have progressed at the moment of the system halt.

The recovery problem to be solved then can be summarized as follows: The effect of incomplete transactions, i.e., transactions which had started but not yet completed at the moment of failure, on the contents of the database must be undone.

To describe the update of a single partition block, let us assume that the whole block will be rewritten. In a technical implementation the unit of information for read and write operations on the backup-store will often be a page. The basic recovery principle can be adopted to this case.

The key of the recovery scheme is the notion of a shadow block [Lor 76]. When a transaction updates a block, the old block - called the shadow - will be kept for the contingency that a failure occurs before the transaction completes and that the shadow is needed for recovery. The shadow will be released only after the new updated block has been properly constructed on the backup store. The main difficulty of such a scheme is the design of the update-commitment operation which performs the switchover from the shadow to the new block. This operation itself may fail and recovery must still be possible.

After a new block has been constructed by an updating transaction two versions of a block reside on the backup store, each representing part of a state of integrity of the database. To perform the update-commitment, the transaction must first assure, that the shadow is no longer used by other transactions. This can be done by either performing updates under an X-lock on the block or by performing updates with an A-lock and converting the A-lock to an X-lock as part of the commitment. After obtaining an X-lock on the block, the new block can then be validated and the shadow can be freed.

Since at any time we may have two versions of a block, we need two address maps defining for each block the physical locations of the shadow and the new block on the backup store. These maps must themselves reside on the backup-store. Let us assume that each map entry is time-stamped, e.g., with the system-time of the moment of creation of the entry. Also associated with each map entry shall be a separately writeable Boolean validation variable. A value true shall mean that the corresponding physical block represents part of a state of integrity of the database. The timestamp of the map entry can be used to identify that state.

With these preliminaries we can now introduce the data objects of the commitment algorithm to be performed by a transaction t_j to update a block B_i:

FL: A list of free storage areas to place new blocks. The details of FL are irrelevant here. FL can be in main or backup store, FL is not needed for recovery purposes.

VO,VI: These are two arrays located on the backup store to represent the two address maps and the timestamps for the physical blocks. $VO[i]$ and $VI[i]$ contain the addresses and timestamps of the shadow and the new block of B_i.

GO,GI: Two Boolean arrays located on the backup store to represent the two validation variables for each block.

Vc: An address map located in main or backup store. $Vc[i]$ contains the address of the currently valid version of block B_i which is made available for read access to other transactions while B_i may be updated by t_j. Vc is not needed for recovery.

To read the block B_i a transaction requests an S-lock on B_i and holds this lock for as long as repeatable reads and the prevention of phantoms in B_i are desired. To update B_i a transaction can request an X-lock on B_i before starting to construct the update. Alternatively, since the shadow of B_i is available until the update is committed, the shadow can be left available for read access while the update is being constructed by requesting an A-lock on B_i first. To commit the update the A-lock is then converted to X. We present the second more complicated update protocol in detail:

1)   Place A-lock on B_i;

2)   Get free slot for new B_i via FL;

3)   Prepare and write new block B_i;

4)   Update and timestamp $VO[i]$ or $VI[i]$;

5)   Validate $GO[i]$ or $GI[i]$;

6)   Invalidate $GI[i]$ or $GO[i]$;

7)   Convert A-lock on B_i to X-lock;

8)   Update $Vc[i]$ with address of new B_i;

9)   Release X-lock on B_i;

10)   Free shadow and update FL

Fig. 4: Locking Protocol for an Updater

The main desirable properties of this update protocol are:

a) For most of the duration of the update block B_i can still be read by other transactions, or equivalently, an update can already be started while the old version of B_i is still locked for read access.

b) An exclusive lock must be held only in steps 7), 8), 9). These steps are very fast, since no operations on backup store are involved.

c) Except for steps 2) and 10), parts of which may have to be programmed as critical regions, updates of different blocks can be performed concurrently, unless prevented by other locks in the hierarchy.

d) The technique of using the shadow blocks for recovery causes only a very small disturbance of the overall operation. No quiescing of the system for taking checkpoints is needed and no extra operations are needed on the backup store beyond the maintenance of the structures VO, VI, GO, and GI.

e) Backup of a single transaction, e.g., because of an integrity violation or a deadlock, although not discussed here in detail, is easily possible without stopping or affecting other transactions.

Recovery: Now let us consider the recovery problem assuming that the system can fail, i.e., halt its operation with an undefined state of the processor and the main memory, at any moment of the update protocol.

Case 1: A failure occurs before step 5). Then exactly one of GO[i] or GI[i] will be true. The corresponding address map entry VO[i] or VI[i] will point to a valid version of block B_i representing a state of integrity.

Case 2: If step 5) itself fails we will not know whether the validation took place or not, and we have two cases:

Case 2a: The validation was not performed, i.e., only one of GO[i] or GI[i] is true and we continue the recovery as in Case 1.

Case 2b: The validation was performed, i.e., both GO[i] and GI[i] are true, we

have two valid versions of B_i and can use the timestamps of VO[i] and VI[i] to
determine the newest version to be used for recovery.

Since step 5) consists of writing only a single bit we can assume that only the
two cases 2a and 2b can arise.

Case 3: Step 6) fails: depending on how step 6) fails, there will be one or two
validated versions of B_i and recovery is performed exactly as in Case 2.

Case 4: A failure occurs after step 6). There will be exactly one validated
version of B_i on the backup store which is used for recovery.

To conclude we want to indicate some of the additional complications arising
in a viable implementation of the techniques presented.

1) The lock protocol presented in Fig. 4 must be generalized to handle
    updating of several blocks within one transaction. This is easily
    possible.

2) The hardware of some machines allows to combine the write operations of
    steps 3) and 4) and the validation of step 5) in a single operation. The
    update protocol can be modified to take advantage of this possibility [Lor
    76].

3) When updating several blocks a generalized conversion operation is
    desirable to convert a set of A-locks in a single operation rather than
    converting A-locks one at a time. Such an operation can increase
    concurrency considerably.

4) Instead of backing up a transaction completely for recovery it may be
    desirable to introduce additional intermediate safe points and to use
    partial backup for recovery. Additional bookkeeping is then necessary to
    inform transactions, how far they have been backed up and how much work
    must be repeated [Lor 76] [ABC 76].

5) An additional level of recovery is needed in reality to guard against
    failures involving the backup store. The techniques presented here can
    be generalized to serve that purpose [Lor 76].

REFERENCES

[ABC 76] M. M. Astrahan, M. W. Blasgen, D. D. Chamberlin, K. P. Eswaran, J. N.
Gray, P. P. Griffiths, W. F. King, R. A. Lorie, P. R. McJones, J. W. Mehl,
G. R. Putzolu, I. L. Traiger, B. W. Wade and V. Watson, "System R: A
Relational Approach to Database Management" to appear in ACM Transactions
on Database Systems, 1, 2 (1976).

[Bay 74] Bayer, R., "Aggregates: A Software Design Method and its Application to
a Family of Transitive Closure Algorithms." TUM-Math. Report No. 7432,
Technische Universität München, September 1974.

[Bay 75] Bayer, R., "On the Integrity of Databases and Resource Locking." In: Data
Base Systems (ed. Hasselmeier, H. and Spruth, W. G.), Lecture Notes in
Computer Science, 39, Springer, 1976.

[Bjo 73] Bjork, L.A., "Recovery Semantics for a DB/DC System." Proceedings ACM
Nat'l. Conference 1973, 142-146.

[CBT 73] Chamberlin, D. D., Boyce, R. F., Traiger, I. L., "A Deadlock-free Scheme
for Resource Locking in a Database Environment." Information Processing
1974, 340-343.

[Cod 70] Codd, E. F., "A Relational Model for Large Shared Data Banks." Comm. ACM
13, 6 (June 1970), 377-387.

[CES 71] Coffman, E. G. Jr., Elphick, M. J., Shoshani, A., "System Deadlocks." ACM
Computing Surveys 3, 2 (June 1971), 67-78.

[Dav 73] Davies, C. T., "Recovery Semantics for a DB/DC System." Proceedings ACM
Nat'l. Conference 1973, 136-141.

[EGLT74] Eswaran, K. P., Gray, J. N., Lorie, R. A., Traiger, I. L., "On the Notions
of Consistency and Predicate Locks in a Database System." IBM Research
Report RJ 1487, December 1974.

[ESC 75] Eswaran, K. P., Chamberlin, D. D., "Functional Specifications of a
Subsystem for Database Integrity. "IBM Research Report RJ 1601, June
1975.

[Eve 74] Everest, G. C., "Concurrent Update Control and Database Integrity." In:
Database Management (ed. Klimbie, J. W., and Koffeman, K. L.), North
Holland 1974, 241-270.

[Fos 74] Fossum, B. M., "Data Base Integrity as Provided for by a Particular
Database Management System." In: Database Management (ed. Klimbie, J.
W., and Koffman, K. L.), North Holland 1974, 271-288.

[GLP 75] Gray, J. N., Lorie, R. A., Putzolu, G. R., "Granularity of Locks in a
Large Shared Database." IBM Research Report RJ 1606, June 1975.

[GLPT75] Gray, J. N., Lorie, R. A., Putzolu, G. R., Traiger, I. L., "Granularity
of Locks and Degrees of Consistency in a Shared Database." IBM Research
Report RJ 1654, September 1975.

[Hab 69] Habermann, A. N., "Prevention of System Deadlocks." Comm. ACM 12, 7 (July
1969), 373-377, 385.

[KiC 73] King, P. F., Collmeyer, A. J., "Database Sharing - an Efficient Mechanism
for Supporting Concurrent Processes." AFIPS Nat'l. Comp. Conf. Proceedings
1973, 271-275.

[LiZ 74] Liskov, B. H., Zilles, S. N., "Progrmaming with Abstract Data Types" ACM
Sigplan Notices, 9, 4 (April 1974), 50-59.

[Lor 76] Lorie, R. A., "Physical Integrity in a Large Segmented Database." IBM
Research Report RJ 1767, April 1976.

[Oll 74] Olle, T. W., "Current and Future Trends in Database Management Systems."
Information Processing 1974, 998-1006.

[Pur 70] Purdom, P., Jr., "A Transitive Closure Algorithm." Bit 10 (1970), 76-94.

[Ram 74] Ramsperger, N., "Verringerung von Prozeßbehinderungen in Rechensystemen."
Dissertation, Technische Universität München, 1974.

[Sch 74] Schroff, R., "Vermeidung von totalen Verklemmungen in bewerteten
Petrinetzen." Dissertation, Technische Universität München, 1974.

[War 62] Warshall, S., "A Theorem on Boolean Matrices." Journal ACM 9, 1 (January
1976), 11-12.

AN ARCHITECTURE FOR HIGH-LEVEL LANGUAGE DATABASE EXTENSIONS

by

C.J.Date

IBM General Products Division
1501 California Avenue, CA 94304

December 1975

Abstract

This paper describes an architecture for a set of database extensions
to the existing high-level languages. The scheme described forms an
architecture in the sense that it is not based on any particular
language: its constructs and functions, or some suitable subset of
them, may be mapped into the concrete syntax of a number of distinct
languages, among them COBOL and PL/I. The architecture includes both
the means for specifying the programmer's view of a database (i.e. for
defining the external schema) and the means for manipulating that
view. A significant feature is that the programmer is provided with
the ability to handle all three of the well-known database structures
(relational, hierarchical, network), in a single integrated set of
language extensions. Another important aspect is that both record-
and set-level operations are provided, again in an integrated
fashion. The objectives of the architecture are to show that it is
possible for relational, hierarchical and network support to co-exist
within a single language, and also, by providing a common framework
and treating the three structures in a uniform manner, to shed some
new light on the continuing debate on the relative merits of each.

The paper is intended as an informal introduction to the architecture,
and to this end includes several illustrative examples which make use
of a PL/I-based concrete syntax.

Disclaimer

The architecture described herein is the responsibility of the author
alone; no particular endorsement or commitment is implied on the part
of his employer.

Reprinted with kind permission from the proceedings of the 1976 ACM
SIGMOD International Conference on the Management of Data.

1.INTRODUCTION

This paper describes an architecture for extending the existing
high-level languages (COBOL, PL/I, ...) to provide direct support for
a wide range of database functions. The scheme described forms an
architecture in the sense that the extensions proposed are not
tailored to any particular language: the general approach taken in the
design has been to define, in a language-independent way, the various
types of data structure to be supported, together with appropriate
operations on these structures, and the detailed problems of mapping
these structures and operations into the concrete syntax of individual
languages have been deferred to a later time. It must be emphasized
that at the time of writing the architecture definition is still
incomplete, so that the paper should be regarded as a status report
rather than as a final specification.

An important goal for the architecture was to support all three of the
well-known data structure classes (relational, hierarchical,
network). An equally important and related aim was to provide this
support via a single general-purpose set of extensions rather than via
three distinct special-purpose sets. A third significant objective
was to provide both record- and set-level operations, again in an
integrated fashion. Thus the architecture described herein represents
an attempt to show that it is possible for relational, hierarchical
and network support to co-exist within a single language. So far as
the author is aware it represents also the first attempt to deal with
all three structure classes in a uniform and consistent manner; it may
therefore also serve to cast some new light on the continuing debate
on the relative merits of the three approaches.

2.THE PROGRAMMER'S VIEW OF A DATABASE

Throughout this paper we are concerned with the database as it is
perceived by the high-level language programmer. To use the
terminology of the ANSI/X3/SPARC Study Group [1,2], we are interested
in the external model (described by an external schema) - and not the
underlying "conceptual" database (described by the conceptual schema),
nor the stored data itself (described by the internal schema). From
here on we shall use the term "database" as synonymous with "external
model".

From the programmer's point of view the significant features of a
database are that it is persistent and shared. By "persistent" we
mean, broadly speaking, that the data is already in existence at the
start of program execution and that it continues to exist after the
program has terminated; by "shared" we mean that the programmer must
in general be aware that other programs may be referencing and
updating the data while his own program is using it. In other
respects a database can be considered as simply a new kind of data
aggregate. The question arises, how should such an aggregate be
presented to the programmer?

Strictly speaking this question is purely syntactic, not
architectural: there are obviously several ways of representing a
database in terms of concrete syntax. However, since it is axiomatic
that the entire syntax will be crucially dependent on the particular

representation chosen, and since in the PL/I-based syntax used in this paper we have selected a slightly unobvious approach, we choose to discuss the issue briefly here. In this syntax a database is represented, not as some new kind of input/output file, but instead simply as part of the program's directly addressable storage area - rather like an array, a queue, or any other "in-core" aggregate - and the programmer is allowed to operate on database data in situ ("direct reference"). Explicit I/O operations are specifically not required. (There is an obvious analogy here with virtual storage systems, in which the programmer is given the illusion of being able to address a large storage area directly and the system handles the necessary I/O operations to make the illusion real.) We present below some reasons for making such a choice.

° The basic point is simply that data in a database is in the system, and from the programmer's point of view it should not be necessary to move it from one place to another in order to process it - he should be able to reference it directly, just as he does "ordinary" (non-persistent, non-shared) or "local" data. A comparative uniformity of reference for local and global data is a great simplifying factor for the user.

° Direct reference automatically provides a great deal of function within existing language. For example, in PL/I, the existing power of operational expressions is immediately available for database data. Thus the database language extensions can be kept to a comparatively manageable size - it is not necessary to have one set of language for database data and one for ordinary data. Retrieval, for example, can be handled by means of an ordinary assignment statement in which the source is a variable in the database.

° As an extension of the previous point, direct reference allows operations of the form

    X=Y;

where X and Y are both references to objects in a database. (Such an operation would require two steps if READ and REWRITE statements were involved.)

° A more specific example:

EMPLOYEE.SALARY=EMPLOYEE.SALARY+500;

EMPLOYEE is a reference to some database record, SALARY is a field in this record. This example shows how the "update but not see" function - sometimes stated as a security requirement - could be handled in the proposed language.

° The foregoing example also shows that field-level access (a major requirement) can be incorporated very naturally into the direct reference language.

° There is an important semantic distinction between assignment operations and READ/WRITE operations, at least as they apply to source/sink devices, which has been obscured in the past by the fact that READ/WRITE operations have also been used for storage devices such as disks. Typically, once a piece of data has been accessed by means of an input operation, it cannot be accessed again (think of a message from a terminal). An assignment operation, on the other hand, may be repeated indefinitely and will normally produce the same result every time. A database retrieval operation will also normally produce the same result every time. Similar remarks apply to output: in particular, once a piece of data - say an output message - has been transmitted, it is generally not possible to access it again, whereas it is generally possible to re-access a piece of data after it has been placed in the database. The direct reference proposal is in line with these semantic distinctions. (As a corollary, I/O statements, not direct reference, should be used for source/sink access. This should not be construed to mean that a program's source/sink data cannot be held on a storage or "database" device.)

　　° The database language extensions also require the introduction of relations [6] as a new kind of local (non-persistent, non-shared) data aggregate. (Relations may also exist in a database.) A local relation may be used, for example, to contain a set of records which are derived in some way (e.g., via a projection operation [6]) from records in the database. It is clearly desirable not to have to use READ/REWRITE statements to access an aggregate which is purely local to the program (a local relation). It is also clearly desirable to be able to access relations uniformly regardless of whether they are local or global (i.e., in a database).

　　° Direct reference to aggregates (as opposed to individual records) permits the specification of operational expressions whose value is another aggregate of the same type: the important property of closure. To illustrate this point we consider the analogy with simple numeric data. If A, B, C, D are numeric data items, it is the property of closure (under arithmetic operations) which tells us that the value of A+B is also numeric, and hence that this value may be multiplied by C - in a nested expression - or may be assigned to D. Returning to the database language, it is the closure property which allows us to write (for example) an assignment statement setting relation X to contain some join [6] of relations Y and Z, or to write a nested expression defining some projection of such a join. Extending the traditional READ statement would not provide the closure property. This would be true even if the READ operation were made powerful enough to retrieve an entire set of derived records - the essence of READ is that it copies data out of a "file" into something which is not a "file".

The programmer, then, is presented with a view of the database as a storage area containing a large amount of data in the form of records. In addition he is given the ability to reference any record he likes by means of a record reference expression (we assume here that he is authorized to access the record concerned). In principle he could make repeated reference to the same record by merely repeating the same expression - although there would be problems over the effect of update operations, particularly if the updates originated in a concurrent program. In practice, therefore, the normal procedure is for the first reference to a record to be in some cursor-setting operation; the effect of such an operation is to set a nominated cursor to point to the record located by evaluating the specified record reference, and subsequent references to the record are made via the cursor. An example will make this clearer.

```
FIND UNIQUE(EMPLOYEE WHERE EMPLOYEE.EMP#='562170') SET(E);
PUT SKIP LIST(E->EMPLOYEE);
E->EMPLOYEE.SALARY=E->EMPLOYEE.SALARY+500;
```

The first of these three statements locates a particular employee record and sets the cursor E to point to it. The PUT statement then prints this record, and the next statement adds 500 to the SALARY field in this record. In the second and third statements E is being used as a cursor qualifier (cf. pointer qualification in current PL/I). Cursor qualification, like pointer qualification, may frequently be implicit, as subsequent examples will show.

The cursor concept is more important than the above rather trivial example might suggest, however. The most significant point about it is that once a cursor has been set to point to a record, that record becomes locked (unless it was so already), and it remains locked at least until such time as the cursor is set to a new value. Thus in the foregoing example the second and third statements are guaranteed to refer to the same record, and this record is guaranteed not to have been altered by a concurrent program. Neither of these guarantees could have been made if the entire record reference expression appeared (and was therefore re-evaluated) in each of the two accessing statements.

Space precludes detailed discussion of locking in this paper. In general, however, the locking features of the language are as proposed by Engles [13]. Several other reasons for the provision of cursors will also be found in [13].

3. THE APPROACH TO COMMONALITY

As explained in section 1, an objective for the proposed language extensions is commonality of language across the three data structure classes. The approach taken to attaining this objective is based on the realization that, in essence, a hierarchy is merely a special case of a network - a network in which each child record has exactly one parent - and a relation is simply a special case of a hierarchy - a hierarchy consisting of a root only. However, this intuitive statement is far too vague to be useful other than as a broad indication of direction; let us immediately make it more precise by considering each of the three data-structure classes in turn and defining in each case the data constructs that the language extensions will permit.

    ° In the relational case the only data construct is the relation [6]. Relations are perceived as having an ordering but such ordering cannot be used to carry information "essentially" [10]. (A construct is "essential" if it carries information that would be lost if the construct were removed. Thus, for example, ordering based on field-values is "inessential" - no information is actually lost if the records are shuffled into a different sequence - whereas ordering based on, say, time of arrival is "essential".)

    ° In the network case there are basically two permitted data constructs, the record-type and the fan set (also called DBTG set [3] or owner-coupled set [10]). Fan sets are usually thought of as coming in two varieties, "singular" and "multiple"; in actuality, however, the two constructs behave very differently; for most of this paper we shall ignore the "singular" case and reserve the term "fan set" for the "multiple" case.

Both record-types and fan sets may be used to carry information
essentially. In this context the record-type may be likened to the
relation (we shall make this statement more precise later). Fan sets
are used to represent certain associations between record-types,
associations which in the relational case would be represented by
means of a common domain in the record-types concerned. For example,
see Fig. 1.

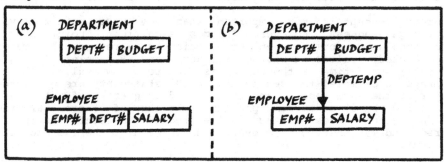

Figure 1: (a) relational representation, and
          (b) network representation,
              of a department-employee structure

It must be emphasized, however, that in general not all such
associations are represented by means of fan sets. For example, in
Fig. 1(b), all employees having the same department are associated via
the fan set DEPTEMP; but all employees having the same salary are
associated, not via a fan set, but via equality of SALARY values in
the EMPLOYEE record-type. This latter method of representing
associations is the only method available in the relational case. It
follows that a network-handling language should be capable of
exploiting both methods of representing associations, whereas a
relation-handling language need only be capable of handling the second
method.

    °   A hierarchy is merely a special case of a network in which
each record-type except one (the "root") is a child in exactly one fan
set; the root is not a child in any fan set. The fan sets are
conventionally un-named, since no ambiguity can result.

The definitions just given, while capturing the most significant
features of the three structure classes, do not cater for certain
features of hierarchies and networks as defined in some systems today,
specifically IMS [14] and DBTG [3]. The features in question are ones
which it is widely felt have no place in a controlled database
environment [5,10,12,15,17], though it must be admitted that there is
a certain amount of contention on this point. Space does not permit
the arguments and counter-arguments to be repeated here. However, we
state briefly those characteristics of hierarchical/network structures
as described above which distinguish them from the corresponding
structures in IMS and DBTG.

    °   No two records of a given record-type may contain exactly
the same values, field for field, and participate as children in
exactly the same fans of the same regular fan sets. (A fan set is
regular if its children are both NONADOPTABLE and NONORPHANABLE; see
section 4 below for an explanation of these terms.)

° Records cannot contain repeating groups.

° Fan sets cannot contain more than one type of child.

° Areas [3]/realms [4] are not supported.

° No ordering is defined between records of different types.

° Ordering across records of the same type cannot be "essential".

Most of these constraints have been imposed on the grounds of intellectual manageability (any one of them could be dropped if sufficient cause were shown, but only at the cost, in each case, of additional language extension). To return to the main argument: if the definitions given earlier for relation, hierarchy and network are accepted, it can be seen that - as stated at the beginning of the section - a relation is a special case of a hierarchy, and a hierarchy is a special case of a network. This observation permits us to define a single set of language extensions encompassing all three structure classes. To be more specific:

° the language extensions required for relational declarations are a subset of those required for hierarchical declarations, which are in turn a subset of those required for network declarations;

° the operators required for relational processing are a subset of those required for hierarchical processing, which are in turn a subset of those required for network processing;

° (for a given operation, as applicable) the operands required for relations are a subset of those required for hierarchies, which are in turn a subset of those required for networks.

The database language extensions thus have an "onion-layer" structure, as illustrated in Fig. 2.

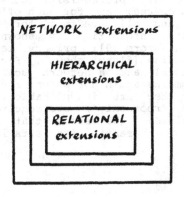

Figure 2: the onion-layer language

4.DECLARATIVE LANGUAGE

As explained in section 2, we are concerned with what is referred to
in [2] as an external schema. Although external schemas may in
practice be written separately from the program(s) using them,
possibly even in a different language [2], a version of the relevant
schema must be available to the programmer when he writes his program
and to the compiler when the program is compiled; and it is this
version which concerns us here. This version of the schema is
conceptually part of the source program, and it must therefore be
expressed in high-level language terms (very likely it will be
INCLUDEd from an appropriate library). Henceforth we shall take
"external schema" to refer to this high-level language version.

We are assuming, incidentally, that at some point (normally prior to
execution) the object form of the external schema will be bound to the
conceptual schema, and also at some point (normally at execution time)
the version of the external schema used at compilation time will be
checked to match the version currently known to the system. We shall
not consider these processes in any detail in this paper.

The basic purpose of the external schema is to define the programmer's
view of the database. To achieve this aim the declarative language
extensions should permit the specification of as many of the
programmer's assumptions about the database as possible. Such
specifications will in turn allow a large number of system checks to
be applied, many of them at compilation time, and will generally help
to prevent programs from executing under false assumptions (and hence
from producing incorrect results). In the design of the declarative
language extensions, therefore, the ground-rule was: be as explicit as
possible.

We present the declarative language by means of an example (based on
an example in [11]). An education database contains information about
an in-house company training scheme. For each training course the
database contains details of all prerequisite courses for that course
and all offerings of that course; and for each offering it contains
details of all teachers and all students for that offering. A
relational schema for this information is shown in Fig. 3 (all
relations in third normal form [9]; primary keys [6] shown by
underlining; underlying domains [6] not shown). Figures 4 and 5 show,
respectively, a hierarchical and a network schema for the same
information (underlying domains again not shown; the concepts of third
normal form and primary key are inapplicable). Note that two
hierarchies (one of them "root only") are required in Fig. 4 if
redundancy is to be avoided. (We assume that all fan sets are
"essential"; the handling of inessential fan sets is beyond the scope
of this paper.)

```
COURSE    (COURSE#, TITLE)
PREREQ    (COURSE#, PRE#)
OFFERING  (COURSE#, OFF#, DATE, LOCATION)
TEACHER   (COURSE#, OFF#, EMP#)
STUDENT   (COURSE#, OFF#, EMP#, GRADE)
EMPLOYEE  (EMP#, NAME)
```

<u>Figure 3</u>: relational schema for the education database

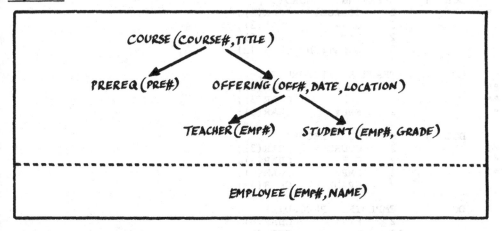

<u>Figure 4</u>: hierarchical schema for the education database

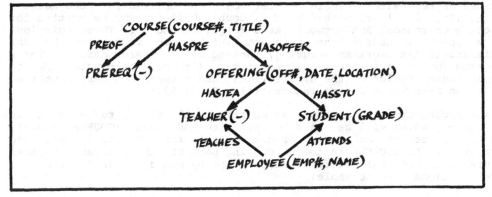

<u>Figure 5</u>: network schema for the education database

In the external schema for this example we first define the record-types by means of appropriate RECORD declarations. (A record is basically the same as a level-one structure in PL/I today, except that the attribute RECORD effectively gives it a new storage class [18].)

```
    DCL  1    COURSE    RECORD(C),
              2    COURSE#   CHAR(3),
              2    TITLE     CHAR(33);

    DCL  1    PREREQ    RECORD(P),
oo            2    COURSE#   CHAR(3),
o             2    PRE#      CHAR(3);

    DCL  1    OFFERING  RECORD(O),
oo            2    COURSE#   CHAR(3),
              2    OFF#      CHAR(3),
              2    DATE      CHAR(6),
              2    LOCATION  CHAR(12);

    DCL  1    TEACHER   RECORD(T),
oo            2    COURSE#   CHAR(3),
oo            2    OFF#      CHAR(3),
o             2    EMP#      CHAR(6);

    DCL  1    STUDENT   RECORD(S),
oo            2    COURSE#   CHAR(3),
oo            2    OFF#      CHAR(3),
o             2    EMP#      CHAR(6),
              2    GRADE     CHAR(1);

    DCL  1    EMPLOYEE  RECORD(E),
              2    EMP#      CHAR(6),
              2    NAME      CHAR(18);
```

Lines marked with a single bullet would be omitted for the network case (Fig. 5); lines marked with a double bullet would be omitted for both hierarchical and network cases (Figs. 4 and 5). These omissions are possible because the relevant information is carried by the hierarchical/network structuring, instead of by fields defined over a common domain as in the relational case. (It would be possible not to omit these fields in the hierarchical and network schemas, but then the fan sets would become inessential. See [10].)

Each record-type has a cursor associated with it. C, for example, is a cursor which will be used to point to individual COURSEs (only). Also, C serves as the default cursor for implicitly-qualified references to COURSE in the processing part of the program. Further cursors may be defined for a record-type by means of explicit cursor declarations - for example:

```
    DCL  C1   CURSOR(COURSE);
```

Every individual cursor is constrained to a single record-type.

Now we can define the database.

```
DCL   EDUCATION DATABASE
      BASESET
      (RECORD(COURSE)       UNIQUE(COURSE#),
       RECORD.(PREREQ)      UNIQUE,
       RECORD(OFFERING)     UNIQUE((COURSE#,OFF#)),
       RECORD(TEACHER)      UNIQUE,
       RECORD(STUDENT)      UNIQUE((COURSE#,OFF#,EMP#)),
       RECORD(EMPLOYEE)     UNIQUE(EMP#));
```

This declaration defines the EDUCATION database as containing six "base sets". A base set is an important special case of a construct that recurs throughout database structures, viz. the record set. A record set is simply a homogeneous (single record-type) collection of records, usually but not always with some defined ordering. A base set is that particular (ordered) record set which consists of all occurrences of some given type of record.

In the example the base sets are un-named (note that the names COURSE, PREREQ etc. are the names of the constituent record-types, not of the base sets themselves), but in general record sets may be given a name if desired. With the declarations as shown each of the six base sets is in fact a relation, and this is all that is required for the relational case. For a hierarchical or network structure additional entries will be required (to be explained below), and in the particular example under consideration UNIQUE would be specified for COURSE and EMPLOYEE only - the other four base sets would not be relations in this case. The meaning of UNIQUE is that each record in the base set has a unique value for the indicated field combination.

Any or all of the six base sets could be defined to have a value-controlled ordering: for example, we could specify ORDER(UP COURSE#) for courses (and such an entry would imply UNIQUE(COURSE#) unless NONUNIQUE were specified in the ORDER entry). For simplicity we have assumed default (system-defined) ordering in every case.

To impose a hierarchical or network structure on the database, the declaration must include a FANSET specification as well as the BASESET specification already shown. For the hierarchical structure of Fig. 4 this could be as follows.

```
      FANSET
      (RECORD(PREREQ)     UNDER(COURSE)     ORDER(UP PRE#),
       RECORD(OFFERING)   UNDER(COURSE)     ORDER(UP OFF#),
       RECORD(TEACHER)    UNDER(OFFERING)   ORDER(UP EMP#),
       RECORD(STUDENT)    UNDER(OFFERING)   ORDER(UP EMP#))
```

The syntax here has been chosen to emphasize the fact that the important thing about a fan is the corresponding set of children, rather than the set of children plus the parent. For example, the scope of a DO-loop - see section 7 - is typically a set of children, not an entire fan. The four fan sets shown above are un-named, though there is no reason why they should not be given a name if desired. Within each fan of each fan set the child records are ordered as indicated. Again each ORDER entry implies a corresponding UNIQUE entry.

For the network structure of Fig. 5 the FANSET entry could be as follows. Notice that here the fan sets have been named, although there is no reason why they should not remain un-named if no name is required. The details of exactly when a name is required are somewhat complex and will not be discussed in this paper.

```
FANSET
(PREOF     RECORD(PREREQ)    UNDER(COURSE),
 HASPRE    RECORD(PREREQ)    UNDER(COURSE),
 HASOFFER  RECORD(OFFERING)  UNDER(COURSE) ORDER(UP OFF#),
 HASTEA    RECORD(TEACHER)   UNDER(OFFERING),
 HASSTU    RECORD(STUDENT)   UNDER(OFFERING),
 TEACHES   RECORD(TEACHER)   UNDER(EMPLOYEE),
 ATTENDS   RECORD(STUDENT)   UNDER(EMPLOYEE))
```

However, the FANSET entries as shown (for both hierarchic and network cases) are not complete. For any given fan set, in general, the child record-type may be (a) TRANSFERABLE or not, (b) ADOPTABLE or not, and (c) ORPHANABLE or not, with respect to that fan set. Each fan set declaration should include a specification of the programmer's assumptions with respect to transferability, adoptability and orphanability, so that appropriate compile- and bind-time checks may be made. Transferability applies to both hierarchies and networks; adoptability and orphanability apply to networks only. In the context of essential fan sets (the only kind we are discussing here), a child record-type is TRANSFERABLE if a RECONNECT statement may be used to move an individual child from one fan to another in the fan set; it is ADOPTABLE if a CONNECT statement must be used to perform the initial linking of an individual child to its first fan in the fan set; and it is ORPHANABLE if a DISCONNECT statement may be used to remove an individual child from one fan without at the same time linking it to another fan in the fan set. (Note that adoptability is not the same as "connectability". A better term would be desirable. For those readers familiar with DBTG, adoptability corresponds to MANUAL membership; orphanability corresponds to OPTIONAL membership [3]. There is at present no DBTG equivalent to transferability.)

5.CURSORS AND CURSOR STATES

A cursor is an object whose primary function is to designate some individual record by means of that record's record identifier (RID). Each record has a unique RID. Before explaining the cursor concept in any more detail, it is first necessary to amplify the associated notion of ordered record set, since the operation of setting a cursor usually involves the selection of a record from such a set.

An ordered record set is simply a set of records with a total ordering imposed on them. A relation is one example; a base set is another (base sets are not necessarily relations). The set of children in a single fan is a third example. The set of all children in all fans of a given fan set is an example of a record set which is only partially ordered (note, however, that exactly the same collection of records may constitute another record set which does have a total ordering).

A given record may participate in any number of ordered record sets simultaneously (every record participates in at least one such set, viz. the relevant base set). We may model this situation as follows. An ordered record set S may be thought of as a closed, directed loop. The loop has a unique point of discontinuity called the zero position (P0), which may be thought of as both the beginning and the end of the loop. At any given time the loop holds a set of n+1 objects (n greater than or equal to zero), located at n+1 discrete positions P0, P1, P2, ..., Pn on the loop. These n+1 positions are such that, with respect to the loop direction, P0 precedes P1, P1 precedes P2, ..., Pn precedes P0. The object at Pi (i in the range 1 to n) is the RID of the record which is ith in the ordering of the record set being modelled. The object at P0 is the "zero RID", i.e. a dummy record identifier which is considered as identifying a fictitious "zero record" (R0), distinct from all real records. Note that R0 appears in every ordered record set. We shall refer to R0 as the zeroth record of such a set, and use 1st, 2nd, 3rd, ... to refer to the 1st, 2nd, 3rd, ... real record of such a set. See Fig. 6.

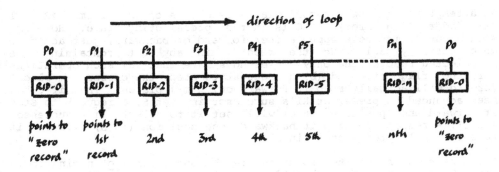

<u>Figure 6</u>: the loop model of an ordered record set

Now let C be a cursor constrained to records of type R (the record-type involved in set S). Then at any given instant C will be either "selecting" or "preselecting" some record of type R (possibly the zero record, which is considered to be of every known record-type).

A cursor that is <u>selecting</u> a given record has the RID of that record as its value. For example, if C has RID-3 as its value, it is selecting the third record in set S. Since records may simultaneously belong to several distinct sets, this record may also be the 10th in set S', the 6th in set S'', and so on. The record concerned may be accessed via a reference of the form C->R, unless it is the zero record: an attempt to access R0 is an addressing error. A cursor which is selecting a record is said to point to that record.

If cursor C currently has the value RID-i (identifying the ith record in S), then it may be stepped forward 1, 2, ... or n-i positions within S to select some other record; however, it cannot be stepped as far as (or past) R0 at the end of the set. Similarly, it may be stepped backward 1, 2, ... or i-1 positions within S to select some other record; however, it cannot be stepped as far as (or past) R0 at the beginning of the set. In general a cursor which is selecting a record can be set to select another record by stepping it any number of positions (providing the zero position is not reached), in either direction, in any ordered set containing the record it is currently selecting.

Now suppose cursor C is currently pointing to record Ri (i nonzero) in set S, and suppose that Ri is the object of an operation which removes it from S or changes its position within S. Examples of such operations are DESTROY; DISCONNECT; RECONNECT; and ordinary field update operations, if the field concerned is an ordering field. In order that the programmer may retain his position within S for use in subsequent operations, DISCONNECT and similar statements allow the specification of an ADV (advance) option. Any cursor named in the ADV option is advanced to preselect the record (possibly R0) which immediately follows Ri's old position in the ordering of the set concerned (which is specified either by the operation or in the ADV option itself). A cursor that is preselecting a given record has the RID of that record, together with a flag, as its value; the flag is set to show that the record is being preselected, not selected.

An attempt to access a record via a reference of the form C->R will fail (addressing error) if C is in the preselecting state. However, such a cursor may be stepped either forward or backward, just as if it were actually selecting the record, in any set containing the preselected record; the only differences are that (a) such operations turn the flag off, and (b) a request to step the cursor m places forward will actually step it forward only m-1 places. Thus if C has been advanced to preselect Ri's successor in set S, a request to step it forward one position (in S) will set it to select Ri's successor (in S); a request to step it backward one position (in S) will set it to select Ri's predecessor (in S).

Any cursor which pointed to Ri before the operation not nominated in the ADV option remains unchanged (i.e. it now points to Ri in its new position), except in the case of DESTROY, where such a cursor is automatically advanced to preselect Ri's successor in the appropriate base set.

6.FREE CURSORS

The importance of the record set construct should be clear from the previous section. The language must allow the programmer to write expressions to denote record sets - not only pre-declared ones, such as the set of all EMPLOYEE record occurrences, but also dynamically generated ones, such as that subset of EMPLOYEE record occurrences where the jobname is 'PROGRAMMER' (for the sake of the example we suppose that EMPLOYEE records include a JOBNAME field).

Formally, we need to be able to write set-defining expressions such as:

X WHERE X is an EMPLOYEE record & X.JOBNAME='PROGRAMMER'

Conceptually this may be thought of as follows: "out of the entire universe of objects X, select just those which satisfy the predicate (the condition following the WHERE)"; and the predicate says "we are interested only in those objects X which are EMPLOYEE records, and the JOBNAME field in these records must have the value PROGRAMMER". X here is a "free variable". In the language we represent free variables by means of cursor-qualified record references - for example:

E->EMPLOYEE WHERE E->EMPLOYEE.JOBNAME='PROGRAMMER'

(the condition "X is an EMPLOYEE record" is implied). If E is the default cursor for EMPLOYEE, and if JOBNAME is unambiguous, this expression can be simplified to:

EMPLOYEE WHERE JOBNAME='PROGRAMMER'

(a more intuitively obvious form). Note that a cursor-qualified reference that represents a free variable is semantically different from a syntactically identical reference in other contexts. Specifically, it is not a reference to the record selected by the indicated cursor. In fact the current value of the cursor is irrelevant (and is not changed); the cursor merely serves as a syntactic device to link references to fields in the predicate to the free variable. As another example, the expression:

E->EMPLOYEE WHERE E->EMPLOYEE.JOBNAME = F->EMPLOYEE.JOBNAME

is a reference to the set of employees having the same jobname as the employee selected by cursor F. Cursor F here is performing its normal selection function; cursor E is a "free cursor" and is being used as part of a free variable reference.

To simplify repeated references to the same set of records, it is possible to CONNECT the records resulting from the evaluation of a set-defining expression to an empty, named "window set". This effectively provides a method of giving a name to a dynamically generated set of records. Space precludes detailed discussion of window sets in this paper.

7.MANIPULATIVE LANGUAGE

In this section we present some of the major features of the manipulative language extensions, primarily by means of examples.

We start with the most important cursor-setting operation, viz. the FIND statement - syntax:

FIND record-reference SET(cursor-name) ;

Example (using the relational schema of Fig. 3):

FIND FIRST(PREREQ WHERE PREREQ.PRE#='322') SET(P);

In this example PREREQ WHERE ... is a set reference, i.e. an expression denoting a record set (actually a subset of the PREREQ base set, with an ordering inherited from this base set), and FIRST is a "built-in reference" which selects the first record in this ordered set. Cursor P is set to point to this record. Note that P is also acting as the (implicit) free cursor in the references to PREREQ (because P is the cursor named in the RECORD declaration for PREREQ). The phrase SET(P) could have been omitted: if no SET option appears in a given FIND statement the appropriate default cursor is assumed.

We can now refer to the selected PREREQ record, and to fields within it, using P as a (possibly implicit) cursor-qualifier.

Examples:

```
LOCALCOURSE#=P->PREREQ.COURSE#;    /*field retrieval */
PREREQ.COURSE#=LOCALCOURSE#;       /*field update    */
LOCALPREREQ=PREREQ;                /*record retrieval*/
PREREQ=LOCALPREREQ;                /*record update   */
IF PREREQ.COURSE#='860' THEN ...
PUT SKIP LIST(PREREQ);
```

The FIND statement may optionally include either a FOUND or a NOTFOUND specification. These options nominate a flag which is to be set if the FIND is successful or unsuccessful (as applicable).

Example (following the previous FIND statement):

```
FIND NEXT(PREREQ WHERE PREREQ.PRE#='322') NOTFOUND(DONE);
```

This statement will step P along to the next PREREQ with PRE# 322. ("Next" here refers to the ordering of the PREREQ base set.) If no more such PREREQs exist the flag DONE will be set. Thus to loop through all such PREREQs:

```
      P=ZERO; /*set P to point to record zero*/
LOOP:FIND NEXT(PREREQ WHERE PREREQ.PRE#='322') NOTFOUND(DONE);
      IF DONE THEN GO TO EXIT;
      .....
      GO TO LOOP;
EXIT: .....
```

Example (the same loop, using a DO statement):

```
DO PREREQ WHERE PREREQ.PRE#='322' SET(P);
    .....
END;
```

This code is defined to be semantically identical to the loop code given above (except that no explicit flag-setting occurs). Again the SET option may be omitted, in which case the cursor assumed is that defined in the relevant RECORD declaration.

Two more important built-in references are UNIQUE and PARENT. PARENT is applicable to hierarchies and networks only.

Example (UNIQUE):

```
FIND UNIQUE(COURSE WHERE COURSE.COURSE#='860');
```

UNIQUE selects the single record in a single-record set; it is an error if the set does not contain exactly one record.

Example (PARENT, using the hierarchical schema of Fig. 4):

```
    FIND FIRST(STUDENT WHERE .....);
    FIND PARENT(STUDENT);
```

Using the network schema of Fig. 5:

```
    FIND FIRST(STUDENT WHERE .....);
    FIND PARENT(STUDENT,HASSTU);
```

In both these examples S is set to point at the first STUDENT (with respect to the ordering of the STUDENT base set) satisfying some criterion, and O is set to point at its parent OFFERING. In the network case a fan set name is required within the PARENT reference, since otherwise it would be ambiguous.

For clarity we allow the built-in reference

```
    PARENT(X)
```

to be written

```
    Y OVER X
```

wh is the declared parent record-type for X.
Similarly,

```
    PARENT(PARENT(X))
```

may be written

```
    Z OVER X
```

where Z is the declared parent of Y, and so on. (Similar simplifications may also be made where X is a child in more than one fan set - i.e. where Y is not unique - under most circumstances, but the details are beyond the scope of this paper.)

Example (using the hierarchical schema, to loop through
        all children of a fan):

```
    FIND UNIQUE(COURSE WHERE COURSE.COURSE#='860');
    DO OFFERING WHERE SAME(PARENT(OFFERING),COURSE);
        .....
    END;
```

SAME(record-reference,record-reference) is a built-in function whose value is _true_ if the two record references denote the same record, _false_ otherwise. Record set references of the form

```
        X WHERE SAME(PARENT(X),Y)
```

are so common that the following is permitted as a shorthand:

```
        X UNDER Y
```

Similarly,

```
        X WHERE SAME(PARENT(PARENT(X)),Z)
```

can be abbreviated to:

    X UNDER Z

and so on. (Again, similar simplifications may usually be made where
X is a child in more than one fan set, but no further details will be
given here.)

The DO statement above can thus be reduced to:

    DO OFFERING UNDER COURSE;

The order in which the OFFERINGs are processed in this example is
determined by the order of the OFFERING base set.

Example (as previous example, but using the network schema):

FIND UNIQUE(COURSE WHERE COURSE.COURSE#='860');
DO OFFERING IN HASOFFER WHERE SAME(PARENT(OFFERING,HASOFFER),COURSE);
    .....
END;

In the DO statement OFFERING IN HASOFFER defines a partially ordered
record set - the set of all OFFERINGs appearing as children in the fan
set HASOFFER - but the WHERE clause restricts this to a totally
ordered subset (it would be an error if it did not).   Default rules
similar to those already mentioned allow expressions of the form

    X IN F WHERE SAME(PARENT(X,F),Y)

to be abbreviated (in most cases) to

    X UNDER Y

Thus, as in the hierarchical case, the DO statement above may be
reduced to

    DO OFFERING UNDER COURSE;

So far all examples have been basically one-record-at-a-time. We now
present an example dealing with an entire record set as a single
operand.

Problem: retrieve all legal course-number/teacher-name pairs
        (a pair is "legal" if a teacher with the indicated
        name teaches at least one offering of the indicated
        course).

We need a local relation to hold the result.

```
DCL 1 CT RECORD(CTC),
      2 COURSE# CHAR(3),
      2 NAME    CHAR(18);

DCL CTR BASESET(RECORD(CT) UNIQUE);
```

Using the relational schema:

```
CTR=(TEACHER.COURSE#,EMPLOYEE.NAME)
      WHERE EMPLOYEE.EMP#=TEACHER.EMP#;
```

Using the hierarchical schema:

```
CTR=(COURSE.COURSE#,EMPLOYEE.NAME)
      WHERE EMPLOYEE.EMP# EQSOME
          (TEACHER.EMP# WHERE
              SAME(PARENT(PARENT(TEACHER)),COURSE));
```

The parenthesized expression "(TEACHER.EMP# ...)" can be unambiguously abbreviated to

```
(TEACHER.EMP# UNDER COURSE)
```

The value of this expression for a given course is the corresponding set of teacher employee numbers. The expression "X EQSOME S" has the value <u>true</u> if the set S contains a member with value equal to that of X.

Using the network schema:

```
CTR=(COURSE.COURSE#,EMPLOYEE.NAME)
      WHERE EMPLOYEE EQSOME
          (PARENT(TEACHER WHERE
              SAME(PARENT(PARENT(TEACHER,HASTEA),HASOFFER),COURSE),
                                        TEACHES));
```

Notice the use of PARENT with an aggregate argument (and hence acting as an aggregate reference). Once again we may unambiguously simplify the expression following EQSOME, this time to:

```
(EMPLOYEE OVER (TEACHER UNDER COURSE))
```

Since EMPLOYEE also appears (with a different denotation) before the EQSOME, however, the two references must have different free cursors to distinguish them, and hence at least one must include an explicit free cursor in the complete simplified expression - for example:

```
CTR=(COURSE.COURSE#,EMPLOYEE.NAME)
      WHERE EMPLOYEE EQSOME
          (F->EMPLOYEE OVER (TEACHER UNDER COURSE));
```

(where F, like E, is a cursor over EMPLOYEEs).

In all three cases the result of the retrieval is in local relation CTR; records in this result can be accessed via record references and cursors, just like records in a database.

Example (updating): change the date and location of offering
        number 3 of course 860 to 21st July 1975, Helsinki.

Using the relational schema:

```
FIND UNIQUE(OFFERING WHERE OFFERING.COURSE#='860'
                         & OFFERING.OFF#   ='  3');
DATE='750721';
LOCATION='HELSINKI';
```

If a program intends to update several fields of a record, as in this
example, it may be preferable to retrieve a copy of the record, make
the changes to the copy, and then update the original record by means
of an assignment from the copy. For example, the sequence:

```
FIND UNIQUE(OFFERING etc.);
TEMPOFFERING=OFFERING;
TEMPOFFERING.DATE='750721';
TEMPOFFERING.LOCATION='HELSINKI';
OFFERING=TEMPOFFERING;
```

may be preferable to the previous code. The advantage is basically
one of performance: it is probably more efficient to perform a single
(record) update than two or more separate (field) updates.   This is
particularly likely to be so if the implementation applies integrity
checks on each update; moreover, "spurious" errors may be signalled if
at some given time the program has updated one field and not another.
On the other hand some programs may not be bothered by such problems,
and for them code sequences such as the first of the two above are
simpler and more natural.

Example (creating a new record): local structure STUDENTAREA
        contains a new student record to be inserted into
        the database.

Using the relational schema:

```
CREATE STUDENT FROM STUDENTAREA;
```

Using the hierarchical schema:

```
CREATE STUDENT FROM STUDENTAREA
    CONNECT(UNDER OFFERING);
```

(We asume here that cursor O already identifies the OFFERING which is
the new student's parent-to-be.)

Using the network schema:

```
CREATE STUDENT FROM STUDENTAREA
    CONNECT(UNDER OFFERING VIA HASSTU,
            UNDER EMPLOYEE VIA ATTENDS);
```

(We assume here that cursors O and E have already been set
appropriately. An UNDER entry must be specified for each fan set in
which STUDENT is NONADOPTABLE. VIA options are used to indicate the
relevant fan sets; they may be omitted if no ambiguity results.)

Example (destroying an existing record):

> DESTROY OFFERING;

We assume here that cursor O has been set to identify the record to be destroyed. In general the operand may be any record reference, or any set reference if it is desired to destroy several records at once. The record(s) specified are destroyed, together with all their NONORPHANABLE children. All cursors which previously identified any of these records are advanced within the OFFERING base set.

Fan set operations

The fan set operations are CONNECT, DISCONNECT, RECONNECT. Their syntax is as shown below (no examples will be given). VIA options (and the FROM option in the case of DISCONNECT) may be omitted if no ambiguity results. The ADV option mentioned in Section 5 is not shown.

CONNECT record-reference UNDER record-reference [VIA fan-set-name];

RECONNECT record-reference UNDER record-reference [VIA fan-set-name];

DISCONNECT record-reference [FROM fan-set-name];

Once again a set reference (rather than a record reference) may appear as the first operand, if it is required to deal with several records at once.

8.SUMMARY

We have presented some major features of the proposed database language extensions. We may summarize the highlights of the proposal as follows.

 °   All three data structure classes are supported.

 °   The database is represented as an extension of the program's storage area.

 °   The programmer can retain multiple explicit positions in the database.

 °   Record selection (via cursor) and record access (via cursor-qualified reference) are separable functions.

 °   Record references permit a wide variety of "navigational" operations (UNIQUE, FIRST, PARENT, plus others not discussed in this paper).

 °   The programmer can deal with entire record sets as single operands.

 °   Record set expressions have the generality and "completeness" [8] of predicate calculus, without involving predicate calculus notation.

In conclusion we list some other features of the proposal which we do
not have room to discuss in this paper.

- °   Locking [13].

- °   Error-handling and feedback (on-conditions).

- °   "Window sets" and associated CONNECT/DISCONNECT operations.
A window set is a record set which is wholly contained within some
underlying set; it acts as a window into the underlying set, through
which some subset of the underlying records may be seen. The records
may be viewed in a different sequence through such a window.
"Singular fan sets" are handled by this mechanism.

- °   Built-in functions such as COUNT and TOTAL [7].

- °   Set comparisons such as SUBSETOF.

- °   Null data values.

- °   Fields, records etc. as arguments and parameters.

ACKNOWLEDGEMENTS

The writer is pleased to acknowledge useful discussions and
communications with a large number of colleagues, especially Bob
Engles, Chris Paradine and John Roskell. Acknowlegements are also due
to Rita Summers, Charlie Coleman and Eduardo Fernandez, who
independently developed language extensions very similar to the
relational portions of the present proposal [19].

REFERENCES

1.   C.W.Bachman: "ANSI/X3/SPARC   Study   Group   on   Data   Base
     Systems: Summary of Current Work" (January 1974).

2.   ANSI/X3/SPARC Study Group on Data Base Systems: Interim
     Report (8 Feb 1975).

3.   Data Base Task Group of CODASYL Programming Language
     Committee: Final Report (April 1971).

4.   Data Base Language Task Group of CODASYL Programming
     Language Committee: COBOL Data Base Facility Proposal (March
     1973).

5.   Proceedings of IFIP TC-2 Special Working Conference: A
     Technical In-Depth Evaluation of the DDL (Namur, Belgium,
     13-17 Jan 1975). North-Holland (1975).

6.   E.F.Codd: "A Relational Model of Data for Large Shared Data
     Banks". CACM 13,6 (June 1970).

7. E.F.Codd: "A Data Base Sublanguage Founded on the Relational Calculus". Proc. 1971 ACM SIGFIDET Workshop on Data Description, Access and Control.

8. E.F.Codd: "Relational Completeness of Data Base Sublanguages". In Data Base Systems, Courant Computer Science Symposia Series Vol. 6, Prentice-Hall (1972).

9. E.F.Codd: "Recent Investigations in Relational Data Base Systems". Proc. IFIP Congress 1974, North-Holland.

10. E.F.Codd, C.J.Date: "Interactive Support for Non-Programmers: the Relational and Network Approaches". Proc. 1974 ACM SIGMOD Debate, Ann Arbor, Michigan (May 1974).

11. C.J.Date: "An Introduction to Database Systems". Addison-Wesley (1975).

12. R.W.Engles: "An Analysis of the April 1971 DBTG Report". Proc. 1971 ACM SIGFIDET Workshop on Data Description, Access and Control.

13. R.W.Engles: "Currency and Concurrency in the COBOL Data Base Facility". Proc. IFIP TC-2 Working Conference on Modelling in Data Base Management Systems, Freudenstadt, Germany, January 1976 (to appear).

14. IBM: Information Management System/Virtual Storage General Information Manual (IBM Form No. GH20-1260).

15. G.M.Nijssen: "Data Structuring in DDL and Relational Data Model". In Data Base Management Systems (ed. Klimbie and Koffeman), Proc. IFIP TC-2 Working Conference, Cargese, Corsica 1974 (North-Holland).

16. G.Held, M.Stonebraker: "Networks, Hierarchies and Relations in Data Base Management Systems". Proc. ACM Pacific Conference, San Francisco, April 1975.

17. R.W.Taylor: "Report on IFIP TC-2 Special Working Conference: A Technical In-Depth Evaluation of the DDL (Namur, Belgium, 13-17 Jan 1975)".

18. ANSI/ECMA: BASIS/1-12 (Draft PL/I Standard), July 1974.

19. R.C.Summers, C.D.Coleman and E.B.Fernandez: "A Programming Language Extension for Access to a Shared Data Base." Proc. ACM Pacific Conference, San Francisco, April 1975.

DATA STRUCTURES AND GRAPH GRAMMARS

P.L. Della Vigna
C. Ghezzi
Istituto di Elettrotecnica ed Elettronica
Politecnico di Milano - Piazza L. da Vinci 32
20133 Milano - Italy

ABSTRACT

This paper is concerned with a formal model for data structure definition: data graph grammars (DGG's).

The model is claimed to give a rigorous documentation of data structures and to suit very properly program design via stepwise refinement.

Moreover it is possible to verify data structure correctness, with regard to their formal definition.

Last, attribute context-free data graph grammars (A-CF-DGG's) are introduced. A-CF-DGG's not only give a complete and clean description of data structures and algorithms running along data structures, but also can support an automatic synthesis of such algorithms.

KEY WORDS AND PHRASES

Data structure, abstraction, stepwise refinement, software reliability, correctness, program synthesis, context-free grammars, attribute grammars, parsing.

1. INTRODUCTION

Programming methodologies which can help in designing correct, easily modifiable, readable and portable software have become an important topic in computer science.

A widely accepted principle is that the quality of software can be considerably improved if the programmer can express his tasks in a free and natural way, without being concerned with details of the machine, which could force him to tailor his solution to some unnatural or unessential features.

Very high-level languages are an ambitious answer to these problems, but it has been argued they cannot exhaust all the needs of programmers. Moreover the serious problems of optimization which arise have not yet received a solution which allows to obtain a code of good quality.

Another attractive attack to this problem consists in successively decomposing a solution through "levels of abstraction". This means that the solution is initially specified by using an abstract machine whose operations and data tailor the problem to be solved. Whenever an abstraction is not directly supported by the language, it is recursively detailed until a level is reached which is directly supported by the system.

We feel that programming through levels of abstraction should not only be considered as a general philosophy to be divulged to non-believers, but should also inspire the design of computer-aided program development systems which allow to test, measure and modify programs at each stage of their stepwise refinement. Our research effort is presently in this area.

Quoting Liskov /1/, two kinds of abstraction are recognized to be useful in writing programs: "abstract operations and abstract data types . Abstract operations are naturally represented by subroutines or procedures, which permits them to be used abstractly (without knowledge of details of implementation). However, a program representation for abstract data types is not so obvious; the ordinary representation, a description of the way the objects of the type will occupy storage, forces the user of the type to be aware of implementation information".

These principles have inspired the definition and implementation of the CLU programming language/system, which is one of the most interesting research efforts towards the definition of a programming system supporting structured programming /2/ and modularity /3/.

We present here another model for data structures definition, abstrac tion and refinement which is based on graph grammars. In particular, we will show how the model can be used for clean documentation of the project and how it can support a computer assisted design of data struc tures,resulting in a considerable improvement of program reliability.

The reader who is interested in this topic is invited to read some re lated works which have appeared in the literature (/4/,/5/,/6/).

2. DATA GRAPH GRAMMARS

A data structure can be viewed abstractly as a set of objects connected by a network of access paths. Thus we can formally define a data graph over Σ (the node alphabet) and Δ (the link alphabet) as a triplet $D = (N, \phi, \psi)$, where N is the set of nodes, $\phi : N \to \Sigma$ and $\psi \subseteq N \times \Delta \times N$ are the node and link labelling functions respectively.

Let $\mathcal{G} = \{D | D \text{ is a data graph over } \Sigma, \Delta\}$; a data graph language $\mathcal{D}$ over Σ, Δ is a subset of $\mathcal{G}$.

Two data graphs $D = (N_D, \phi_D, \psi_D)$ and $F = (N_F, \phi_F, \psi_F)$ are equivalent $(D \equiv F)$ if a one-to-one equivalence function $e : N_D \to N_F$ can be found such that

1) $\phi_D(n) = \phi_F(e(n))$, $\forall n \in N_D$

2) $(n_1,a,n_2) \in \psi_D$ iff $(e(n_1), a, e(n_2)) \in \psi_F$

Languages of graphs, as an extention of the well-known languages of strings, have been studied by researchers in pattern-recognition in a number of papers (/7/,/8/,/9/,/10/,/11/). Applications to language de finition and translation are explained in /12/ by Pratt, from whom we borrow some formalism.

Also if it appears that the theory of graph grammars may be developed along lines similar to the theory of string grammars, many problems re main yet to be studied; for example :

a) connections with graph-automata;

b) parsing;

c) definition of meaningful restricted classes of grammars.

We shall consider here mainly context-free graph grammars, without trying to give any answers to the questions above for which we refer to /10/, /11/. We shall rather restrict our attention to their use as a tool for data definition.

Let $D = (N, \phi, \psi)$ and $n_i, n_j \in N$; the interpretation of $\phi(n_i) = X_i$

and $\phi(n_j) = X_j$ is that object n_i and n_j are of type X_i and X_j respectively. $(n_i, Y, n_j)\epsilon \psi$ means that object n_j can be accessed by n_i following the access link Y.

Links should not be considered as pointers, as well as nodes do not represent memory locations; rather they are abstract ways of referencing
objects whose definition can be recursively given in terms of other
links. In practice, for example, links could represent a simple reference or even a search algorithm.

A top-down design of a data structure should be considered as a set of
operations which recursively detail the description of types and links.
In particular, we shall concentrate here on data type refinements:
link refinements could also be taken into account with minor changes
to the model.

Node type refinements are represented here as production rules which
describe the structure of a type in terms of lower level component data types.

Formally, a <u>data graph grammar</u> DGG is a 5-tuple G = $(\Sigma_n, \Sigma_t, \Delta, S, R)$,
where the <u>nonterminal node alphabet</u> Σ_n, the <u>terminal node alphabet</u>
$\Sigma_t (\Sigma = \Sigma_t \cup \Sigma_n$ is the <u>total alphabet</u>) and the <u>link alphabet</u> Δ are finite non-empty mutually disjoint sets, S $\epsilon \Sigma_n$ is the <u>starter</u> (the <u>axiom</u>)
and R is the set of <u>production rules</u>. Each element r ϵ R is a 5-tuple
r = (A, D, I, O, W) such that

1) A $\epsilon \Sigma_n$

2) D = (N, ϕ, ψ) is a connected graph over Σ and Δ $^{(°)}$

3) I ϵ N is the <u>input node</u>

4) O ϵ N is the <u>output node</u>

5) W $\subseteq$ N .

Before defining how productions are used to derive data graphs, we introduce the operation <u>join</u> which, applied to two graphs, gives a set
of graphs as result. Let $D_1 = (N_1, \phi_1, \psi_1)$, $D_2 = (N_2, \phi_2, \psi_2)$, $D' = (N', \phi', \psi')$
be graphs over Σ, Δ and $\bar{N}_2$ a (possibly empty) subset of N_2. D' ϵ <u>join</u>
$(D_1, D_2, \bar{N}_2)$ if D' is equivalent to a graph D = (N, ϕ, ψ) such that :

1) N = $M_1 \cup M_2 \cup M_3$ where M_1, M_2, M_3 and M_4 are mutually disjoint
   set such that $N_1 = M_1 \cup M_2$, $N_2 = M_3 \cup M_4$, $\bar{N}_2 \subseteq M_3$, $\eta : N_2 \to M_2 \cup M_3$

(°) Let $D' = (N, \phi, \psi')$ be the undirected graph associated to D, such
that $\psi' = \{(n_1, a, n_2) | (n_1, a, n_2) \epsilon \psi \vee (n_2, a_1, n_1) \epsilon \psi\}$: D is connected if
   D' is connected.

is a surjective application satisfying the conditions

a) $\eta(n) = n \quad \forall n \in M_3$

b) $\eta(n) \in M_2 \quad \forall n \in M_4$ such that $\phi_2(n) = \phi_1(\eta(n))$

2) a) $\phi(n) = \phi_1(n) \quad n \in N_1$

b) $\phi(n) = \phi_2(n) \quad n \in M_3$

3) $(n,a,m) \in \psi$ iff n, m $\in N_1$ and $(n,a,m) \in \psi_1$ or n', m' $\in N_2$ can be found such that $n = \eta(n')$, $m = \eta(m')$ and $(n', a, m') \in \psi_2$.

Intuitively, each resulting graph of <u>join</u> $(D_1, D_2, \bar{N}_2)$ can be viewed as a juxtaposition of D_1 and D_2 where nodes of D_2 not in $\bar{N}_2$ can be identified with nodes in D_1 with the same label.

If e is the equivalence function e : N $\rightarrow$ N', the <u>joint function</u> j : $N_1 \cup N_2 \rightarrow$ N' is defined as follows :

1) $j(n) = e(n) \quad \forall n \in N_1$

2) $j(n) = e(\eta(n)) \quad \forall n \in N_2$

The operation <u>join</u> is <u>simple</u> (<u>s-join</u>) if $\bar{N}_2 = N_2$. In such a case the result of the <u>join</u> operation is a single graph formed by the pair of graphs D_1 and D_2.

The <u>derivation set</u> Y(G) defined by the data grammar G is a set of graphs over Σ and Δ which can be recursively defined as follows :

i. Y(G) contains all the graphs D_0 (the <u>start graphs</u>) equivalent to $(\{n\}, \phi, \varepsilon)$, where $\phi(n) = S$ and ε is the empty link labelling function

ii. let $D_1 = (N_1, \phi_1, \psi_1) \in$ Y(G), $\bar{n} \in N_1$, $\phi_1(\bar{n}) = A \in \Sigma_n$, $(A, D_2, I, O, W) \in R$, $D_2 = (N_2, \phi_2, \psi_2)$. Y(G) contains also the graphs D' equivalent to D = (N, ϕ, ψ) constructed as follows:

1. let $D_1' = (N_1', \phi_1', \psi_1')$, where

    a) $N_1' = (N_1 - \{\bar{n}\}) \cup \{n_I, n_0\}$, $n_I, n_0 \notin N_1$

    b) $- \phi_1'(n) = \phi_1(n) \quad \forall n \in N_1 - \{\bar{n}\}$

       $- \phi_1'(n_I) = \bar{X}, \bar{X} \in \Sigma$

       $- \phi_1'(n_0) = \tilde{X}, \tilde{X} \in \Sigma$

    c) $- (n_1, a, n_2) \in \psi_1' \quad \forall n_1, n_2 \in N_1 - \{\bar{n}\}$
       such that $(n_1, a, n_2) \in \psi_1$

       $- (n_0, a, n_I) \in \psi_1'$ if $(\bar{n}, a, \bar{n}) \in \psi_1$

       $- (n, a, n_I) \in \psi_1' \quad \forall n \in N_1 - \{\bar{n}\}$ such that $(n, a, \bar{n}) \in \psi_1$.

       $- (n_0, a, n) \in \psi_1' \quad \forall n \in N_1 - \{\bar{n}\}$ such that $(\bar{n}, a, n) \in \psi_1$.

2. let $D_1'' = (N_1'', \phi_1'', \psi_1'') \in$ <u>join</u> (D_1', D_2, W)

3. if j is the joint function j : $N_1' \cup N_2 \rightarrow N_1''$

then

    a) $N = N_1'' - \{j(n_I), j(n_0)\}$

    b) $\phi(n) = \phi_1''(n)$, $\forall n \in N_1'' - \{j(n_I), j(n_0)\}$

    c) $-(n_1, a, n_2) \in \psi \ \forall n_1, n_2 \in N_1'' - \{(j(n_I), j(n_0)\}$

       $-(n, a, j(I)) \in \psi \ \forall n \in N_1'' - \{j(n_I), j(n_0)\}$ such that

       $(n, a, j(n_I)) \in \psi_1''$

       $-(j(0), a, n) \in \psi \ \forall n \in N_1'' - \{j(n_I), j(n_0)\}$ such that

       $(j(n_0), a, n) \in \psi_1''$

       $-(j(0), a, j(I)) \in \psi$ if $(j(n_0), a, j(n_I)) \in \psi_1''$

In general, the application of a rule to a graph D in Y(G) gives a result which depends on D, i.e. the operation is context dependent.

A DGG is a <u>context-free data graph grammar</u> (CF-DGG) if all the rules (A, D, I, O, W) where D = (N, ϕ, ψ) are such that W = N.

The <u>data graph language</u> (DGL) defined by a grammar G is :

$$L(G) = \{H|H = (N_H, \phi_H, \psi_H) \in Y(G) \wedge \phi_H(n) \in \Sigma_t \ \forall n \in N_H\}$$

<u>Example 1</u>

The following grammar $^{(0)}$ defines the set of binary directed acyclic graphs over $\Sigma = \{a\}$ and $\Delta = \{x_1, x_2\}$.

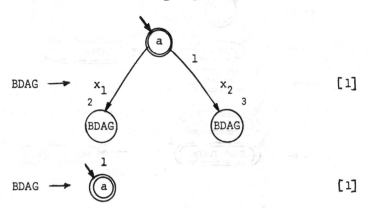

$(^{0})$ The rule (A,(N, ϕ, ψ), I, O, W) is represented as A $\rightarrow$ (N, ϕ, ψ), where the input node is marked by an arrow, and the output node by a double circle.
The set of nodes W is bracketed by [and] . In the sequel, if no set W is listed, W = N is assumed.

Example 2

The following grammar generates the data structure shown in fig. 1, re‑
presenting the employee file of a firm. Employees are grouped accord‑
ing to their sex.
If an employee is married, the name of the wife must be known; more‑
over, the system should record married couples of employees.

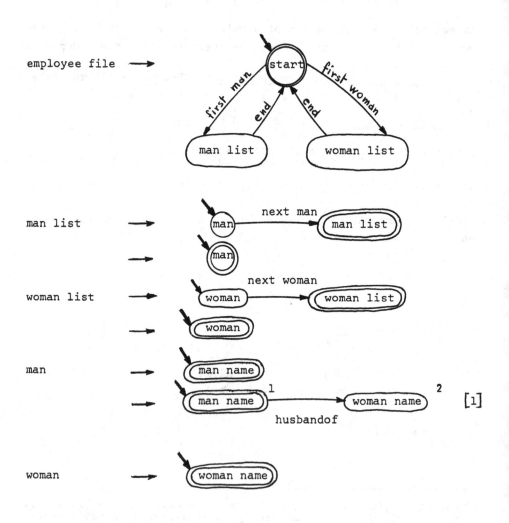

[1]

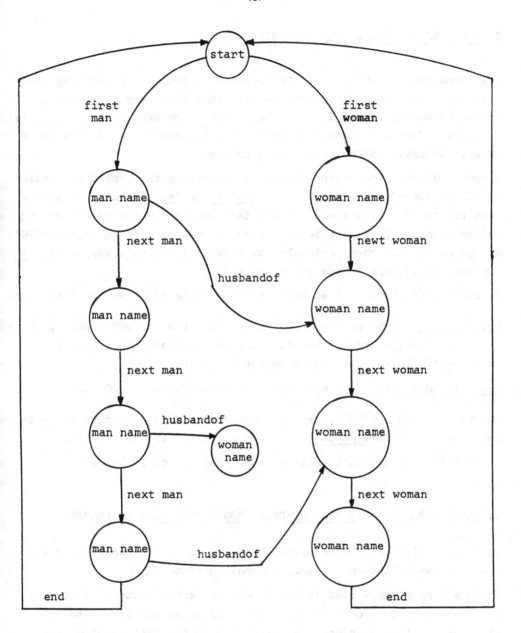

Figure 1

3. THE PARSING PROBLEM FOR DATA STRUCTURES

The formalism of DGG's should be viewed as a tool for describing data structures in a clean and rigorous way. This is a very important property, because it is well known that a clean documentation can greatly increase software reliability, as it becomes much more easy to prove program correctness and to maintain programs.

A number of questions naturally arise concerning the formal properties of DGG's. One of them regards the parsing problem for DGG's, i.e. the possibility of deciding whether a data structure is correct according to its formal definition. Several results on such problems for CF-DGG's are given in /11/ where suitable subclasses of CF-DGG's supporting efficient parsing algorithms are also studied.

As for the models described here it is possible to prove the following:

Proposition 1 - The parsing problem is decidable for DGG's having rules
(A,D,I,O,W), where D = (N, ϕ, ψ), such that cardinality (W) $\geq$ 1.
In particular, it is decidable for CF-DGG's.

Proposition 2 - The parsing problem is undecidable for DGG's.

Moreover, given a CF-DGG, programs which test data structure correctness (data structure parsers) can be automatically constructed.

In what follows we shall restrict out attention to CF-DGG's

4. DATA GRAPH GRAMMARS AND TOP-DOWN PROGRAM DESIGN : AN EXAMPLE

In this section we give an example showing how DGG's can be used in the stepwise refinement of program construction.

Given a library organized in sections of different matters we develop an algorithm which computes ε, the set of empty sections. The data structure will be developed in parallel with the refinement of the search algorithm.

The program is written in an Algol-like language, with the following conventions for operations on the data structure: if A is an object of type α and a is a link exiting A, then :

1. B:=a(A) means that the data structure control leaves object A following link a and the object reached by A under a is denoted by B;
2. is-link (A,a) is a boolean function which is true iff a link label-

led a leaves A;

3. if A denotes an object at step i whose type α is detailed by the
   rule   α→D at step i+k (k ⩾ 1), then A denotes the input node of
   graph D at step i+k.

Data structure	Program

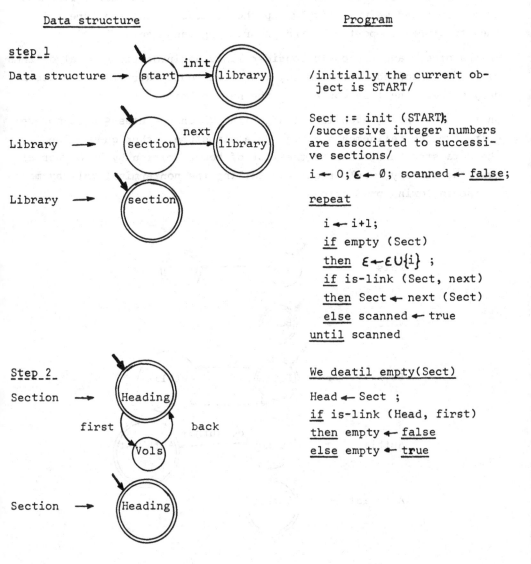

step_1

Data structure → (start) —init→ (library)

/initially the current object is START/

Library → (section) —next→ (library)

Sect := init (START);
/successive integer numbers
are associated to successive sections/

Library → (section)

$i \leftarrow 0; \varepsilon \leftarrow \emptyset$; scanned ← <u>false</u>;

<u>repeat</u>

   $i \leftarrow i+1$;
   <u>if</u> empty (Sect)
   <u>then</u> $\varepsilon \leftarrow \varepsilon \cup \{i\}$;
   <u>if</u> is-link (Sect, next)
   <u>then</u> Sect ← next (Sect)
   <u>else</u> scanned ← true
<u>until</u> scanned

Step_2

Section → (Heading)

first ⌣ back

(Vols)

Section → (Heading)

<u>We deatil empty(Sect)</u>

Head ← Sect ;
<u>if</u> is-link (Head, first)
<u>then</u> empty ← <u>false</u>
<u>else</u> empty ← <u>true</u>

The reader should note that further refinement is required to detail step 4. The refinement implies:

1) definition and possible refinement of links;
2) concrete implementation of the data structure.

If we consider each link as a simple reference, no further refinement is required and we must simply map the abstract data structure onto the structures supported by the programming language.

On the other hand, we could consider links as invocations of algorithms yet to be detailed. For example, link next could extract from a secondary storage the file containing the next section.

On the other hand, even if the algorithm which computes ε does not require further refinements of the data structure, other queries about the data structure, such as the list of books written by an author all over the library, would require detailing the nonterminal Vols by means of the following productions

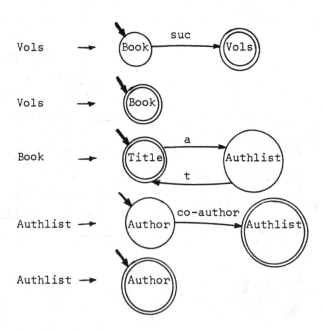

5. DATA GRAPH GRAMMARS AND PROGRAM SYNTHESIS

In this section we show how data graph grammars can be used for automatically synthesizing algorithms which perform computations running along the data structure.

We introduce here the formalism of Attribute-CF-DGG's which can be con
sidered as an extension of similar concepts of /13/ /14/.

For each symbol X ε Σ there is a set I(X) of inherited attributes and
a set S(X) of synthesized attributes. The evaluation of the attributes
is defined within the scope of a single production, by means of attributes rules. Attributes of the lefthand side nonterminal of the produc
tion are synthesized while attributes of the righthandside elements are
inherited; attribute rules specify how a given attribute can be comput
ed in terms of attributes of other elements in the same production.

As to the example described in section 4, we introduce the following
synthesized attributes :

- ε, giving the set of empty sections;
- ʊ, giving the set of books written by a given AUTHOR;
- α, which is true iff AUTHOR has at least one book in the library;
- in, which is true iff AUTHOR is in the authorlist of a book;

and the inherited attribute

- n, which numbers each section of the library.

The Attribute-CF-DGG which represents the example is shown in fig. 2.
The indices which appear in the attribute rules relate attributes to
the elements of the productions.

Attributes can be evaluated by an algorithm which runs along the parse
structure of the data structure; the values computed for the attributes
of the starter of the grammar are the result of the data structure.
In our example the evaluation of attribute ε of the nonterminal
"Data structure" gives the same result as the program described in sec
tion 4.

The reader should note that using the formalism of Attribute-CF-DGG we
simply specify, for each rule, how to compute an attribute, in terms
of other attributes. In other words we do not give the formal specifica
tion of an algorithm, because the evaluation sequence of the attributes
is not specified. The only constraint which must be satisfied by an ef
fective algorithm is that an attribute can be evaluated only if the va
lues of the attributes from which it depends are known.

It is possible to design an algorithm which, given the attribute-CF-DGG
and a data structure satisfying the grammar, is able to find a suitable
evaluation sequence (if it exists /13/) which allows:

a) to compute all the attributes in an interpretative scheme,

    or

b) to generate an object program which computes the attributes.

In both cases, data types and operators used in attribute rules must be directly supported by the interpreter or by the programming language in which the object program is written.

In the example, we have supposed that the object language supports data of type integer and boolean.

If we do not have a computer aided program design system, which is able to automatically construct a program which evaluates attributes, Attribute-CF-DGG's seem to play an useful role in giving a complete and clean documentation of data structures and algorithms which run along data structures.

It must be emphasized that this model is not suitable to represent operations which dynamically change data structures. Therefore whenever a data structure is modified it is necessary to re-parse the structure in order to obtain the new values of its attributes.

Attributes can also be used to impose restrictions on the class of data structures defined by a CF-DGG which cannot be specified by a CF-DGG or could be with a rather complicated grammar.

In the sequel we present an Attribute-CF-DGG for the example in Sec. 4

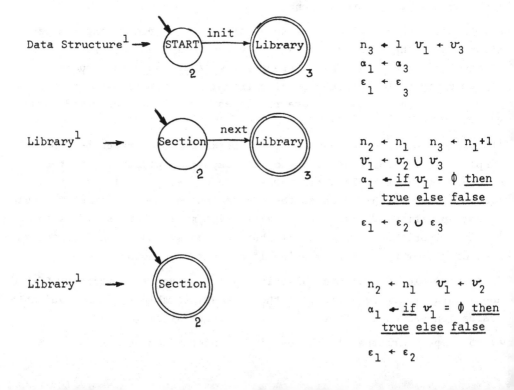

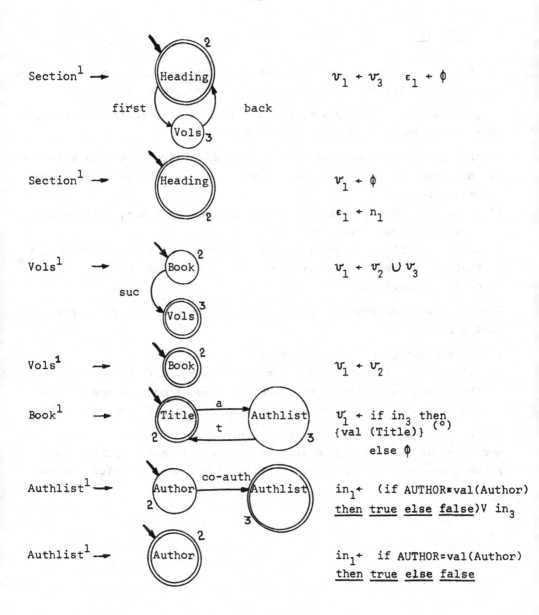

$$v_1 \leftarrow v_3 \qquad \epsilon_1 \leftarrow \phi$$

$$v_1 \leftarrow \phi$$

$$\epsilon_1 \leftarrow n_1$$

$$v_1 \leftarrow v_2 \cup v_3$$

$$v_1 \leftarrow v_2$$

$$v_1 \leftarrow \text{if } in_3 \text{ then}$$
$$\{val\ (Title)\}\ ^{(\circ)}$$
$$\text{else } \phi$$

$$in_1 \leftarrow (\text{if AUTHOR} = val(Author)$$
$$\underline{then}\ \underline{true}\ \underline{else}\ \underline{false})\lor in_3$$

$$in_1 \leftarrow \text{if AUTHOR} = val(Author)$$
$$\underline{then}\ \underline{true}\ \underline{else}\ \underline{false}$$

($\circ$) Val (a) gives the value of the terminal a

6. CONCLUSION

In this paper we have given a formal definition of data graph grammars and we have discussed their relevance to data structure design.

In particular, we have restricted our attention to context-free data graph grammars, and we have shown that:

1) they give a complete and rigorous documentation of a data structure;
2) they describe in a clean and natural way stepwise refinements of data structures;
3) it is possible to verify data structure correctness, with regard to their formal (syntactic) definition;
4) it is possible to associate attribute rules to each production, so that algorithms which walk along a data structure can be automatically synthesized.

Further investigations are currently going on with regard to the following points:

1) dynamic change of data structures
2) data graph realization in a computer memory, with respect both to the automatic choice of efficient storage structures and restrictions on CF-DGG's which derive graphs more easily implementable /6/.

These points and a deeper insight into the practical relevance of the model are worth studying to support our belief that attribute data graph grammars can play an useful role in computer assisted program design.

REFERENCES

/1/ Liskov, B. "An introduction to CLU", Computation Structures Group
     Memo 136, MIT Project MAC, 1976.

/2/ Dahl, O.J., Dijkstra, E.W., Hoare C.A.R. "Structured programming"
     Academic Press New York, 1972.

/3/ Parnas, D.L. "On the criterion used in decomposing systems into
     modules", CACM 15, 12, 1053-58, 1972.

/4/ Earley, J. "Toward an understanding of data structures", CACM 14,
     617-626, 1971.

/5/ Shneiderman, B., Scheuermann, P. "Structured data structures",
     CACM 17, 10, 583-587, 1974.

/6/ Rosengerg, A.L. "Addressable data graphs", JACM 19, 2, 309-340,
     1972.

/7/ Pfaltz, J.L., Rosenfeld, A., •"Web grammars"Proc. 1st Intl. Joint
     Conference on Artificial Intelligence, Washington, 609-19, 1969.

/8/ Montanari, U.C. "Separable graphs, planar graphs and web grammars",
     Information and Control, 16, 243-67, 1970.

/9/ Pavlidis, T. "Linear and context-free graph grammars", JACM 19,
     11-22, 1972.

/10/ Milgram D.I. "Web automata", University of Maryland, Computer
     Science Center Technical rep. 271, 1973.

/11/ Della Vigna, P., Ghezzi, C. "Context-free graph grammars", Inter-
     nal rep. 76-1, Istituto di Elettrotecnica ed Elettronica, Po-
     litecnico di Milano, IEEPM, 1976.

/12/ Pratt, T.W. "Pair grammars, graph languages and string to graph
     translations", JCSS 5, 560-595, 1971.

/13/ Knuth, D. "Semantics of context-free languages", Math. Systems
     Theory, 2, 127-145, 1968; Correction: Math.Systems Theory 5,
     95-96, 1971.

/14/ Bochmann, G.V. "Semantic evaluated from left to right", CACM 2,
     19, 55-63, 1976

Selecting an optimal set of secondary indices

Theo Härder, Technische Hochschule Darmstadt

1. Introduction

An important design problem concerning the effectiveness of data base systems is the selection of access paths (secondary indices) supporting the fast access to sets of records qualified by transactions. However, the exploitation of access paths is useful only when they save processing time compared with the serial scan of the total data base. Consequently, an access path must essentially reduce the response time of a query, because it involves additional expenses with respect to storage and maintenance.

In a data base system the global optimization of the selection problem regarding all transaction types and their frequencies captured for all heterogeneous applications is necessary for economic reason. The indexing problem can be stated in the following way:
Invert a subset of attributes such that the total expected costs resulting from all transactions are minimized or, conversely, the gain is maximized with respect to the serial scan of all queries. The index optimization can be subject to the additional constraint that in case of storage restrictions only a limited number of secondary indices is available.

A number of studies have appeared in reference literature considering this problem. Lum has taken an empirical approach (Lu71), while others (Ki74, St74, Sk74) use stochastic models concerning probabilities for retrieval and update to obtain analytic solutions. In our refined model there are some additional means to describe transaction types and different kinds of processing. Essentially, the following characteristics and parameters allow a detailed description when considering design questions:

- query, update, insert and delete operations,
- statistical queries without access to the records,
- access time as a function of a transaction's hit ratio,
- random processing according to random and random-sorted lists,
- sequential processing in case of high hit ratios,
- storage costs for access paths,
- storage characteristics of real devices.

2. Model assumptions

Let A_1, A_2, ..., A_n be nonempty sets, not necessarily distinct. A subset R of the Cartesian product $A_1 \times A_2 \times \ldots \times A_n$ is called a relation, and A_i is designated a domain or attribute of R. Let r be an element of R, then r is a n-tuple $(r_1, r_2, \ldots, r_n)$ where r_i belongs to A_i. The attribute or minimal group of attributes which guarantees the uniqueness of tuples is called primary key. The physical occurrences of a relation and of a tuple are denoted respectively as file and record.

We assume that the N_{REC} records of the file are randomly stored in secondary memory and are not clustered according to any criteria. The records are uniformly distributed over neighbouring cylinders of a disk, and access to them is performed with equal probability for all transactions. The assumption of clustered records (Ro74) is not useful when dealing with arbitrary transactions.

The selection problem of access paths is discussed concerning one relation. In case of independence between relations the results can be directly extended to a multi-relational data base.

We distinguish two classes of access paths. Obtaining access via primary key one record is found at the most. In comparison to this a secondary key qualifies n records. The corresponding access path is called secondary index. A primary key access path is necessary for an efficient support of batch processing. The following three operation primitives are important for its implementation:

- random access to any record,
- sequential processing of all records in a particular order,
- efficient maintenance.

To support the processing of ad hoc queries secondary indices are suitable. An index on the i-th attribute of R is a mapping from elements in A_i (attribute values) into those tuples in R for which that element in the i-th attribute occurs, i.e., a mapping $I_i : A_i \rightarrow 2^R$ (Ki74). We assume the existence of atoms for the domains (Wo71) so that each attribute has a finite set of elements. The attribute A_i has j_i attribute values with the frequencies N_1, N_2, ..., N_{j_i}, where

$$\sum_{k=1}^{j_i} N_k = N_{REC} \text{ is valid.}$$

To describe the distribution we use the resolution factor (Wa73) $Rf_i = N_{REC}/j_i$ as the expected value, which is justified under the consideration of various transaction types.

A two level hierarchical organization for the index consisting of the catalogue for
the attribute values and the corresponding target lists is considered. The catalogue
entries (attribute values) contain the actual frequencies N_{ik} for statistical information purposes, besides the address of the target list. The catalogue of A_i is
organized as a B-tree implemented in physical blocks of length B in secondary storage. In order to find the target list of a particular value of A_i a B-tree of
height h must be traversed. Assuming the length of an attribut value entry to be
D ($D \approx B/100$) the number of necessary accesses to locate the target list is

$$h_i = \begin{cases} 1 \text{ for} & j_i \leqslant B/D & \approx 10^2 \\ 2 \text{ for } B/D & < j_i \leqslant (B/D)^2 & \approx 10^4 \\ 3 \text{ for } (B/D)^2 & < j_i \leqslant (B/D)^3 & \approx 10^6 \end{cases}$$

The target list itself can contain primary keys, tids or record addresses in case of
a vector implementation or logical or physical marks when packed boolean arrays are
taken. The storage requirement for one entry or mark be S_M. Then a target list is
consequently stored in

$$N_{Bi} = \left\lceil \frac{N_{REC} \cdot S_M}{j_i \cdot B} \right\rceil$$

physical blocks.

In order to express the storage costs C_{ST} of an index we introduce a cost factor c
which is related to storage unit and time. The dimension of c should be chosen such
that storage costs and access costs are comparable. Neglecting the storage space for
catalogue information the costs for the inversion of one attribute are

$$C_{ST} = c \cdot S_M \cdot N_{REC},$$

since N_{REC} target entries exist for each attribute in normalized relations.

In our model four different types of transactions are considered. First of all we
restrict ourselves to read and update operations which extend only to one attribute.
Hence a "decoupled" transaction model follows in which all attributes can be analysed
separately.

In a retrieval transaction Q_{Ri} all records with a given attribute value for the i-th
attribute are selected. All qualified records must be looked up and placed to the
user's disposal. The probability of this transaction type be p_i. In many applications
only statistical information is retrieved which refers to the frequency of certain
elements of a data base. The search for the actual records is not necessary if frequency information is contained in the catalogue or the target list of an index.
Assuming the probability s_i of that query type, the probability r_i of a retrieval
transaction for the i-th attribute follows

$$p_i + s_i = r_i.$$

The total retrieval probability in a normalized relation with n attributes as candidates for inversion is given by

$$\sum_{i=1}^{n} (p_i + s_i) = \sum_{i=1}^{n} r_i = R$$

Three different types of maintenance operations are distinguished:

- update of an existing record,
- deletion of an existing record,
- insertion of a new record.

In all three transaction types it is assumed that the operation is restricted to one record which is identified by primary key. The update of a record requires the search via the access path of the primary key and the rewrite of the updated record. Insertions and deletions are performed via primary key. With respect to our model only the overhead caused by a secondary index is relevant.

In an update transaction Q_{Ui} the value of the i-th attribute of a record is changed. In case of inversion the maintenance of the index requires reading and rewriting of two target lists and catalogue entries. Assuming an update probability u_i for the i-th attribute the total probability of an update transaction is given by

$$\sum_{i=1}^{n} u_i = U$$

In an insertion or deletion transaction Q_I resp. Q_D the storage address of the record is found via the access path of the primary key and the corresponding operation is performed. For all inverted attributes the corresponding target lists and catalogue entries must be updated. Given the probabilities I and D for these transactions, then

$$R + U + I + D = 1.$$

To estimate the costs of index operations the following general assumptions are made. The catalogue with all attribute value entries and all target lists are stored on disk. In any case a head movement with an average seek time t_{sav} must be performed in order to find the catalogue. Another one is needed to locate at the beginning of the target list. The transfer of data from disk is done block after block where $\bar{t}_o$ is the average time for rotational delay and transfer of a block or page.

For a transaction of type Q_{Ri} the cost of transferring the total target list is

$$C_{pi} = 2 \cdot t_{sav} + (h_i + N_{Bi}) \cdot \bar{t}_o .$$

In case of a statistical query only the corresponding entry of the attribute value must be searched. Thus,

$$C_{si} = t_{sav} + h_i \cdot \bar{t}_o .$$

For the maintenance operations (Q_U, Q_I, Q_D) it is supposed that the update in the target lists can be done locally so that in each case only one block has to be transferred to main storage and written back to the original bucket of the disk. In addition the changed attribute value entry containing the actual sum (N_{ik}) has to be rewritten. The index costs for insertion and deletion of a record are always equal. The expense per inverted attribte A_i is given by

$$C_{Mi} = 2 \cdot t_{sav} + (h_i + 3) \cdot \bar{t}_o .$$

Since two catalogue entries and target lists are always involved in an update operation the overhead $C_{Ui} = 2 \cdot C_{Mi}$ arises with a transaction of type Q_{Ui}.

If no index exists for an attribute the total file has to be read and examined sequentially in case of qualification. Since the order of accessing records does not matter a physical sequential processing will be chosen for economic reasons. In our model the pages are transferred continuously from the external storage medium at maximal channel speed. By application of a synchronizing buffer technique the internal computing times for the selection of the qualified records can be overlapped. It is assumed that speed and availability of the central processor do not affect the sequential processing. This serial scan may possibly be delegated to a peripheral specialized computer (Ka75).

Assuming a cost constant K_{seq} for one record the total cost of scanning the whole file is given by

$$C_{seq} = K_{seq} \cdot N_{REC} .$$

The cost C_A for the random processing of a transaction depends mainly on the number of records (N_{qual}) accessed on disk ($C_A = N_{qual} \cdot \bar{t}$). Therefore we introduce the hit ratio of a transaction by

$$HR = \frac{N_{qual}}{N_{REC}} \cdot 100 \% .$$

In our simple transaction model N_{qual} corresponds to the resolution factor Rf. The expected hit ratio of a transaction Q_{Ri} is

$$HR_i = \frac{100}{j_i} \cdot \% \ .$$

The total cost for the random accesses of a transaction increases with the hit ratio, while it remains constant in the course of sequential processing. Hence, random processing is only preferable for $C_A < C_{seq}$. The hit ratio must be less than the critical boundary $HR_o = \frac{100}{j_o} \%$ with $j_o = \frac{t}{K_{seq}}$ otherwise sequential processing is more advantageous, even if an access path exists.

Random access is considered in two different cases:

1) The seeks are not coordinated. Any cylinder is entered with equal probability in random order. The average access motion is a function of the number of occupied cylinders N_{CYL}. An average access time $\bar{t}_r$ results independent of the hit ratio. The cost of this processing according to random lists is given by

$$C_{Ai} = \frac{N_{REC}}{j_i} \cdot \bar{t}_r$$

2) Since all record addresses are known to the data base system at the beginning of a random transaction processing, the access pattern to the external storage may be determined in such a manner that the access motions are performed only in one direction und thus become minimal. The average seek is a function of N_{CYL} and HR. The average access time $\bar{t}_s$ to a record diminishes with increasing hit ratio. The cost of this processing according to random-sorted lists is given by

$$C_{Ai} = \frac{N_{REC}}{j_i} \cdot \bar{t}_s(j_i) \ .$$

3. **Selection of attributes for simple transaction types**

Since the attributes appear to be single and independent in our transaction model they can be considered separately. The resulting costs are shown in the following table in which sequential processing is compared to random processing supported by an index. The common overhead in maintenance operations is omitted.

costs	no secondary index for A_i	secondary index for A_i
Retrieval: C_{Ri}	$r_i \cdot C_{seq}$	$p_i \cdot C_{Ai} + s_i \cdot C_{si} + p_i \cdot C_{pi}$
Update: C_{Ui}	0	$u_i \cdot C_{Ui}$
Insertion: C_{Ii}	0	$I \cdot C_{Mi}$
Deletion: C_{Di}	0	$D \cdot C_{Mi}$
Storage: C_{STi}	0	C_{ST}

The basic demand for the inversion decision is the reduction of costs to realize a gain G compared with the physical sequential processing. Thus,

$$G_i \quad = r_i \cdot C_{seq} - p_i \cdot C_{Ai} - C_{ST} - C_{Index} > 0 \qquad (3.1)$$

with $\quad C_{Index} = p_i \cdot C_{pi} + s_i \cdot C_{si} + u_i \cdot C_{Ui} + (I+D) \cdot C_{Mi}$

In order to find the lower boundary of attribute values j_i for the inversion of A_i we replace C_{Index} with 0. From equation (3.1) follows

$$j_i > j_{\ell i} \quad = \frac{p_i \cdot \bar{t}}{r_i \cdot K_{seq} - c \cdot S_M} \qquad \text{with } \bar{t} = \bar{t}_r \text{ resp. } \bar{t}_s (j_{\ell i}) \qquad (3.2)$$

Hence, the lower boundary of j is determined by

- the probability of retrieval operations,
- the average random access time,
- the speed of sequential processing,
- the storage costs.

This characteristic can be considered independent of N_{REC}, if the weak influence of N_{REC} on $\bar{t}_r$ is neglected. A critical parameter for the lower boundary of j is the length of a record R_ℓ , because the speed of sequential processing is linearly dependent on this factor, while the average random access time for $R_\ell < B$ remains approximately constant. It is shown in (Hä75) that the lower boundary of j is a useful parameter, which is easy to determine and of sufficient precision for practical applications. Note that j_o derived from relation (3.2) with c = 0 and $r_i = p_i$ has considerable values. Assuming the characteristics of a disk IBM 2314, $N_B = 3$ (pages per track) and load factor $\beta = 1$, some values of j_o are given in the following table.

	$\bar{t} = \bar{t}_s(j_o)$	$\bar{t} = \bar{t}_r$
$R_\ell = 80$	$j_o = 57$	$j_o = 270$
$R_\ell = 400$	$j_o = 12$	$j_o = 54$

The selection of indices without storage restrictions is obtained by inversion of n' < n attributes with $j > j_\ell$ oder $G > 0$. When merely m < n' attributes can be inverted, those with the highest gain contributions should be adopted. A_i is preferred to A_k, when

$$\Delta_{ik} = G_i - G_k > 0 \tag{3.3}$$

holds. Relation (3.3) is discussed for the case $r_i = p_i$. Because of $C_{Mi} \approx C_{Mk}$ it can be simplified to

$$r_i \cdot (C_{seq} - C_{Ai} - C_{pi}) - 2 \cdot u_i \cdot C_{Mi} > r_k \cdot (C_{seq} - C_{Ak} - C_{pk}) - 2 \cdot u_k \cdot C_{Mk} \tag{3.4}$$

In a given application with fixed characteristics for storage structure, file allocation and type of random processing, the three parameters $\{j, r, u\}$ of each attribute must be considered when selecting the optimal set. The comparison of pairs of triples can be achieved graphically by curve bundles in the r-j-plane. It can be shown that the update probability u is of minor importance in this respect. For sufficient large files ($N_{REC} > 10^4$) N_{REC} has no influence on the outcome of the selection, which is checked by further evaluation of relation (3.4), that is, the decision for an appropriate set of indices remains valid in case of growth or shrinkage of the file too. It should be underlined that the parameters j and r exert the dominant influence on the solution of the index problem.

4. Selection of attributes for complex transaction types

In our extended model, complex operations are admitted for retrieval and update. Disjunctions and conjunctions of search criteria are allowed in a query. For an attribute A_i it is conceivable to specify $1 \leqslant q_i \leqslant j_i$ attribute values which are connected by V (OR). Note also that when $q_i = j_i$, the i-th attribute in no way restricts qualifying tuples and can be dropped consequently from the query. q_i is the complexity of the attribute condition (Ca73). The disjunctions of all attributes with $q_i \neq j_i$ are associated mutually by the boolean operator $\bigwedge$(AND). The number of the $q_i \neq j_i$ conditions denotes the complexity of the tuple condition (Ca73). Formally the transaction type Q_R is described by

$$Q_R = (q_1, q_2, \ldots, q_n) \text{ with } 1 \leqslant q_i \leqslant j_i, \quad i = 1, 2, \ldots, n$$

In case of queries related to different relations or which enforce recursions for their evaluation, Q_R can be viewed as a query primitive, which should be embedded in an appropriate non-procedural language (As74).

The access to the target lists of the specified attribute values is performed according to the model of section 2. The single lists are merged in main storage according to the applied boolean operators. It is assumed that the resulting costs of the final target list can be neglected. If all attributes specified in Q_R are inverted, the target list T(L) contains exactly the entries for the qualified tuples. In other cases only a list S(L) specifying a superset of the searched tuples can be derived. Based on the cardinality of T(L) or S(L) the decision is made whether random or sequential processing is preferable. The examination and selection of records achieved in case of a list S(L) in core is neglected in our cost model.

In case of statistical queries the answer is completed as soon as a target list T(L) is constructed. If only a list S(L) is derived all records according to this list have to be read and examined.

In case of complex transactions the expense for an attribute cannot be separated from the total costs, which depend on the set of existing indices SI respectively. With regard to section 2 the costs for index operations are obtained likewise:

Retrieval:
$$C_{pk} = \sum_{i \varepsilon SI \wedge (q_{ik} < j_i)} (2 \cdot t_{sav} + (h_i + N_{Bi}) \cdot \bar{t}_o) \cdot q_{ik}$$

Update:
$$C_{Uz} = \sum_{i \varepsilon SI \wedge (q_i = 1)} 2 \cdot C_{Mi}$$

Insertion and Deletion:
$$C_I = C_D = \sum_{i \varepsilon SI} C_{Mi}$$

For statistical and normal retrieval transactions the access costs to the records must be distinguished with regard to the list types T(L) or S(L). If the necessary access rate exceeds

$$AR \geqslant HR_o = \frac{100}{j_o} \quad \%,$$

physical sequential processing is performed, because the time factor is more favourable than in random processing. Otherwise, random processing is provided for the subsetting of records. When a complete list T(L) is established for a statistical query, the access to the records is not required. Hence, the following expression for access costs holds for normal retrieval operations

$$
C_{A_{pk}} = \begin{cases} \dfrac{\bar{t}}{\displaystyle\prod_{i \epsilon SI} \left(\dfrac{j_i}{q_{ik}}\right)} \cdot N_{REC} & \text{for } AR_k < \dfrac{100}{j_o} \text{ \%} \\[4ex] C_{seq} & \text{for } AR_k \geqslant \dfrac{100}{j_o} \text{ \%} \end{cases}
$$

and for statistical retrieval operations

$$
C_{A_{s\ell}} = \begin{cases} 0 & \text{for } AR_\ell = HR \\[2ex] \dfrac{\bar{t}}{\displaystyle\prod_{i \epsilon SI} \left(\dfrac{j_i}{q_{i\ell}}\right)} \cdot N_{REC} & \text{for } AR_\ell < \dfrac{100}{j_o} \text{ \%} \\[4ex] C_{seq} & \text{for } AR \geqslant \dfrac{100}{j_o} \text{ \%} \end{cases}
$$

In normalized relations the target lists with regard to one attribute are distinct. Therefore the disjunction of those lists corresponds to an addition. The expected hit ratio of A_i is given by

$$
HR_i = \frac{q_i}{j_i} \cdot 100 \text{ \%} .
$$

For the conjunction of attributes stochastic independence is assumed between their values so that the hit ratio of Q_R can be described by

$$
HR = \frac{100}{\displaystyle\prod_{i=1}^{n} \left(\frac{j_i}{q_i}\right)} \text{ \%}
$$

For the computation of costs an access rate AR must be applied, which is determined for a given set SI of secondary indices by

$$
AR = \frac{100}{\displaystyle\prod_{i \epsilon SI} \left(\frac{j_i}{q_i}\right)} \text{ \% \quad with } AR \geqslant HR
$$

The transactions of type Q_R are separated in r_s statistical and r_p normal retrieval types with the probabilities s_ℓ resp. p_k. Hence,

$$\sum_{\ell=1}^{r_s} s_\ell + \sum_{k=1}^{r_p} p_k = R.$$

An update transaction Q_U is performed on one record, which is accessed via primary key PK. Several changes of attribute values are allowed. Formally the transaction type Q_U is described by

$$Q_U = PK : (a_1, a_2, \ldots, a_n) \quad \text{with } a_i \; \epsilon \; \{0,1\}$$

$a_i = 1$ denotes the update of A_i. For each changed attribute value the operations described in section 2 are accomplished, if an index exists. The total probability of an update follows from the probabilities u_z of the single transaction types by

$$\sum_{z=1}^{w} u_z = U.$$

Analogous to equation (3.1) the costs resulting from all transactions in case of existing indices are gathered and compared to the results obtained if no access paths are available to support direct access. The following global gain function is received, which comprises all transactions types, their probabilities and the storage costs for indices.

$$G = R \cdot C_{seq} - \sum_{k=1}^{r_p} p_k \cdot (C_{A_{pk}} + C_{pk}) - \sum_{\ell=1}^{r_s} s_\ell \cdot (C_{A_{s\ell}} + C_{p\ell}) - \sum_{z=1}^{w} u_z \cdot C_{Uz} - (I+D) \cdot C_D - \sum_{i \epsilon SI} C_{ST} \quad (4.1)$$

To solve the selection problem the gain G is to be maximized, that is, the set SI of secondary indices must be found such that the total gain resulting from all applications is maximal. Generally, the gain is to be computed for all possible subsets SI from the n candidates among the attributes. Only the examination of the powerset with 2^n sets guarantees an optimal solution, because no index sets can be excluded a priori. Besides the number of attribute values j_i of an attribute A_i, its links to other attributes in the single transactions of type Q_R determine, above all, its membership to the optimal solution. Global retrieval probabilities are no adequate means to describe a transaction load (Sk74, St74). It is shown in (Hä75) that generally no proper solutions can be obtained under model simplifications of this kind.

In special cases the number of the index candidates for the optimal solution can be reduced a priori to improve the computation overhead. We discuss applications without statistical queries ($s_\ell = s = 0$). When the hit ratio of a transaction k exceeds the critical limit HR_o described by

$$HR_k \geqslant HR_o \quad \text{or} \quad \prod_{i=1}^{n} \left(\frac{j_i}{q_{ik}}\right) \leqslant j_o \qquad (4.2)$$

then the transaction is handled in any case in a sequential manner. If condition (4.2) holds for all transactions in which A_i happens to qualify ($q_{ik} < j_i$), than A_i is no candidate for the optimal index set IS, because no efficiency is derived comparing it with sequential processing.

$$\forall \ Q_{Rk} : \ (A_i \mid (q_{ik} < j_i) \wedge (\prod_{\ell=1}^{n} (\frac{j_\ell}{q_{\ell k}}) \leqslant j_o)) \Longrightarrow A_i \notin IS$$

This condition is independent of application parameters such as transaction probabilities.

In a second example the costs for index operations and storage space are assumed to be negligible ($C_{Index} = 0$, $c = 0$). This assumption allows a good approximate solution in many applications. Furthermore, the following relation holds

$$\frac{j_i}{q_{ik}} > j_o \quad \text{for } j_i \neq q_{ik},$$

that is, all attributes improve the total gain in case of inversion independent on each other.

Under these assumptions equation (4.1) yields

$$\frac{G}{N_{REC}} = R \cdot K_{seq} - \sum_{k=1}^{r_p} P_k \cdot \frac{t}{\prod_{i \in SI} (\frac{j_i}{q_{ik}})}$$

In order to maximize the gain the cost of random processing is to be minimized. Hence,

$$\sum_{k=1}^{r_p} P_k \cdot \frac{t}{\prod_{i \in SI} (\frac{j_i}{q_{ik}})} \overset{!}{=} Min$$

The minimum is attained, if the single terms of the sum are minimized or if the expressions

$$\prod_{i \varepsilon SI} (\frac{j_i}{q_{ik}}) \, , \, k = 1, \, 2, \, \ldots, \, r_p$$

are maximized. Since $j_i \geqslant q_{ik}$, the single products are maximal, if the index set SI is maximal. Hence, all n attributes are to be inverted in this special case without storage restrictions. If only a limited number m of indices is allowed, the selection is reduced to a combinatorial problem, where the number of combinations of n attributes taken m at a time without repetitions must be examined. This is because the total gain increases constantly in this special case with the cardinality of optimal index sets. The number of index sets to be computed is given in this limited selection by

$$Z = \binom{n}{m} = \frac{n!}{m! \, (n-m)!}$$

as opposed to 2^n in the normal case.

5. Dynamic evaluation of secondary indices

Even in the case of an optimal index set, existing access paths are not used in any transaction to support retrieval, because sequential processing is preferable for high access rates. Therefore the data base system needs appropriate rules for rapid decision making. Here we discuss a procedure for predicting access rates with different degrees of precision. In queries which are formulated in a non-procedural language the qualifying predicates can be divided so that they can be represented by a binary predicate tree (As74). Three cases are distinguishable for their evaluation. A predicate is represented by a list T(L) or S(L), otherwise there is no way of locating the qualified tuples so that N_{REC} tuples must be considered. The evaluation of the predicate tree starts at the leaves, which consist of the single attribute values, and is continued recursively up to the root.

According to (As74) the possible links of these cases by AND- and OR-nodes are given in the following table. The recursive application of these connections on all non-leaf nodes permits the computation of the expected access rate. For this reason the list lengths related to N_{REC} are invented as hit probabilities p_i under the assumption of stochastic independence. On the level of the leaves these probabilities can be directly expressed by the parameters of the value distributions j_i. For disjunctions of values concerning one attribute in a normalized relation, $p_1 \cdot p_2 = 0$ yields.

list of left subtree

AND	$T(L2)$	$S(L2)$	N_{REC}
$T(L1)$	$T(L1 \wedge L2)$	$S(L1 \wedge L2)$	$S(L1)$
$S(L1)$	$S(L1 \wedge L2)$	$S(L1 \wedge L2)$	$S(L1)$
N_{REC}	$S(L2)$	$S(L2)$	N_{REC}

list of right subtree

hit probability of left subtree

AND	$T(p_2)$	$S(p_2)$	1
$T(p_1)$	$T(p_1 \cdot p_2)$	$S(p_1 \cdot p_2)$	$S(p_1)$
$S(p_1)$	$S(p_1 \cdot p_2)$	$S(p_1 \cdot p_2)$	$S(p_1)$
1	$S(p_2)$	$S(p_2)$	1

hit probability of right subtree

list of left subtree

OR	$T(L2)$	$S(L2)$	N_{REC}
$T(L1)$	$T(L1 \vee L2)$	$S(L1 \vee L2)$	N_{REC}
$S(L1)$	$S(L1 \vee L2)$	$S(L1 \vee L2)$	N_{REC}
N_{REC}	N_{REC}	N_{REC}	N_{REC}

list of right subtree

hit probability of left subtree

OR	$T(p_2)$	$S(p_2)$	1
$T(p_1)$	$T(p_1+p_2-p_1 \cdot p_2)$	$S(p_1+p_2-p_1 \cdot p_2)$	1
$S(p_1)$	$S(p_1+p_2-p_1 \cdot p_2)$	$S(p_1+p_2-p_1 \cdot p_2)$	1
1	1	1	1

hit probability of right subtree

The expected hit probability for the root is needed to determine the kind of further processing. The outlined procedure renders the expected value of the access rate of a transaction type. In order to improve the accuracy of the forecast the actual list lengths N_{ik} stored in the catalogue can be taken to process a particular query. However, additional overhead is imposed to acquire this information. The most expensive way to support the decision is finally the actual merging of target lists, which provides the actual access rate.

6. Conclusion

The problem of finding an optimal set of secondary indices for a given transaction load is considered. In our model the description of queries, updates, insertions and deletions, which are characterized by their type and probability, is provided. For simple transaction types, which refer only to one single attribute, a "decoupled model" is established. Each attribute can be considered separately so that simple analytic solutions are obtained. With respect to inversion a lower boundary depending on detailed storage and processing characteristics exists for the number of attribute values per attribute.

For complex transaction types their exact attribute combinations and their probabilities are taken into account. To find an optimal index set, in the general case the powerset of all attributes must be examined. In special cases one can get simple solutions.

A prediction procedure for the estimation of the access time behavior during the dynamic evaluation of secondary indices is given.

References

(As74) Astrahan, M.M., Chamberlin, D.D.: Implementation of a Structured English Query Language, IBM Research Report, RJ 1464, San José, Oct. 28, 1974.

(Ca73) Cardenas, A.F.: Evaluation and Selection of File Organization - a Model and System, in: CACM, Vol. 16, No. 9, Sept. 1975, pp. 540-548.

(Co70) Codd, E.F.: A Relational Model of Data for Large Shared Data Banks, in: CACM, Vol. 13, No. 6, June 1970, pp. 377-387.

(Hä75) Härder, T.: Auswahl optimaler Indexmengen, Research Report DV 75-2, FG DVS, TH Darmstadt, Sept. 1975.

(Ka75) Karlowsky, I., Leilich, H.-D., Stiege, G.: Ein Suchrechnerkonzept für Datenbankanwendungen, in: Elektronische Rechenanlagen 17 (1975), No. 3, pp. 108-118.

(Ki74) King, W.F.: On the Selection of Indices for a File, IBM Research Report, RJ 1341, San José, 1974.

(Lu71) Lum, V.A., Ling, H.: An Optimization Problem on the Selection of Secondary Keys, in: Proc. of ACM National Conference, 1971, pp. 349-356.

(Ro74) Rothnie, J.B., Lozano, T.: Attribute Based File Organization in a Paged Memory Environment, in: CACM, Vol. 17, No. 2, Feb. 1974, pp. 63-69.

(Sk74) Schkolnick, M.: Optimizing Partial Inversions for Files, IBM Research Report, RJ 1477, San José, Nov. 21, 1974.

(St74) Stonebraker, M.: The Choice of Partial Inversions and Combined Indices, appears in Journal of Computer and Information Sciences.

(Wa73) Wang, C.P.: Parametrization of Information System Application, IBM Research Report, RJ 1199, San José, April 11, 1973.

(We73) Wedekind, H.: Systemanalyse, Carl Hanser Verlag, München 1973.

(Wo71) Wong, E., Chiang, T.C.: Canonical Structure in Attribute Based File Organization, in: CACM, Vol. 14, No. 9, Sept. 1971, pp. 593-597.

A MODEL FOR DATA STRUCTURES

Mila E. Majster
Institut für Informatik
Technische Universität München

INTRODUCTION

Using a computer for the solution of problems - either by programming
some algorithm or by performing retrieval operations in a data bank
system usually involves at each level of abstraction data items as
well as structured data, i.e. collections of data items which are somehow related to each other. If we group data items together into a set
and endow this set with certain operations we get the concept of the
elementary data type. If we now group structured data together and want
to endow this set with certain operations, we can destinguish between
three kinds of operations: those which consider structured data as a
whole (without referring to their structure or to their components
explicitly), those which deal only with the structure between the data
items ("structural operations") and those which concern a data item
itself. In this paper we want to restrict ourselves to structured data
and structural operations.

At this point I should like to motivate the need of a formalization of
structured data and structural operations. The arguments can be summarized as follows:

(1) Structured data are used at each level of abstraction. The desrip-
    tion of these data varies considerably from one level to the other.
    Even at the same level, e.g. in high level programming languages,
    it is seldom uniform. The question, e.g., as to whether the oper-
    ations which can be applied to the data should be part of the de-
    scription has no uniform answer. Thus communication is difficult.

(2) The design and efficiency of an algorithm depend strongly on the
    choice of the data structure which represents the objects to be
    manipulated. In certain areas this dependency has been early rec-
    ognized (e.g. for sorting and searching problems) and led to the
    development of specific structured data (e.g. different kind of

trees, binary trees, balanced trees, B-trees, etc.) These structured data have been formally described and analysed. Until now,
however, there exist very few approaches to the definition of
general data structures.

(3) A rigorous definition of the notion "realization" presupposes the
formalization of the concept "data structure".

(4) For proofs of correctness of programs the involved data structures
must be formally describable.

Our formalism is chosen such that it is independent of a specific programming language and a specific computer model.

I. FORMAL MODEL

When we speak of structured data we usually think of a composite entity consisting of "simpler" constituents which are related somehow.
The nature of the relation may differ considerably in the different
levels of abstraction. It may be e.g. an order relation in a set, a
relation describing a family tree, a relation describing the access
mechanism in a computer memory etc. In general, the relation is the
appropriate mathematical concept for handling composite data. As
usually more than one relation is involved in describing structured
data we choose the extended directed graph for our purposes. Our claim
is that there is an extended directed graph corresponding to any structured data.

DEFINITION 1.
An extended directed graph is a pair (N,P) consisting of a nonempty
set N of nodes which is at most countable and a finite set P of partial
mappings from N to N.

If p is a partial mapping from N to N which is defined for some n∈N
then np denotes the value of p at n.

DEFINITION 2.
By H(P) we denote the semigroup with identity generated by P under
functional composition.

There is a simple way to represent an extended directed graph graphically. If $p \epsilon P$ and $n \epsilon N$ and $m = np$ we display the nodes by circles and express the fact that $m = np$ by an arrow from n to m with designation p.

We want now to give some examples of extended directed graphs.

1. Let $N = (n_{ij})_{\substack{i = 1...8 \\ j = 1...8}}$

$P = \{p_1, p_2, p_3, p_4\}$

where

$$n_{ij} \, p_1 = n_{ij+1} \qquad j = 1...7; \forall i$$

$$n_{ij} \, p_2 = n_{ij-1} \qquad j = 2...8; \forall i$$

$$n_{ij} \, p_3 = n_{i+1j} \qquad i = 1...7; \forall j$$

$$n_{ij} \, p_4 = n_{i-1j} \qquad i = 2...8; \forall j$$

(N,P) is represented in the plane as follows

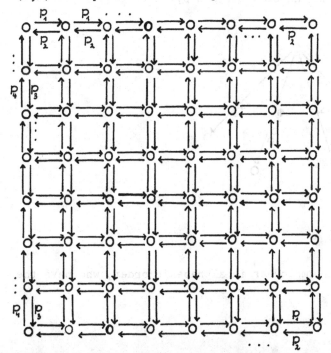

(N,P) can be thought of as one possible representation of a chessboard.

2. Let $N = (n_i)_{i \in \mathbb{N}}$ and
$P = \{p_1, p_2\}$ where
$n_i p_1 = n_{2i}$ $i = 1, 2, \ldots$
$n_i p_2 = n_{2i+1}$ $i = 1, 2, \ldots$

Hence

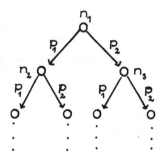

(N,P) is an infinite binary tree.

3. Consider the following mode declaration in Algol 68

mode **employee** = (**string** name, **real** salary, **ref** **employee** boss,
ref **employee** next)

An object of this mode can be described by

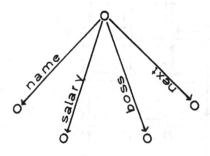

We consider now three employees in alphabetic order, who have the same boss

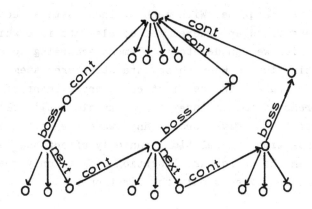

If we are only interested in the relations between the four employee
we get

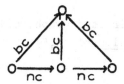

Extended directed graphs can be investigated similarly as directed
graphs. Typical results are: decomposition of an extended directed
graph into disjoint constituents, determination of generating sets,
maximal constituents and so on. For these questions the reader is referred to [1].

II. DATA STRUCTURES

We have now introduced our basic concept, the extended directed graph.
We have seen how structured data can be described using these graphs.
Until now, the relations between the data items - these are represented by the nodes in the graph - were supposed to be given a priori
and fixed. Note that we never mentioned something like an "operation"
on the data. We are now interested in the dynamic behaviour of structured data. Before going into detail in the discussion of operations
let us first consider three well-known examples of data structures:

a list, a pushdown-list, a queue. With each of these data structures
we have basically associated an ordered set of elements into which we
can insert or from which we can delete an element according to specific rules. The distinction between these data structures stems from
the different kinds of rules: in the first case, any element of the
ordered set can be removed and an insertion of an element is allowed
between (with respect to the given order) any two elements. In the
second case both, insertion and deletion, can only affect the last
element of the set. In the third case insertion affects only the last
element, whereas deletion affects only the first one.

Thus, informally we can say that a data structure - as opposed to
structured data - is not only determined by the relations between its
data items but also by the operations which can be performed on the
structured data. We are going to suggest a definition of the notion
data structure based on our previous model in which the above considerations have been taken into account. In order to do so we need
a series of auxiliary definitions.

DEFINITION 3.
Let $\Gamma = (N,P)$ be an extended directed graph, $\omega \notin N$. A pair (Γ,m), where
$m \in N \cup \{\omega\}$, is called a <u>configuration</u> of (N,P).

DEFINITION 4.
Let G be a set of finite extended directed graphs and τ a set of configurations of elements of G. A partial mapping

$$o : \tau \longrightarrow \tau$$

is called an elementary

1) <u>access operation</u>, if

$$(\Gamma,m)o = (\Gamma', m')$$

   implies $\Gamma = \Gamma'$ and either

   i) there are no edges starting from m and $m' = \omega$

or

   ii) there exists a mapping q which is defined at m, such that

$$m' = mq$$

   In this case we say that we access m' along a path named
   q starting from m.

2) <u>node-insert operation</u>, if

$$(\Gamma,m)o = (\Gamma',m')$$

implies

  i) $m' \neq \omega$

 ii) card (N) = card$(N')-1$

iii) the subgraph of Γ' which is defined by $N' \smallsetminus \{m'\}$ is - up
  to renaming - a partial graph of Γ such that $n_1 p = n_2$
  $n_i \varepsilon N$ $p \varepsilon P$ implies $\overline{n}_1 \overline{p} = \overline{n}_2$, where n_i (resp. p) corresponds
  to $\overline{n}_i$ (resp. $\overline{p}$) according to the renaming.

 iv) $m = \omega$ or $\overline{m}$ (i.e. the element corresponding to m) is connected to m' by a single edge.

In the same way we can define node-deletion, edge-insertion, and -de-
letion.

There are some interesting features of the above definitions. Looking
e.g. at the definition of the access operation we see that we can permit or prohibit the access to some element by defining the mapping O
in the right way. Moreover, our definition guarantees that a node n
can be accessed from a node m only if n and m are related in the graph.

Having defined what an elementary operation should be we can now construct the data structures.

DEFINITION 5.
Let $\mathfrak{m}$ be a set of finite extended directed graphs. An extended directed
graph
$$\mathfrak{K} = (\mathcal{C}_{\mathfrak{m}}, T)$$
consisting of

 i) a set of configurations of elements of $\mathfrak{m}$, such that for each
  graph $\Gamma \varepsilon \mathfrak{m}$ there is at least one configuration of Γ in $\mathcal{C}_{\mathfrak{m}}$.

ii) a finite set T of elementary operations on $\mathcal{C}_{\mathfrak{m}}$
  is called a data structure class. The elements in H(T) are called
  operations.
  A pair $(\Gamma, \mathfrak{K})$, where Γ is an extended directed graph
  and $\mathfrak{K}$ a data structure class is called a data structure, if
  there is a configuration of Γ which is a node of $\mathfrak{K}$.

EXAMPLES.
Let $\mathfrak{m}' = \{(N,P) : (N,P)$ is extended directed graph, $P = \{p\}$ and
$p^t = \overset{\infty}{\underset{i=1}{\bigcup}} p^i$ is an order relation on $N\}$.

For each natural number k we choose exactly one graph Γ_k with k nodes.
Then we put

$$\mathcal{M} = \{\Gamma_k : k \in \mathbb{N}\}$$

(Here $\Gamma_k = (N_k, \{p_k\})$ with $N_k = \{n_{k1}, \ldots n_{kk}\}$

$$n_{ki}p_k = n_{ki+1} \quad i = 1 \ldots k-1)$$

Based on this set of graphs we construct now the following data structure classes.

1. Let $\mathcal{T}_{\mathcal{M}}^L$ be the set of all possible configurations of all elements
of $\mathcal{M}$. We choose the elementary operations as:

$$t_i : \mathcal{T}_{\mathcal{M}}^L \longrightarrow \mathcal{T}_{\mathcal{M}}^L \quad i = 1,2,3$$

$$t_1 : (\Gamma_k, n_{k1}p_k^m) \longmapsto (\Gamma_{k+1}, n_{k+1,1}p_{k+1}^m) \text{ for } k>0, \ k-1 \geqslant m \geqslant 0 \quad \text{and}$$

$$(\Gamma_k, \omega) \longmapsto (\Gamma_{k+1}, n_{k+1,1}p_{k+1}^k), \ (\Gamma_0, \omega) \longmapsto (\Gamma_1, n_{11})$$

t_1 is the operation "insert one element in front of the one at
which you point now.

$$t_2 : (\Gamma_k, n_{k1}p_k^m) \longmapsto (\Gamma_k, n_{k1}p_k^{m+1}) \text{ for } k>0 \quad k-1 \geqslant m \geqslant 0 \quad \text{and}$$

$$(\Gamma_k, n_{k1}p_k^{k-1}) \longmapsto (\Gamma_k, \omega)$$

t_2 is the operation "go to next element"

$$t_3 : (\Gamma_k, n_{k1}p_k^m) \longmapsto (\Gamma_{k-1}, n_{k-1,1}p_{k-1}^m) \quad k>0 \quad k-1 \geqslant m \geqslant 0$$

$$(\Gamma_k, n_{k1}p_k^{k-1}) \longmapsto (\Gamma_{k-1}, \omega) \quad k>0$$

t_3 is the operation "delete the element which is pointed at".

The extended directed graph

$$\mathcal{L} = (\mathcal{T}_{\mathcal{M}}^L, \{t_1, t_2, t_3\})$$

is called list class. A pair

$$(\Gamma_n, \mathcal{L})$$

is called <u>list</u> <u>of</u> <u>length</u> <u>n</u>.

Γ_n is graphically illustrated by

$$n_{n1} \quad O \xrightarrow{\ p_n\ } O \xrightarrow{\ p_n\ } O \ \cdots\cdots O$$

$$\underbrace{\hphantom{n_{n1} \quad O \xrightarrow{\ p_n\ } O \xrightarrow{\ p_n\ } O \ \cdots\cdots O}}_{n \text{ nodes}}$$

The graph $\mathcal{L}$ which describes the list class is illustrated by

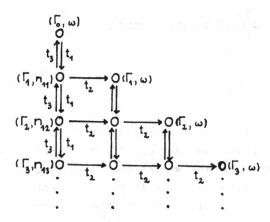

$\mathcal{L} = (\tau_{m}^{L}, \{t_1, t_2, t_3\})$ is an __infinite__ extended directed graph with entry. Please note that a list can only be traversed in one direction.

2. Let

$$\tau_{m}^{K} = \{(\Gamma_k, \ n_{k1}) \quad k \geqslant 1\} \ \cup \ \{(\Gamma_0, \omega)\}$$

we choose the following operations

$$k_i : \tau_{m}^{K} \longrightarrow \tau_{m}^{K}$$

$$k_1 : (\Gamma_k, \ n_{k1}) \longmapsto (\Gamma_{k+1}, \ n_{k+1,1}) \quad k \neq 0, \quad (\Gamma_0, \omega) \longmapsto (\Gamma_1, n_{11})$$

$$k_2 : (\Gamma_{k+1}, \; n_{k+1,1}) \longmapsto (\Gamma_k, \; n_{k1}) \quad k \neq o, \quad (\Gamma_1, n_{11}) \longmapsto (\Gamma_o, \omega)$$

The extended directed graph

$$\gamma = (\; \mathcal{C}^K_m, \{k_1, k_2\})$$

is a data structure class describing the cynamic behaviour of pushdown lists. The class is illustrated by

For more complicated examples we refer to [1] where a large number of interesting data structures has been described using our model of extended directed graphs. Here we restrict ourselves to point at some of the benefits of our model: The fact that a configuration of an extended directed graph can be a node in two different data structure classes enables one to construct a "connection" between these two classes. Let be

$$\mathfrak{K}_1 = (\mathcal{C}^1_{m_1}, T_1)$$

$$\mathfrak{K}_2 = (\mathcal{C}^2_{m_2}, T_2)$$

two data structure classes. We set

$$\mathfrak{K}_1 \cup \mathfrak{K}_2 = (\mathcal{C}^1_{m_1} \cup \mathcal{C}^2_{m_2}, T_1 \cup T_2)$$

If a configuration occurs in $\mathcal{C}^1_{m_1}$ and in $\mathcal{C}^2_{m_2}$ then in $\mathfrak{K}_1 \cup \mathfrak{K}_2$ - which is also a data structure class according to our definition - the operations of both T_1 and T_2 can be applied to that configuration. Thus, starting from some given classes new datastructure classes can be created.

Another point to be mentioned is that equivalence of data structures

as well as questions concerning the simulation of one data structure
by another data structure can be treated within this model.

Moreover, those data structure classes which can be defined by specific methods, e.g. so-called definition only by operations, can be
characterized with the help of our model.

III. REALIZATIONS OF DATA STRUCTURES

How can we formally define the realization of data structures? As a
data structure is given by a pair

$$(\Gamma, \mathbf{\mathfrak{L}})$$

one part of our task will be to allocate storage to Γ. The other part
of our task will then be to declare how the operations have to be
treated. As time is lacking, we will here concentrate on the first
project.

DEFINITION 6.
Let (N,P) be an extended directed graph an A a set, $|A| \geq |N|$. A pair
(r,ρ) consisting of an one-to-one mapping

$$r : N \to A$$

and an one-to-one homomorphism of semigroups

$$\rho : H(P) \to A^{(A)} \qquad (A^{(A)} \text{ is the set of partial mappings}$$
$$\text{from } A \text{ to } A.)$$

such that
  i) $np \in N \quad \mathbf{X} \quad (nr)(p\rho) \in Nr$
 ii) $(np)r = (Nr)(p\rho)$, if p is defined at n.

REMARK.
Restricted to strongly connected extended directed graphs this definition coincides with the one given in [2].

We can interpret our definition as follows: Let A be a contiguous set
of addresses, i.e. $A = \{x \in N : a \leq x \leq b\}$ for some $a,b \in \mathbb{N}$. If the elements of N are considered as external names, the mapping r can be considered as the addressbook for the structured data. It assigns a unique

address to each element of N. Pρ is both a representation for the edges
of (N,P) and a mechanism for calculating the address of np from the
address of n according to

$$(np)r = (nr)(pρ).$$

When using structured data we often do not refer explicitly to an element by an external name but we refer to by its relation to some other
element. Imagine for example the use of binary trees, where in most
cases a node is referred to as "son of node n", n being its father
node. In this case we need not keep the whole addressbook r in memory.
We just keep

$$n_o r$$

where n_o is the root of the tree. The address of some element in the
tree can be calculated with the help of

$$pρ \qquad p \, ε \, P$$

IV. DISPLACING OF REALIZATIONS

As one can easily see, any extended directed graph (N,P) can be real-
ized in any set $A, |A| \geq |N|$. The question which interests us now is:
What happens if such a realization has to be shifted within our memory
A? In the worst case we must set up a completely new addressbook r and
redefine ρ. For a big class of extended directed graphs, however, there
exists a possibility to avoid this effort of complete redefinition.

DEFINITION 7.
A node n_o of an extended directed graph is called entry, if for every
nεN there exists a mapping p such that $n_o p = n$.

DEFINITION 8.
Let (N,P) be an extended directed graph with entry n_o. (N,P) is said
to have a displacement mapping in A, $|A| \geq |N|$, if there exists

$$δ* : N \to A^A$$

with the following properties
i) δ* is one-to-one

ii) for any a ε A there exists a realization (r_a, ρ_a) such that

   a) $n_o r_a = a$

      $nr_a = a(n\delta*)$

   b) the mapping β_a

      $\beta_a : \{t \, \varepsilon \, H(P)\rho_a : at \, \varepsilon \, Nr_a\} \rightarrow A^A$

      which is defined by for all b ε A

      $b(p\rho_a)\beta_a = (n_o p)r_b$

      is well defined and one-to-one onto $N\delta*$.

If an extended directed graph with entry n_o has such a displacement mapping $\delta*$ we proceed in the following way: Instead of maintaining information about a specific realization which has to be updated all the time we keep $\delta*$ in memory. Then, if one specific value a ε A is given, which is supposed to be the future address of n_o we can easily calculate the position of n ε N with respect to the realization (r_a, ρ_a)

$$nr_a = a(n\delta*).$$

Property ii,b constructs an intrinsic correspondence between the partial transformations in $H(P)\rho_a \subset A^{(A)}$ which do not lead out of the realization r_a of (N,P) and the total transformations in $N\delta* \subset A^A$. Via this correspondence all realizations are related in the following way: Let a,b ε A and β_a, β_b the corresponding mappings. Then we get for p ε $Fun(n_o)$

$$p\rho_b = (p\rho_a)(\beta_a \, \beta_b^{-1})$$

and hence have built up a relation between ρ_a and ρ_b.

EXAMPLES.

1. The first three examples of section I have a displacement mapping.
2. An extended directed graph with entry which has no displacement mapping is given by

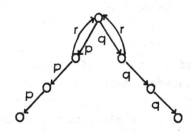

We proceed now in the investigation of extended directed graph with
displacement mappings and look for a simple criterion for determining
whether an extended directed graph has such a mapping.

PROPOSITION 1.

Let (N,P) be an extended directed graph with entry n_o. $|A| \geqslant |N|$;
the following statements are equivalent
i) (N,P) has a displacement mapping $\delta^* : N \to A^A$ such that
    $n_o\delta^* = id_A$.
ii) for all p,q defined at n_o $n_op = n_oq$ implies $p = q$.

Proof:
i) implies ii). Let us assume that $n_op_1 = n_op_2$ and $p_1 \neq p_2$.
    Then for all $b \varepsilon A$ $b(p_1\rho_a)\beta_a = (n_op_1)r_b = (n_op_2)r_b = b(p_2\rho_a)\beta_a$.
    Hence we get $(p_1\rho_a)\beta_a = (p_2\rho_a)\beta_a$.
    As β_a and β_a are one-to-one we get $p_1 = p_2$.

ii) implies i). For any $a \varepsilon A$ let us choose a realization (r_a,ρ_a)
    with $n_or_a = a$.
    Let $n \varepsilon N$ be given. There is a unique $p \varepsilon H(P)$ such that
    $n = n_op$.
    We put for all $a \varepsilon A$ $a(n\delta^*) := a(p\rho_a)$.
    $\delta^* : N \to A^A$ is a displacement mapping.

Proposition 1 gives us an useful criterion to decide if an extended
directed graph has a displacement mapping. Moreover, if we once found
out that n_o is an entry which satisfies ii) and choose for each $a \varepsilon A$
a realization (r_a,ρ_a) with $n_or_a = a$ we can construct a displacement
mapping δ^*. This is described in the following corollary.

COROLLARY 1.

Let n_o be an entry satisfying ii). Let for each $a \varepsilon A$ a realization
(r_a,ρ_a) with $n_or_a = a$ be given. We define

$$a(n\delta^*) := a(p\rho_a)$$

where $n = n_op$. δ^* is a well defined mapping from N to A^A and satisfies the conditions of a displacement mapping.

In order to make the involved concepts clear to the reader we demonstrate our techniques for the case $A = \{0,1,2,...M\}$.

PROPOSITION 2.

Let (N,P) be an extended directed graph with entry n_o.

$$A = \{0,1,\ldots M\}, \quad M \geqslant |N|.$$

Let $(r_o\rho_o)$ be any realization with $n_o r_o = 0$. Then there exists a displacement mapping $\delta^* : N \to A^A$ such that

$$a(n\delta^*) = a + nr_o \bmod |A|$$

(i.e. the total function

$$n\delta^* : A \to A$$

is additive).

<u>Proof:</u>

Let $n = n_o p$ then $nr_o = O(p\rho_o) =: k_n \in A$. We put

$$a(n\delta^*) := a + k_n \bmod |A|.$$

Then we get

$$nr_o = k_n = 0 + k_n = O(n\delta^*).$$

For each $a \in A$ we define now r_a, ρ_a, β_a. First we make the following observations.

1. $n\delta^* : A \to A$

   $n\delta^*$ is a total mapping and $a(n\delta^*) \in A$ for any a. Hence
   $$\delta^* : N \to A^A$$

2. δ^* is one-to-one: Suppose that
   $$n\delta^* = n'\delta^*,$$

   then

   $$nr_o = O(n\delta^*) = O(n'\delta^*) = n'r_o. \text{ Hence } n = n'.$$

We put now for $a \in A$

$$n_o r_a := a \quad nr_a := a \, n\delta^* = a + k_n \bmod |A|.$$

Surely r_a is a one-to-one mapping from N to A. By defining

$$p\rho_a = r_a^{-1} \, p \, r_a$$

we complete the proof.

COROLLARY 2.

Let n_o satisfy ii) in proposition 1. We define

$$\delta_o : N \longrightarrow A^{(A)}$$

$(n_o p)\delta_o := p\rho_o$, then for the mappings δ^*, r_a, ρ_a which are given in proposition 2 the following equations hold:

$$n\ r_a\ = a + (0)(n\delta_o)\ \text{mod}|A|$$

$$(np)r_a = a + (n\ r_o)(p\rho_o)\ \text{mod}|A|$$

$$= a + (0)(np\delta_o)\ \text{mod}|A|$$

We can now make the following conclusions:

1. It follows from corollary 2 that we can make use of the existence of a displacement mapping $\delta*$ without explicitly calculating it. Once we found a realization (r_o, ρ_o) of (N,P) with $n_o r_o = 0$ for which moreover

$$n\ \delta_o$$

is easily determined and $n\ \delta_o$ is a "simple" function from A to A (e.g. additive) then for each a ϵ A we get a nice realization (r_a, ρ_a) if we use

$$n\ r_a\ = a + (0)(n\delta_o)\ \text{mod}|A|$$

$$(np)r_a = a + (0)(np\delta_o)\ \text{mod}|A|$$

$$= a + (0)(n\delta_o)(p\rho_o)\ \text{mod}|A|$$

2. It is clear that the above propositions can also be stated if we choose a realization (r_s, ρ_s) with $n_o r_s = s$ as a starting point instead of (r_o, ρ_o).

3. If we define for each a ϵ A

$$(n_o p)\delta_a := p\rho_a$$

(where n_o is a basic entry)

$$\delta_a : N \rightarrow A^{(A)}$$

and

$$h_a : N\delta_a \rightarrow N\delta_o$$

$$h_a\ /\ p\rho_a \rightarrow p\rho_o$$

then

$$\beta_a = h_a \cdot \beta_o.$$

In this section we showed that there is an interesting technique for realizing structured data such that relocations can be easily performed. This technique works for extended directed graphs with basic entry. In [1] we demonstrate how these techniques can be easily adapted to the more general case. To give you an idea how this works: we introduce auxiliary "imaginary" edges and nodes which only appear

when addresses are determined. These auxiliary elements are n o t
part of the structured data.

REFERENCES

[1] Mila E. Majster: Extended directed graphs, a model for data struc-
    tures and data structure classes. Ph.D. thesis, Technische Univer-
    sität München, 1975.

[2] A. L. Rosenberg: Data graphs and addressing schemes. Journal of
    Computer and Systems Sciences 5, 193-238 (1971).

Further references on this subject:

E. F. Codd: A relational model of data for large shared data banks.
CACM, 13, No. 6, 1970.

J. Earley: Towards an understanding of data structures. CACM, 14,
No. 10, 1971.

C.A.R. Hoare: Notes on data structuring. APIC Studies in Data
Processing No. 8: Structured Programming.

B. Liskov, S. Zilles: Programming with abstract data types.
SIGPLAN Notices, Vol. 4, 1974.

W. Turskii: A model for data structures and its applications I, II.
Acta Informatica, 1, 1972.

FAST ACCESS SEQUENTIAL STRUCTURES

G. Martella   F.A. Schreiber

Istituto di Elettronica - Politecnico di Milano

P. Leonardo da Vinci, 32 - 20133 Milano - Italy

1. INTRODUCTION

The minimization of the product (time x storage) is a very common goal
to be achieved in many problems in the world of data management. Unfor-
tunately very often the requirements for minimizing one of the two factors are in contrast with those for minimizing the other one, so that
a compromise must be looked for according to the peculiar problem or
application in concern. This is the case of query-oriented information
systems in which large amounts of data have to be searched for retrieving the records answering some particular questions, expressed in terms
of the value taken by some attributes of those records, called keys.
If the amount of data to be examined is very large and/or the storage
medium is a slow one, the time to give the answer can be very long if
an appropriate storage organization is not chosen. One of the most widely used techniques to solve this problem is the *file inversion* with
respect to one or more of the relevant attributes, creating secondary
indices which put in relation the key value with the storage locations
[1].
This concept can be extended to obtain Query-inverted File Organizations
in which the addresses of all the storage blocks containing the records
answering a particular request are put in relation with the request itself (fig. 1). All the records are stored in contiguous storage locations in order to reduce the access time to answer the query [2].

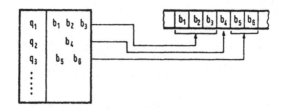

Fig. 1

This organization, however, requires a lot of storage since records answering more than one query are to be stored in a redundant way.
In [1,3] the *consecutive retrieval property* (CR) has been defined for

a query set as the peculiarity of keeping the storage consecutiveness
of all records answering a query, while avoiding the duplication of
any of them. Such an organization clearly minimizes both storage space
and retrieval time, but it is not applicable to whatever set of queries on whatever set of records. So it becomes of interest the consideration of consecutive retrieval *with redundancy* (CRWR) while trying to
keep the redundancy as low as possible.
In [3] it has been investigated the possibility of organizing a file
on a CR basis only by examining the set of queries and their structure,
extending then this organization to dynamic files.
In this paper we shall present a solution to the CRWR problem in dynamic files with fast access properties to be used in real-time systems
and we shall give some comparison data with other data organizations.

2. - THE QUERY GRAPH

In this section we introduce some definitions about the notion of covering of two queris and a graph representation of the query set; a
formal treatment of this subject can be found in [3], from which
paper we report some conclusions.

Given a set $\{Q\} \equiv (q_1, \ldots, q_2)$ of *queries*, a set $\{A\} \equiv (a_1, \ldots, a_N)$ of
attributes, a set $\{V\} \equiv (v_{a_1 1}, \ldots, v_{a_1 k}, \ldots, v_{a_N 1}, \ldots, v_{a_N p})$ of *va-*
lues which can be given to each attribute, a query q_1 is identified
as a string of one value from $\{V\}$ for each one of the attributes of
the set $\{A\}$ which uniquely specifies a set of records in a file (characteristic values). A value $v_{a_j i}$ of an attribute a_j may make another
attribute a_k meaningless; an *indifference condition* X is entered
as value of an attribute a_i whenever the value of a_i is not essential in answering a particular query q_1 (notice that no more than n-1
indifference conditions can be specified in a query).
The set $\{Q\}$ of all allowable queries can then be built knowing the
set of values of each attribute and their characteristics. We should
give each attribute all its possible values, the indifference condition
included; owing to the aforesaid uncompatibility among the values of
some different attributes, the corresponding "theoric" queries must be
deleted, thereby reducing the dimensions of the set $\{Q\}$.
Let us consider now a query q_1 with only m attributes having some
specified value, being the other n-m indifference conditions. Be $\{R\}$
the set of records constituting the whole file; be $\rho(q_1) \in \{R\}$ the
set of records answering q_1; the set $\rho(q_1)$ then is constituted by all
the records identified by the assigned values for the key attributes

and by any possible configuration of values for the remaining attributes.

It is possible now to build a *Covering Table* C as a matrix the colunms of which correspond each to an attribute a_j and the rows to a query q_i. Entries c_{ij} represent the value taken by the attribute a_j in the query q_i.

Def.: A query q_i is said to *cover* a query q_k (simbolically $q_i > q_k$) if and only if, for each attribute a_j $1 \leq j \leq n$,

either:

$$c_{ij} = c_{kj}$$

or

$$c_{ij} = x$$

Obviously, whenever two distinct queries q_i, q_k are expressed with the same number of indifference conditions, no covering possibility exists between them.

It is possible to demonstrate that the covering operation is transitive [3]. If a subset $\{q_l\}$ of $\{Q\}$ exists such that $q_{l_1} > q_{l_2} > \ldots > q_{l_s}$ it is called a *covery chain*.

A *covering graph* can be built from a *covering table* under the following rules :

1. - to each query $q_i \in \{Q\}$ a node corresponds in the graph;
2. - whenever $q_i > q_k$ and there is no q_j such that $q_i > q_j > q_k$, there is an oriented edge from q_i to q_k.

In [3] it has been proved that whenever the covering graph, we call hereafter the "query-graph", is a treee, a CR organization is possible; moreover, whenever $\{Q\}$ can be subdivied in subsets such that the "root-queries" of the various subsets are all disjoint and all the covering graphs for the subsets are trees, a CR organization is still possible. Let now C be a general covering table. The associated *covering graph* will have some source nodes corresponding to queries not covered by any other query (at least one of such nodes always exists) and some sink nodes corresponding to the lowest level queries. However it is possible to consider only *covering graphs* with a single source node without limiting the generality of the related considerations. It is in fact possible to add to the query set a "dummy" query covering all the others, this query being described by the intersection set of the characteristic values of attributes for all the source nodes. Would this set be empty, the dummy query could be represented as: "read the whole file".

We consider now in a general covering table two queries q_i and q_j such that:

$$q_i \nmid q_j \quad \text{and} \quad q_j \nmid q_i$$

$$\rho(q_i) \cap \rho(q_j) \neq \phi$$

The two following conditions must then be met

a) if attribute a_k has non indifferent values both for q_i and q_j it must be

$$c_{ij} = c_{jk} \ (\neq x)$$

b) for at least two attributes a_1, a_m it must be

$$c_{i1} = x \neq c_{j1} \quad \text{and} \quad c_{jm} = x \neq c_{im}$$

These conditions are expressed in the covering graph by the existence of a node, corresponding to the query consisting of all the specified values of q_i and q_j, with two incident edges; the covering graph then is no more a tree.

Even if there are some instances of non-tree query-graphs still allowing a non-redundant CR organization, these graphs correspond to the existence of two one-dimension CR organization with *conjunctive ends* (see theorem 4 in [1] and Fig. 2), this property is not generally true for any general query-graph.

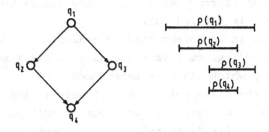

Fig. 2

The problem then is to look for a CRWR organization which assures a fast access-time by multiplexing the records answering some subsets of queries.

3. - REDUNDANT CR ORGANIZATIONS

We have already noticed that the query graph is always a cycle-free o-
riented graph (acyclic digraph) in which all paths leave from a single
"source" node to reach one or more "sink" nodes. For acyclic digraphs
the possibility exists of ordering the nodes in several different *levels*
on the base of their distance from the source node; for query-graphs,
for which the condition 2 of section 2 holds, this fact corresponds to
assigning to each level all the queries having the same number of indifference conditions in a decreasing order. Therefore the source will represent the query with the maximum number of indifference conditions,
while the sinks will represent queries with no indifference condition.
In the following we propose two different approaches to the definition
of a redundant CR organization by transforming general query-graphs in
query-trees.
The first approach can be called the "natural splitting" since the query-tree is obtained by splitting and multiplexing all the nodes having
more than one incoming edge as in the following algorithm.

A_1 - The root of the query-tree is made to coincide with the source
     node of the query-graph;
A_2 - At the next level, nodes having more than one incoming edge are
     multiplexed, together with all their outgoing edges to the lower
     level, as many times as the number of the input edges;
A_3 - On the graph, modified as in step A_2, step A_2 is repeated until
     the sink nodes are reached.

Fig. 3 shows a graphical representation of the algorithm while in Fig.
4 a complete example is carried out.
For such an approach it is interesting to evaluate how many copies of
each node are produced, since this value gives a first measure of the
amount of redundancy which has been introduced.
We can notice that the nodes belonging to levels 1 (the root) and 2
are never multiplexed. At level 3, each node is multiplexed as many
times as the number of its "fathers". At subsequent levels, each node
is multiplexed as many times as the number of its fathers having a
single "grandfather" plus the number of grandfathers of the fathers having more than one grandfather and so on.
To formalize this "tongue twister" calculation let us call:

    $P_s(t_i)$ - the number of fathers of node t_i having a single grand-
            father
    $P_m(t_i)$ - the number of fathers of node t_i having multiple grand-

fathers

l - the level the node t_i belongs to

$P^k(t_i)$ - the father(s) on the k-th generation starting from (t_i)

$\#(t_i)$ - the number of copies of node (t_i)

then

$$\#(t_i) = \sum_{o^k}^{l-1} P_s \ (P^k_m \ (t_i))$$

with the obvious conventions that: $P^o_m(t_i) = t_i$,

$P^k_m(t_i) = 0$ if no father with multiple grandfathers exists,

$P_s(t_i) = 0$ if no father with single grandfather exists (i.e. the root),

$P_s(0) = 0$.

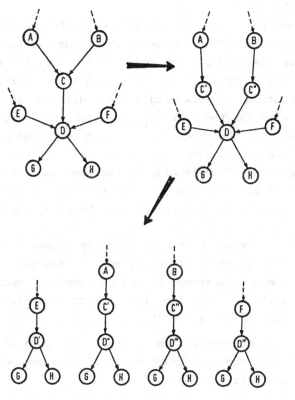

Fig. 3

A more exact definition for the redundancy of a data organization in query-oriented systems has been proposed by Ghosh [1]. Let us indicate by $|\rho(q_i)|$ the number of different records answering a query q_i, by m the number of distinct records in the file, and by m_1 the number of records in a particular file organization. The redundancy is defined to be

$$R = \frac{m_1 - m}{m}$$

where $m = \left| \bigcup\limits_{i=1}^{N} \rho(q_i) \right|$

In our case the value of m_1 can be recursively evaluated on the query-tree in the following way:

$$m_1 = \left| \rho(t_1) \right| \quad , \quad \left| \rho(t_i) \right| = \left| \rho(t_i) \bigcap (\cup \rho(\phi_{t_i})) \right| + \sum \left| \rho(\phi_{t_i}) \right| \quad i = 1, \ldots, N$$

where ϕ_{t_i} denotes the sons of node t_i and N is the number of nodes in the query-tree.

In Fig. 4 a possible organization of the records on the storage medium is shown. To retrieve the records an index must be built giving the set of queries answered by each node of the tree, the nodes representing the initial address of a subfile, and the number of blocks occupied on the storage. In answering a particular query, a search must be made in the index for the node t_i at which the query is at the highest level, so that only the needed records are retrieved with a single access. But we can save a very large amount of time mainly in replying to a set of queries all belonging to the same subtree. In fact, choosing the node in the tree answering to the highest level query, we can retrieve the records also answering all the other queries with a single access.

The index for this kind of organization can become a rather large table depending on the nature of the query set so that the research in it can become lenghty and cumbersome. So let us examine a second approach, based on the notion of spanning tree, for transforming the general query-graph in a set of trees $\{T\} \equiv (t_1, \ldots, t_q)$.

B_1 - Take a spanning tree for the query-graph. This tree will have a root $t_1 \equiv q_1$ and will leave a set of co-trees for the remaining part of the query-graph.

The choose of the spanning tree must be made in such a way as to minimize the number of disjoint rooted co-trees.

This condition corresponds to minimize the repetition of the already considered paths as imposed by step B_3. To build the other trees, the following steps are needed:

B_2 - leaving from the root of the next cotree follow the path on the cotree until the last node of the cotree itself is reached.

B_3 - if the node reached in step B_2 is a leaf, repeat step B_2. If it
is not a leaf, move further on the spanning tree either until the
leaves are reached or until the root of a new cotree is reached,
then repeat step B_2.

Query	Attribute values
q_1	α_1 × × × × ×
q_2	α_1 × β_1 × × ×
q_3	α_1 γ_1 × × × ×
q_4	α_1 × β_1 δ_3 × ×
q_5	α_1 γ_1 β_1 × × ×
q_6	α_1 γ_1 × × ϑ_1 ×
q_7	α_1 γ_1 β_1 δ_3 ϑ_1 ×
q_8	α_1 γ_1 β_1 × ϑ_1 ε_1
q_9	α_1 γ_1 β_1 δ_3 ϑ_1 ε_2
q_{10}	α_1 γ_1 β_1 δ_3 ϑ_1 ε_1

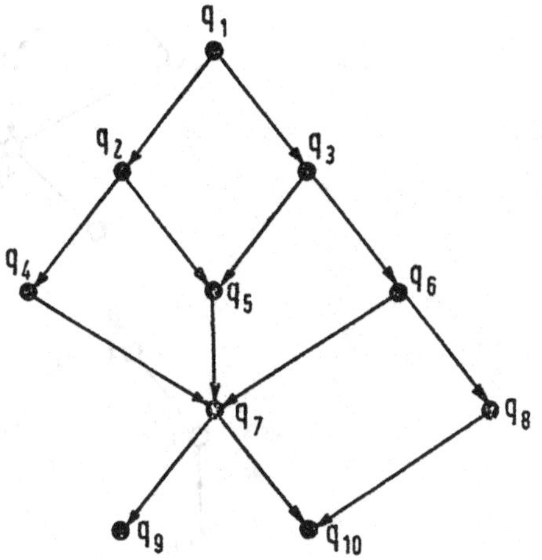

the query-graph

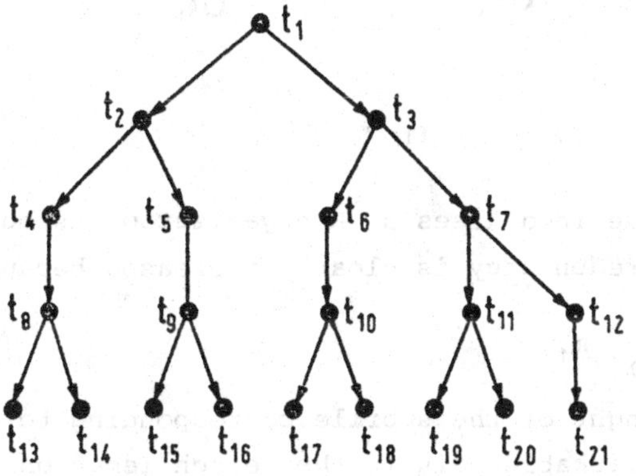

the derived
query-tree

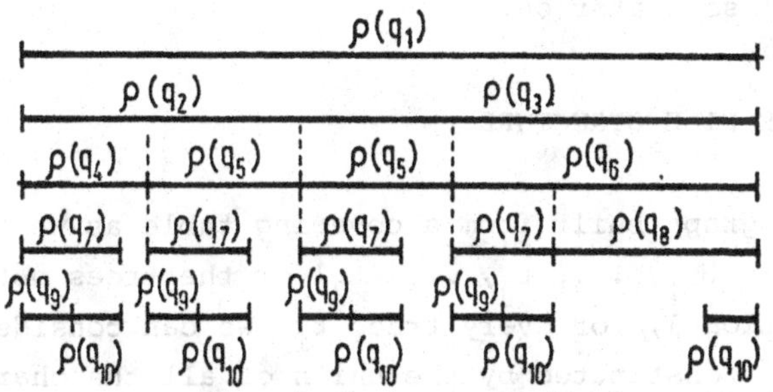

the physical organization

Fig. 4

An example of such a procedure is shown in fig. 5 for the same query-graph of fig. 4.

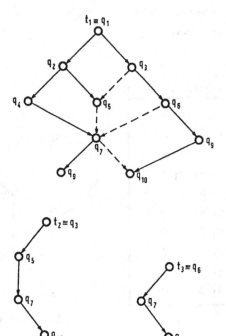

Fig. 5

For each one of the defined trees a CR organization is built on the storage medium. The redundancy is clearly increased because we must consider now

$$m_1 = \sum_{i=1}^{n} m_{1i} \, ,$$

where m_{1i} is the lenght of the subfile corresponding to the i-th tree. However we have a remarkable gain in the search lengh on the index table as we shall see later on.

4. - BUILDING THE FILE STRUCTURE

Given a covering graph built from a covering table as we saw in section 2 and the set $\{T\} \equiv \{t_1, \ldots, t_j, \ldots, t_2\}$ of the trees obtained by algorithm B in section 3, for every tree t_i we can consider a characteristic string S_i constituted by the union of all the characteristic values of the L_i queries belonging to t_i, i.e.:

$$S_i = \bigcup_{j=1,L_i} \{v_{a_{1j}}, \ldots, v_{a_{kj}}\}$$

As seen in section 3 for every t_i it is possible to have a CR organization constituting a subfile stored at address I_i.

An index can be built in which the associations S_i, L_i, I_i are listed for all the t_i (Fig. 6).

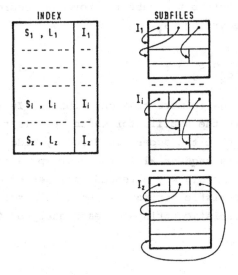

Fig. 6

The first block of the subfile, at address I_i, contains only the pointers to the beginning of the $\rho(q_k)$ ($k=1, \ldots, L_i$), while data are stored beginning from the second block.

5. - FILE MANIPULATION

Let us now examine how some operations can be performed on the proposed structure.

5.1. - SEARCHING

Let $q_k \in \{Q\}$ be a query with characteristic string

$$S_{q_k} \equiv \{v_{a_1 K}, \ldots, v_{a_N k}\}$$

If there is an S_i such that

$$S_{q_k} \cap S_i \neq \phi \qquad\qquad i=1, \ldots, z$$

the query can be answered.

Moreover, if

$$S_{q_k} \cap S_i > S_{q_k} \cap S_j \neq \phi \qquad\qquad j=1,\ldots, z \quad i \neq j$$

the set $\rho(q_k)$ belongs to the subfile stored at address I_i, associated in the index to the string S_i.
If

$$S_{q_k} \cap S_i \equiv S_{q_k} \cap S_j \neq \phi \qquad\qquad j=1,\ldots, z \quad i \neq j$$

the set $\rho(q_k)$ belongs to more than one subfile. In this case the access will be made in the subfile for which L_i is the smallest.
It must be noticed that the access is directly made to the address I_i then the retrieval is sequential in the corresponding subfile.
This method can be immediately extended to a set of queries $\{Q^x\}$. In this case a characteristic string must be considered built as the union of the characteristic strings of each query of the set $\{Q^x\}$.

5.2. -. UPDATING

An updating operation can consist in:

a - insertion of new records
b - deletion of existing records
c - modification of some values in existing records.

These operations can be performed in the proposed organization in the following way:

a - *Insertion*

Let ρ^x be the record to be inserted, described by the characteristic string

$$S_{\rho^x} = \{v_{a_1}\rho^x, \ldots, v_{a_N}\rho^x\}.$$

The following cases can be considered:

a.1, - $\qquad\qquad S_{\rho^x} \cap S_i = \phi \qquad\qquad\qquad i=1, \ldots, z$

In this case the complete reorganization of the file structure seen in section 4 is necessary. Actually such a case is seldom encountered in very large files.

a.2. -
$$\left.\begin{array}{l} S_{\rho^{\times}} \cap S_i \neq \phi \\ S_{\rho^{\times}} \cap S_j = \phi \end{array}\right\} \qquad 1 \leq i \leq k \leq j \leq z$$

In this case $\rho^{\times}$ must be inserted in all the k subfiles for which the intersection is not empty. It must be noticed that anyway the index is not affected by the operation.

b - *deletion*

A search operation must be triggered as in a.2, then the record is deleted from the k subfiles in which it was stored.

c - *modification*

Let $S_{\rho j} = \{v_{a_1 j}, \ldots, v_{a_N j}\}$ be the characteristic string of the record ρ_j to be modified.
In all the instances for which

$$S_{\rho_j} \cap S_i \neq \phi \qquad i=1, \ldots, z$$

the modified value is substituted to the old one.
Let now $S_{\rho_j}^{\times}$ be the modified characteristic string. A search in the index must be made until

$$S_{\rho_j}^{\times} \cap S_j \neq \phi \qquad i \neq 1, \ldots, z$$

and an insertion operation of all the modified records must be performed while deleting the old instances.

6. - PERFORMANCE EVALUATION

The proposed data organization is suitable for applications having the following features:

- the structure of queries is unknown a-priori
- the response time is a critical parameter
- each query is answered by more than one record
- batches of queries have often to be answered at the same time
- mass storage occupation is not critical
- sequential processing of the stored data is to be made

A comparison can be made with other data structures on the base of some figures of merit such as access time, storage occupation, file manipulation and updating operation complexity, etc.

The proposed data structure belongs to the class of secondary index organizations [4], however, under certain conditions, it offers better efficiency than other structures of the same class.

Since, among the structures of this class, that having characteristics the most similar to the proposed one is the inverted list structure, we are going to compare their performance with respect to access time and manipulation complexity.

As to the access time for the inverted list structure we have:

$$T_{acc} = T_{ind} + M \times T_D$$

where

T_{acc} = Access time

T_{ind} = time spent in sequentially retrieving, in the index file, all the values of the characteristic string, in extracting for each value the list of the addresses at which the records having the particular value are stored, then in intersecting all these lists.

T_D = Direct access time

$M \times T_D$ = Access time to the M different addresses resulting from the intersection of the address lists.

For the proposed organization

$$T^x_{acc} = T^x_{ind} + 2 T_D + (M^x - 1) T_s$$

where

T^x_{acc} = access time

T^x_{ind} = time spent in matching S_{q_k} against all of the S_i, as already seen in section 5.1., for extracting the address of the required subfile.

T_D = Direct Access time for the first block of the subfile

T_s = Sequential Access time

$(M^x - 1) T_s$ = Sequential Access time for the part of the subfile concerning q_k.

We can notice that generally $M < B$, if B is the number of all the blocks in the subfile.

Under certain conditions $T^x_{acc} < T_{acc}$. In fact: $T^x_{ind} < T_{ind}$ always

$M^x < M$ if the blocking factor >1. This is a frequently verified condition.

$T_s \leq T_D$ always. The equal sign applies in the condition (statisti-
cally seldom occuring) in which next direct address in the
following in the sequential organization.

The complexity of updating operations of the two structures is nearly
equal. In fact in the inverted list structure every kind of updating
operation requires an expensive updating of the index file. In the
proposed CR organization the index file is never affected, but updating operations can require the expensive task of inserting records
in a sequential file.

7. - CONCLUDING REMARKS

We have proposed a sequential data structure with secondary index with
fast access properties which can be fruitfully used in applications requiring:

- a high dynamics of the data file
- a-priori unknown query structures
- multiple access keys
- sequential data processing
- low response time
- batches of queries to be simultaneously processed.

Under these requirements the performances of the proposed structure is
better with respect to other structures of the same class. A comparison
example has been given with inverted list structure.

It must be noticed that the method for the analysis and the implementation of the data bank structure can be completely automatized. This
makes possible the use of the computer not only in the data management
phase but also in the design and implementation of the data bank itself.

1. - GOSH S.P. "Consecutive Storage of Relevant Records with Redundan-
              cy", Communications ACM - August 1975 pp. 464-471

2. - WAKSMAN, A., and GREEN, M.W.:
              "On the consecutive retrieval property on file organi-
              zation" - I E E E Trans. on Computers - C-23 1974,
              pp. 173-174

3. - MARTELLA G., and M.G. SAMI:

"On the problem of Query-Oriented File Organization"
XXII Rassegna Internationale Elettronica Nucleare Aero-
spaziale - Roma March 1975

4. - BRACCHI, G., MARTELLA, G.:

"Sistemi Generalizzati per la Gestione delle Informazio-
ni: Le tecniche di organizzazione dei dati". Rivista
di Informatica, Vol. II, n. 3, 1971, pp. 1-48.

DATABASE SYSTEMS ANALYSIS AND DESIGN

E. E. Tozer, Software Sciences Limited

April 1976

ABSTRACT

Developments in the database field have tended to
emphasise programming technology, with a dearth of
accompanying progress in systems analysis and design
methods. This paper puts forward an overall view of
system design which is intended to act as a constraining
framework. It is based upon a pragmatic approach and is
presented in a form which could be (and is being) used on
large scale implementation projects.

Orderly analysis and design procedures are encouraged.
The taking of premature design decisions is discouraged,
especially through the recognition of three distinct
views of data: conceptual, implementation and storage,
and through recognition of distinctions between design
of each of these, specification of mappings between them,
and design of programs and run sequences. It is
envisaged that specific procedures developed elsewhere
(see references) could be incorporated into the methodology
described here.

Software Sciences Limited
Abbey House
282/292 Farnborough Road
Farnborough, Hampshire
Telephone: 44321
Telex: 858228

1. INTRODUCTION

As the computer systems of an organisation develop, there is
an increase in the degree of overlap between originally distinct
systems. Further, increased confidence and familiarity leads
to the individual systems being enriched in power and
sophistication. The combined result is a vast increase in the
complexity of the system design task, at that very point in
time when greater reliance is being placed upon the
performance, reliability and accuracy of the computer systems.

The programming aspects of this situation have been recognised
for some time, and have been tackled with partial success in
the form of "Database Management" systems. Traditional
systems analysis and design procedures are being outstripped
both by the complexity of requirements, and also by the
developing programming technology. This paper proposes an
overall view of the processes involved in analysis and design,
with particular emphasis upon the data, as opposed to the
processing aspects. Different, partially overlapping, aspects
of this field have been tackled in a theoretical manner by
Bramhill & Taylor (1975), Brown (1974), Robinson (1974), and
many others. Whether or not a theoretical basis exists for
the taking of a design decision, a system designer "in the
field" has to take that decision, and he had to live with the
results.

Rather than offering precise formulae for each and every stage
of the progress, this paper puts forward an overall framework,
which identifies important stages, and draws the necessary
distinctions between them. This framework is most important,
as it ensures that premature design decisions are avoided,
and gives direct guidance as to the actual sequence and purpose
of particular analysis and design procedures. There is no
intention to over-constrain the particular techniques or
their variants which individual practitioners would embed in
this framework; the only criterion is that the technique
should be adequate for the purpose, and consistent with the
overall methdology. However, in the interest of being as
specific and as helpful as possible, descriptions of, or

references to, suitable techniques are included where
appropriate.

The analysis and design approach proposed is seen as being
applicable to DP systems in general. Only in the latter
stages does it become dependent upon use of a particular
DBMS. Projects using conventional files or non-Codasyl
DBMS would benefit considerably from adoption of the design
approach put forward, with appropriate variants in the latter
stages.

Section 2 explains the overall viewpoint taken, which is that of
viewing systems analysis and design themselves as a system.

This system is explained in detail in section 3, and each of
the main processing functions is examined in turn in more
detail in sections 4 to 11.

Except where it is explicitly stated otherwise, flowcharts in
sections 2 and 3 show data flow:-

Signifies a data container (file, document etc).

Signifies a process.

Signifies data flow, which may only be from
container to process or process to
container.

2.   VIEWS OF DATA

There are several distinct views of data which are relevant to
the process of analysis and design. This view is not
coincident with that adopted by ANSI SPARC/DBMS Study Group
(1975).

The areas of classification chosen are:-

(i) Level of abstraction
 a) Conceptual
     The view of data held by the organisation. This
     view is purely a function of the mode of operation
     of the organisation and the policies of its
     managers. It is independent of the existence of
     any computer systems, and should be expressed in a
     form most suitable to end-users in the organisation.

 b) Implementation
     All or some subset of the conceptual data view may
     be used by computer systems. The implementation
     view is a representation of that subset. It is
     designed and encoded into machine-readable form for
     this purpose. The implementation view remains as
     independent as possible from c, the storage view.

 c) Storage
     Actual data, described to programs by b, must be
     held on backing store in some form. The storage view
     is a complete description of such data on backing
     store.

(ii) Breadth of view
 a) Global, or corporate.

     The complete view of data, relevant to all processes
     carried out in the organisation.
 b) Specific, or functional.

     The view of data relevant to a particular function of
     the organisation.

(iii) Existence
     Whether or not it is necessary for occurrences of data items
     to exist in some particular form.

VIEWS OF DATA

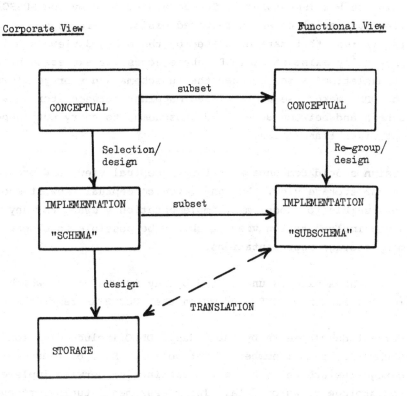

Fig.2.1

The combination of these views of data is shown in Figure 2.1.

The terms SCHEMA and SUBSCHEMA are defined by CODASYL DDLC (1973). They are used subsequently in this paper in the sense shown in 2.1.

All of the data described by the Storage view must actually exist on backing storage. The data described by the SUBSCHEMA view must exist on an as-required basis. There is no requirement that data described by the other 3 views should physically exist at all. Database access is expressed by the "translation" arrow between the subschema and storage views. The DBMS makes use of specified mappings between storage and schema and between schema and subschema, to carry out (hopefully) optimised translation.

Design should commence with the conceptual view, and progress to the storage view. For any given conceptual view it should be possible to choose many implementation views. For any given implementation view it should be possible to choose many storage representations.

A SUBSCHEMA view is unaffected by any SCHEMA change which results in a new SCHEMA of which the SUBSCHEMA remains a subset.

Current developments by the Codasyl DDLC include division of SCHEMA DDL into a number of categories. Some of these categories are relevant to the distinction between implementation and storage views of data. The measurement, tuning, resource allocation and storage categories between them relate to the storage view of data.

The CODASYL DDLC DBAWG (1975) have proposed a more complete separation of the storage view into a Storage Definition Language (DSDL).

3. THE ANALYSIS AND DESIGN PROCESS

3.1 Introduction

This section outlines the method of analysis and design which
is discussed in more detail in the remainder of the paper.
Figure 3.1 shows the process in flow-diagram form, and can
be regarded as a guide to the paper.

Analysis and design is iterative. The need for iteration
pervades almost every data path shown in 3.1. It is not shown
explicitly because to do so would make the diagram excessively
complicated.

3.2 Relationship between Analysis and Design

Traditionally, where system design is recognised as taking
place at all, it is regarded as a process which occurs after
analysis is complete, and before programming commences. It
is more useful to regard both analysis and design as each
taking place at a number of different levels of refinement.
At each level, the order is analysis (or hypothesis
or some blend of the two) leading to definition of functional
requirements, leading to design of a process to meet those
requirements.

During the design process, at each successive stage of
refinement, additional opportunities may be realised, and the
unpleasant truth may emerge concerning the severity of some
constraints. Either at one stage, or through a number of
stages, iteration may take place, by means of presenting
the originator of the requirements with the highlights of the
results of the design process, and offering the opportunity
to modify the requirements in the light of these.

3.3 The Nature of Design

The design process consists of two distinct stages: generation
of a range of possible solutions to a problem, and selection
from the range of a best-fit, according to a pre-defined set

of criteria. Failure to achieve a good enough solution may result in iteration involving alteration of some of the initial conditions and repetition of both stages.

3.4 Development Stages

The processes described in 3.2 and 3.3 take place at each of a number of stages, representing successive levels of refinement. Some of these stages are related to the differing levels of abstraction of views of data.

THE ANALYSIS & DESIGN PROCESS

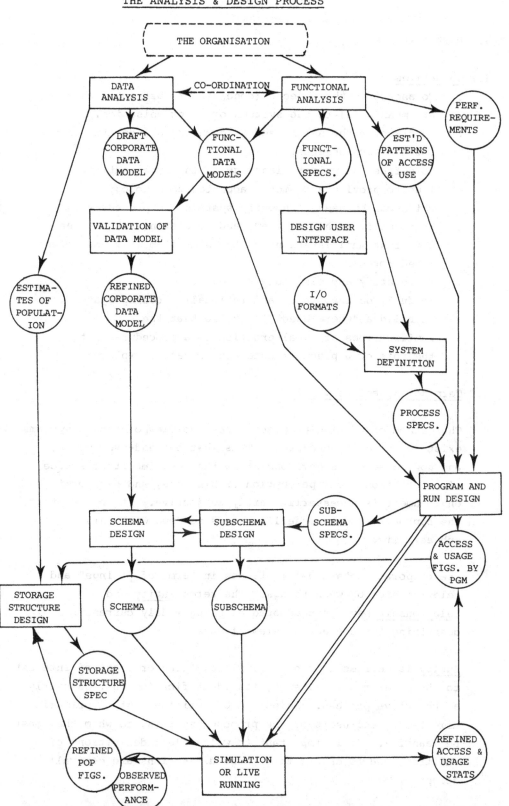

4. DATA ANALYSIS

4.1 Objectives

- To ascertain the objects (concrete or abstract), which are meaningful to the systems of an organisation.
- To discover the nature and relevant of all relationships between such objects.
- To define the private language of the organisation. Thus to provide a commonly accepted terminology which can be used to specify systems and procedures.
- To identify each data item, and to distinguish between different manifestations of the same item (e.g. different coded forms).
- To identify and eliminate synonyms.
- To fully define, unify and rationalise coding systems.
- To build a "where used" index, so that the ramifications of an alterantion to a procedure or to the role of a piece of data can be easily explored.

4.2 Terminology and Conventions

The method of working proposed takes the viewpoint that systems exist to serve the end-user. Thus what the end-user wants, and how he sees his environment is the most important source of information. His perception of his role, and his working environment is necessarily partly subjective. It follows that the approach to data modelling needs to cope with this subjectivity.

The corporate data model is framed in terms of "things" and relationships between things. The terms entity and relationship have been adopted as being widely current for describing the conceptual view of data.

Entity is defined as a person, place, thing or event of interest to the enterprise. As such, its identification must be partly a subjective process. Selection of entities must be primarily directed by end-users of the proposed systems, to whom they must be meangful. It is important to write clear definitions of entities, and to ensure that these definitions are generally accepted.

It is necessary to distinguish between entity types and entity
occurrences. An example of an entity type is "Vehicle".
Occurrences of this type are:

      "Blue Ford Cortina XYZ 132K"

      "Red Honda Motorbike ABC 789J"

Entity types may be shown on data relationship diagrams as
named rectangular boxes.

e.g.
> VEHICLE

Relationships exist between entities. (Use of the term
relationship does not imply any connection with the specialised
terminology of the relational data model). Relationship may
be 1 to 1, 1 to many, or many to many where 1 or "many"
refers to the number of occurrences of the entity type
which may be involved in the relationship.

They can be shown in the following way:

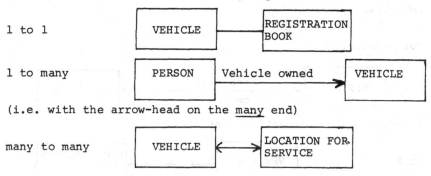

1 to 1   VEHICLE — REGISTRATION BOOK

1 to many   PERSON → Vehicle owned → VEHICLE

(i.e. with the arrow-head on the many end)

many to many   VEHICLE ←→ LOCATION FOR SERVICE

Very often, many to many relationships can be analysed into
two one-to-many relationships.

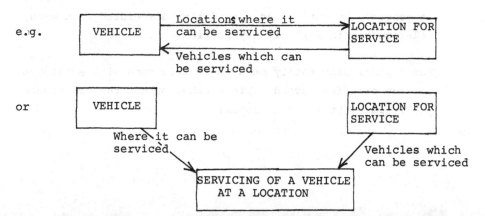

e.g.   VEHICLE → Locations where it can be serviced → LOCATION FOR SERVICE

← Vehicles which can be serviced

or   VEHICLE   LOCATION FOR SERVICE

Where it can be serviced   Vehicles which can be serviced

SERVICING OF A VEHICLE AT A LOCATION

may be more appropriate representations for the purpose of a particular application system.

An entity must have at least one type of data value associated with it, and will usually have several. These data items types are termed <u>attributes</u>.

For example the entity type vehicle may have the attribute types colour, chassis-no, engine-no, date of purchase, registration-no, seating capacity, weight, and possibly many others.

One or more of the attributes of an entity may have unique values which can be used to distinguish between different occurrences of the entity. This attribute or collection of attribures is called the <u>identity</u> of the entity. For example, vehicle may be identified by chassis-no, or by registration-no.

Participation of an entity in a specified relationship may be optional.

For example, in:

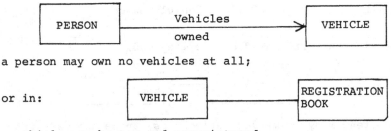

a person may own no vehicles at all;

or in:

a vehicle may be new and unregistered.

In general, an entity has a <u>condition</u> associated with each relationship in which it may participate.

For a particular entity occurrence this condition evaluates to true or false according to whether or not the occurrence participates in the relationship.

In one-to-many or many-to-many relationships, it is necessary
to attempt to quantify the "many". Thus for each relationship
in which it participates in a "many" role, an entity has
associated with it a population. Because data analysis itself
proceeds in a number of stages of refinement, it is desirable
to permit the expression of this population in several forms,
e.g.

```
*       - many
m-n     - range
m,n     - average
n       - absolute value
```

The population may depend upon a specified population condition.

For example, in

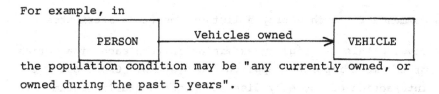

the population condition may be "any currently owned, or
owned during the past 5 years".

There may be any number of relationships between entities.

For example:

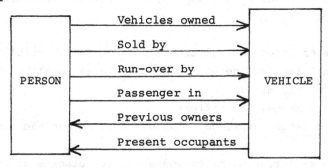

Shows only a small range of the known relationships between
person and vehicle.

For this reason, it is always important to write a clear
definition of each relationship when it is identified.

Relationships may exist between entities of the same type.
e.g.

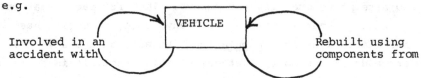

Involved in an   Rebuilt using
accident with   components from

4.3 Method of Working

4.3.1 Develop and discuss a series of draft entity diagrams,
showing only:
Entity, Relationship/description.

4.3.2 Maintain in parallel a working set of entity and relationship
descriptions.

4.3.3 Commence for each entity a list of important attributes.

4.3.4 Develop this material by examining in turn each of a series
of the most important application systems. Check-out the
interaction of these by discussing the overall diagram with
line management at a sufficiently high level for there to be
a broad understanding of all the features.

4.3.5 Document what <u>should</u> happen, rather than what actually takes
place.

4.3.6 When entities and relationships seem fairly stable and well-
identified, refine and augment the data model by showing in
diagram form:
.   Entities, identifiers
.   Relationships, description, populations and conditions.

Such a digram can be called an <u>entity diagram</u> or <u>entity model</u>.

4.3.7 Supporting documentation should now include:
.   Entity Definitions.
.   Attribute lists for entities.
.   Attribute definitions, including meaning of coding systems.
.   Relationship descriptions, populations and conditions.
.   An overall name-directory, showing entities, attributes
and relationships, organised for easy reference.

4.3.8 The complete set of information required to document the corporate data model is:

Entity Data

Definition	Name, description, synonyms, existence rules
Ownership	Where appropriate, that division of the organisation responsible for all occurrences.
	NB Ownership is more often appropriate to specific occurrences; this is an application-dependent requirement.
Statistics	Expected population Overall growth rate
Relationships	Degree, sequence, nature/meaning
Integrity requirements	Privacy Availability
Archival	Number of versions or time-span to be covered

Of these elements, only definition, relationships and approximate statistics are relevant to initial formulation of the entity model.

Attribute Data

Definition	Name, description, synonyms, existence rules, data type and characteristics, coding structure, permissible time-lag between event and updating of the value.
Ownership	(Where different from the entity).
Statistics	Expected population Overall growth rate
Relationships	Cross-reference to entities Derivation/consistency rules
External formats	Inputs, outputs
Integrity	Privacy, Availability, Validation rules,
Controls	Default value, Tolerance on accuracy.

Of this data, only definition is relevant to formulation of the entity model.

Relationship Data

Populations if 1:n or m:n.

Conditions under which entity occurrences particpate.

Conditions governing populations.

Description of the relationship.

5. FUNCTIONAL ANALYSIS

5.1 Objectives

To identify and define the requirements for particular application systems.

To produce for each system identified:
  i)   A functional requirements definition.
 ii)   A definition of the data model appropriate to the application function.
iii)   A definition of likely ranges for system performance and usage traffic.

This section concentrates on items (ii) and (iii).

5.2 Relation to Other Processes

This consists of definition of the processing requirements of each application function, and definition of the associated conceptual data model. This process proceeds in parallel with data analysis, and close co-ordination is necessary.

It is taken as read in this paper that initial selection of application areas is subject to rigorous examination by senior management. A system is only developed if its value outweighs the cost of having it; in the (normal) situation of making optimum use of scarce resources, the systems having highest urgency, and the most favourable value/cost ratios are of course those developed.

5.3   Describing the Functional Data Model

Each functional data model will be a subset of the corporate
data model, with additional information added, concerning:
- patterns of usage;
- access paths;
- attribute subsets actually used;
- sequencing and selection criteria.

In detail, for each entity, and for each function in which
it is accessed, information required is:

Attribute subset accessed

Frequency   How often, hit distribution

Turnaround   Time, tolerance

Access paths   Relationships used, key attributes,
                    ordering, selection/search criteria

Traffic by   Retrieval rate, Creation rate, Modification
access path   rate, Deletion rate.

Integrity   (over and above those defined in data
Controls   analysis).

Of this data, attribute subset and access paths are relevant
to refinement and validation of the entity model; the
remainder have more bearing upon database and storage design.

For each attribute, and for each function in which the
attribute is used as a data item:

Usage   Source, destination, usage mode

Traffic   Retrieval rate, Creation rate, Modification
                    rate, Deletion rate.

Input format	Decoding
Output format	Report heading, editing, encoding
Internal format	Base, scale, precision
Integrity Controls	(Over and above those defined in basic data analysis).
Relationships	Derivation/Consistency rules.

Format information is relevant to potential generation of text or code from the information if it is stored in a data dictionary system.

5.4 Functional Data Model Diagrams

The entity diagram for the relevant subset of the corporate data model should be augmented to show:
Access paths, sequencing and selection criteria,
keys, approximate populations, approximate access traffic.

The remainder of the information specified in 5.2 should be documented in narrative or tabular form.

6. VALIDATION AND REFINEMENT OF THE DATA MODEL

6.1 Purpose

Although the specification of corporate and functional data models is co-ordinated, their features are present for different reasons, and they may be inconsistent in several ways. For this reason they should be cross-checked rigorously.

It is also desirable, having developed these models on a
necessarily partly subjective basis, to apply relevant formal
methods of analysis to the results. In this way it is possible
to find the simplest versions of the data structures.

6.2   Stages of Validation and Refinement

   i)   Completeness
      Does the corporate data model contain features to
      accommodate all required functional data models?

  ii)   Consistency
      Is the c.d.m. self-consistent?
      Is the c.d.m. consistent with each f.d.m.?
      Is each f.d.m. consistent with all the others?

 iii)   Access paths
      Access paths and their relative importance should be
      represented in the c.d.m. Relevant features of an
      access path are:
      -    Traffic for - add, modify, retrieve, delete.
      -    Search keys
      -    Selection criteria
      -    Population from which selection is to take place
      -    Sequencing requirements

  iv)   Normalisation
      Reduction of data structures to 3rd normal form is a
      powerful tool for elimination of unnecessary complexity,
      and for finding the simplest possible form of those
      structures.

      However, such a form is not necessarily the clearest
      or the most appropriate either for end-users or for
      programming. Hence after normalisation has been
      carried out, it may be appropriate to "de-normalise"
      the structures by recreation of hierarchies and
      repeating groups, where this can be firmly justified
      on the grounds of usefulness and clarity.

7.   SYSTEM DEFINITION

7.1   Objectives

This is the stage at which a particular system is designed at
an overall level. Constitutent work units are identified, and
are embedded in a control framework which constrains the
system to operate in a meaningful manner.

7.2   Identification of Processes

"Natural" units of work are identified from the requirements
specification. These units, as yet, bear no relation to
computer programs, but instead represent the user's view of
specific integral jobs which the system is performing for
him.

Examples of processes are:
.   production of a report;
.   the application of a specific transaction to the
         database;
.   the computation, e.g. of a sales forecast, according
         to a specific algorithm.

Characteristics of processes are:
.   they operate upon data; thus process inputs and
         outputs are "logical records", which may be:
         - transactions, reports, units of the database,
           transient data item groupings in memory.

Thus also, the operation of the system may be represented by
a data flow chart showing related processes and their
connecting data paths. (Figure 3.1 in Section 3 is an
example of such a flow chart.)

Where there is value in doing so, processes may be themselves
subdivided into processes; (e.g. considering the example above
of processes, production of a report may consist of
computation of a number of forecasts, and their ranking in
some order).

The subdivision of processes in a data-flow sense loses its values at a point where:

. the units of work lose meaning for the user;
. the relationships between the units of work is more strongly that of a procedural or scheduling nature.

7.3 Design of System Behaviour and Controls

Knowledge of the user's expectations of the system permits the design of a logical framework into which the system processes can be fitted, and which will control their operation in a secure manner.

Particular attention should be paid to useability of those system control parameters provided for users.

7.4 Specification of Processes

English plus decision tables is the most appropriate specification medium. Data flow diagrams are also appropriate, but procedural diagrams and charts should be eschewed except where vital, because they tend to impose premature design decisions.

Essential scheduling requirements between and within processes must be identified and fully defined at this stage. A strong mandatory scheduling relationship between work units indicates that they should be regarded as part of a process.

Care should be exercised to avoid jumping the gun on detailed design work through inclusion at too early a stage of "how" decisions on mechanisms for achieving the results required of the processes. However, certain "how" decisions are appropriate at this stage: e.g. selection of computational methods of performing forecasting or optimisation calculations which are integral parts of the system. Such decisions are necessary at this stage because they affect the system's behaviour towards the user, and have an impact upon the data models.

7.5 Specification of Constraints

The value of each process to the system should be ascertained;
some processes are optional, and inclusion of these has to be
justified. For each function performed, there may be
alternative options, e.g. simple or sophisticated.

Some form of ranking based on priority, cost and flexibility
should be carried out, in order to select the actual
constituents of the first version of the system, and to lay
the guidelines for subsequent development phases.

Tolerances of ranges should be defined for:
 accuracy of results, performance, consumption of resources
 (both development and operating), scheduling.

8.   PROGRAM AND RUN DESIGN

8.1 Objectives

The primary aim of this stage is to select suitable groupings
of system processes, to be formed into programs and program
sequences. The resulting work-units are intended to make
effective use of the resources of the computer by, for example,
avoiding unnecessary repeated transfer of data, whilst at the
same time meeting the performance requirements specified.

8.2 Method

Each system process should have defined:
  i)   Usage frequency;
  ii)   Desired turnaround time;
  iii) Data access requirements, including sequencing;
  iv)   Scheduling relationship to - date/time,
                                   - other processes.

There is a trade-off to be exercised between keeping processes
separate, which makes inefficient use of the computer, but
which retains flexibility, and the binding together of
processes into programs which can make more effective use of
the computer, but which will need to be redesigned if new
processes are introduced.

Stages of the procedure are:
  i)   Choose program groupings according to:
        . I/O - Database access
              - Non database "batch" I/O; TP message handling
        . Scheduling Functions
        . Common service functions
        . Liability to be invoked in a co-ordinated manner
           (i.e. function occurrences part of the same process).
        . Close similarity of associated functional data
           models
        . Similarity of scheduling requirements - e.g. end-month.
 ii)   Specify inter-program scheduling relationships;
iii)   Specify overall frequency and scheduling requirements;
 iv)   Specify the data-access needs of each program in terms
        of:
        - subset of the schema data model,
        - access paths,
        - sequencing,
        - selection criteria,
        - frequency of access.

9.   SCHEMA DESIGN

9.1 Objective

The aim is to design an effective implementation view of the
corporate data model. The effectiveness is judged in terms of:
   .   Clarity and appropriateness
   .   The provision of facilities to enable the definition
        of effective forms of the necessary sub-schemas.
   .   The schema's suitability as a basis for the definition
        of an efficient storage structure.

9.2 Relationship Between Design of SCHEMA and SUBSCHEMA

The details of the method for SCHEMA design are dependent upon
the nature of the file-handler or DBMS in use. In particular,
if a conventional file-handler is used, the drawing of meaningful
distinctions between
- SUBSCHEMA
- SCHEMA
- Storage

may prove difficult.

The simulation of sub-schema using a conventional file handler
is described in 10.2.

In this section, design methods are proposed which are appropriate
to use in Codasyl-type DBMS. (CODASYL DDLC 1973).

The Schema must be designed in principle before subschemas can
be designed. This is because the choise of structural facilities
in a Codasyl SUBSCHEMA is limited to those already present in
the SCHEMA. At the same time, one of the main inputs to SCHEMA
design is a definition of the needs of those SUBSCHEMAS.
Hence it is most likely that there will be several cycles of
iteration between schema and subschema design before
satisfactory designs are achieved.

When modifying the SCHEMA in response to altered or new
SUBSCHEMA requirements, care must be exercised to avoid changes
which would invalidate other existing SUBSCHEMAS. In particular,
it is necessary to take great care to avoid subtle changes,
which would leave the SUBSCHEMAS and DML syntactically valid,
but which would alter the semantics.

9.3   Method for Design of a CODASYL SCHEMA

9.3.1 Translation of the entity representation of the corporate data
      model involves exercise of the following choices:
          Representation of entities:
          - as record-types,
          - as several record types, associated in some way,
          - as group items within a record type.
      .   Representation of relationships:
          - as set types,
          - as several set types, possibly with additional
            record types, e.g. as is required for many-many
            relationships,
          - as repeating groups,
          - as loose associations of records, e.g. by common
            search keys.
      .   Association of attributes with entities.

9.3.2 The information produced in the design process can be classified
      by:
      a)   To be encoded in schema DDL
          i)   Relevant to structure e.g. RECORD, SET, AREA
          ii)   Relevant to mode of use e.g. ORDER, KEY
          iii) Relevant to storage design e.g. LOCATION MODE,
                ACTUAL, VIRTUAL
      b)   To be documented for reference by application programmers.
          e.g. Record occurrence rules
                Record retrieval modes
                Record selection rules
                Processing necessary to maintain consistency when
                each record is STORED, MODIFYed or DELETEd.

A subset of the type a) information can usefully be shown in
diagram form. Successive, not necessary complete, forms of
such a diagram can be used as working notes during the design
process.

9.3.3 Choice of Records and Sets

The most basic choice in SCHEMA design is "what are to be
the record types and set types".

Stages:
  i)   Make each entity-type a record type, including all
       attributes of the entity data items within the record.
       Represent relationships between entities as set types.
  ii) Many-to-many relationships, treated as in (i) above,
       will yield a record/set structure which is invalid in
       a CODASYL DBMS. This is overcome by breaking any such
       relationship into two one-to-many relationships,
       possibly making use of an additional "intersection"
       record, as indicated in Section 4.2.

It is possible that several alternative structures will result
from stages (i) and (ii). There is no harm in this; the
alternatives should be carried forward until there are grounds
for choosing between them. The design (or designs) represent
a "first draft" and are now subject to a number of stages of
refinement.

  iii) Where different subsets of the attributes of an entity
        have different access needs (i.e. are used in different
        subschemas, and/or have different access paths), consider
        their division into 2 or more record types.

        NB Data items common to these record types are redundant,
        and must be kept consistent in some way.

  iv)   Where, within a record type, there is a repeating group
        which has a large, variable population, it may be better
        to make the elements of the repeating group the member
        records of a set, and thus make the DBMS responsible for
        the space management problem.
  v)   Where record types are very small, and several record
        occurrences are commonly accessed together, then it may
        be worthwhile to consolidate record types, so that the
        structure is represented by group items within a record
        type.

vi)   Where a relationship is used rarely or not at all it may be that the overheads involved in sets are not justifiable. In this case, the set-type can be eliminated. Instead, the record occurrences can be associated by a selection process based on like data item values.

vii)   Grouping of several record types by making them members of the same set type is appropriate where this reflects the common patterns of access.

9.3.4 Choice of declared record keys, and record sequences in sets, is governed by the most popular sub-schema usage.

9.4   Information from Data Analysis

Choice of record types, and of the access paths to them, is governed by the relative frequency with which a group of items is accessed in a particular manner.

Thus an analysis procedure is required which:

i)   For each item, determines the relative popularity of different access paths to it.

ii)   For each access path, lists, ordered by popularity, the data items to which access is requested.

Storage structure design (Section 11) requires that these figures should be dissected by:

i)   Type of access -
batch,   where economy of resources is paramount
online,   where response time is paramount

ii)   Insert/delete/modify/retrieve operation.

10.   SUBSCHEMA DESIGN

10.1   Objectives

The aim of this stage is to achieve a program-view of data
which is:
  i)   Appropriate to the needs of the program.
  ii)   Unlikely to be sensitive to alterations in other
        systems, the schema, or the storage structure.
  iii) Consistent with the schema, and derivable from it.

10.2   Method

10.2.1 Using conventional data management

By "conventional" is mean any system in which programs normally
access directly real files resident on backing storage.
  i)   For each record-type in each file on backing storage,
        write a subroutine to perform each of four functions:
        - create;
        - delete;
        - modify;
        - read.
        These subroutines should embody any processing
        necessary to maintain consistency.
  ii)   Design the program view of data, including selection
        and search procedures.
  iii) Define the data mainpulation operations to be carried
        out by the program.
  iv)   Write subroutines for (ii), using (i) as primitive
        operations.

10.2.2 Using a Codasyl style DBMS

The problem is to translate a sub-schema requirement, framed in
terms of access to the entities in possibly several functional
data models, into a record/set subschema, with associated
access path details.

As stated in Section 9, Schema and Subschema design are closely
interrelated.

Select a subset of the schema which most closely meets the
subschema needs.   (This is probably best shown in diagram
form, based upon the conventions shown in Figure 9.1).

If this is unsatisfactory, determine whether the discrepancy is
to be met by modification of the schema, or by special purpose
programming to derive the desired data from a feasible
subschema.

Any modification of the schema should be subject to the
safeguards mentioned in Section 9.2.

There will always be a certain amount of processing which cannot
be expressed in schema or subschema DDL.

This falls into two classes:
   i)   Processing which is generally applicable to operations
         carried out on a particular part of the database;
         e.g. maintenance of consistency when a particular
         record is created or deleted. This is best embodied
         in general purpose subroutines, which are made
         available as part of the database documentation.
   ii)   Processing which is specific to a particular program;
         e.g. selection criteria applied on a particular access
         path.

Both sorts of special purpose processing should be clearly
documented; the latter may be shown on the subschema structure
diagram.

11.   STORAGE STRUCTURE DESIGN

11.1   Objectives

The aim of this stage is to design a representation of the
database on backing storage which efficiently meets the
specified pattern of access and usage, and which also keeps
within specified constraints upon use of resources.

11.2 Statistics Required

The performance of the overall combination of database, DBMS
and application programs is expected to be "optimal" in
some way.

Some combined function of:
- backing storage;
- main storage;
- channel time;
- processor time;
is to be minimised.

Of these only backing storage is not dependent upon usage traffic

The two necessary sets of information for the design process
are:

. The relative weightings of the four main resources
  to be conserved.
. Statistics defining:
   - for each database record
     frequency and hit distribution of:
      . add;
      . delete;
      . modify;
      . retrieve operations
   - for each access path used in the database,
     frequency of use in each of batch and on-line modes.

11.3 Method of support for access paths

Access paths should be ranked according to their level of usage.
The most heavily used paths should then be given highest
priority for efficient access.

On-line access paths require rapid response, possibly at some
cost in consumption of resources. Batch-mode access paths
require support at a minimal consumption of resources, at the
expense of elapsed time if necessary.

Heavily used access paths should be supported by appropriate indexes and pointer mechanisms where the accompanying overheads can be justified.

11.4   Summary of Choices

For a Codasyl-style DBMS, the range of choices which must be exercised at the stage of storage design are:

Database Access Strategy

- Record placement mode - CALC or VIA.
- Record retrieval modes to support, and how efficiently.
- Real or virtual representation of derived data.
- Set representation mode and linkage options.
- Indexing.
- Search keys.

Storage Usage

- AREA placement.
- Schema record to storage mapping;
  - data item representation,
  - data item distribution.

Storage Characteristics

- Device type.
- Page size.
- Space allocation;
  - amount of overflow,
  - growth rate.

ACKNOWLEDGEMENTS

Although the impetus for this work has come from several years
experience gained on a variety of projects, the encouragement to
document it in its present form occurred while the author was
under contract to the Ministry of Defence.   Thanks are due to
my MOD colleagues for this encouragement.

The author is also especially indebted to Bill Waghorn of SCICON
and Ian Palmer of CACI, who have both contributed significantly to
the ideas through extensive discussions.   For comments upon drafts
of this paper, thanks are due to many colleagues within the
Ministry of Defence, and ICL.

REFERENCES

1.   ANSI X3 SPARC/DBMS Study Group Interim Report,
  -    February 1975.
2.   CODASYL DDLC Journal of Development 1973.   Revised 1975.
3.   CODASYL COBOL JOD as modified by the DBLTG Database
      Facility Proposal, March 1975.
4.   Brown, A.P.G. "Entity Modelling" IFIP TC/2 Conference 1975
      (Pub. North Holland Book Co.)
5.   Robinson, K.A. "Description of stored data, using modified
      NCC Standards", Private communication, 1974.
6.   Bramhill, P.S., and Taylor G. "Database Design.   From Codd
      to Codasyl".   To be published in "Database Journal", 1976.
7.   BSC/CODASYL DDLC DBAWG June 1975 Report.

FORMAL TECHNIQUES AND SIZEABLE PROGRAMS

Edsger W.Dijkstra

Burroughs

Plataanstraat 5

NL-4565 NUENEN

The Netherlands

By now we know quite convincing, quite practical and quite effective methods of proving the correctness of a great number of small programs. In a number of cases our ability is not restricted to a posteriori proofs of program correctness but even encompasses techniques for deriving programs that, by virtue of the way in which they have been derived, must satisfy the proof's requirements.

This development has taken place in a limited number of years, and has changed for those who are familiar with such techniques their outlook on what programming is all about so drastically, that I consider this development both fascinating and exciting: fascinating because it has given us such a new appreciation of what we already knew how to do, exciting because it is full of unfathomed promises.

This development is the result of a very great number of experiments: experiments in programming, in axiomatizing, and in proving. It could never have taken place if the researchers in this field had not shown the practical wisdom of carrying out their experiments with small programs. As honest scientists they have reported about their actual experiences. This, alas, has created the impression that such formal techniques are only applicable in the case of such small programs.

Some readers have exaggerated and have concluded that these techniques are primarily or exclusively applicable to so-called "toy problems". But that is too great a simplification. I do not object to describing Euclid's Algorithm for the greatest common divisor as a "toy problem" (in which capacity it has been a very fertile one!). But I have also seen perfectly readable and adequate formal treatments of much less "toyish" programs, such as a binary search algorithm and a far from trivial algorithm for the computation of an approximation of the square root, which would be ideal for a microprogram in a binary machine. I call this last algorithm "far from trivial" because, although it can be described in a few lines of code, from the raw code it is by no means obvious what the algorithm accomplishes.

The question that I would like to address here is what we may expect beyond those "small examples". Hence the adjective "sizeable" in my title.

The crude manager's answer to my question is quite simple: "Nothing.".   He will argue that difficult problems require large programs, that large programs can only be written by large teams which, by necessity, are composed of people with, on the average, n-th rate intellects with n sufficiently large to make formal techniques totally unrealistic.

My problem, however, is that I don't accept that answer, as it is based on two tacit assumptions. The one tacit assumption is that difficult problems require large programs, the second tacit assumption is that with such a Chinese Army of n-th rate intellects he can solve the difficult problem. Both assumptions should be challenged.

On challenging the second assumption I don't need to waste many words: the Chinese Army approach --also called "the human wave"-- has been tried, even at terrific expense, and the results were always disastrous. OS/360 is, of course, the best known example of such a disaster, but please, don't conclude from NASA's successful moonshots that in other cases it has worked. There is plenty of evidence that the data processing associated with these NASA ventures was full of bugs, but that the total organization around it was, however, so redundant that the bugs usually did not matter too much. In short, there is plenty of experimental evidence that the Chinese Army approach does not work; and as a corollary we may conclude that the perfection of Chinese Army Generals is a waste of effort. At the end of my talk I hope that you will agree with me that, in order to reach that conclusion, said experimental evidence was superfluous, because a more careful analysis of the tasks at hand can teach us the same.

                    *   *   *

For my own instruction and in order to collect material for this talk I conducted an experiment that I shall describe to you in some detail. I do so with great hesitation because I know that, by doing so, I shall sow the seed of misunderstanding. The problem of a speaker is that, if he does not give examples, his audience does not know what he is talking about, and that, if he gives an example, his audience may mistake it for his subject! In a moment I shall describe to you my experiment and you will notice that it has to do with syntactic analysis, but, please, remember that syntactic analysis is not the subject of my talk, but only the carrier of my experiment for which I needed an area for computer application in which I am most definitely not an expert.

I wrote a paper with the title "A more formal treatment of a less simple example.". Admittedly it was still not a very large example: the final solution consisted of four procedures, of which, in beautiful layout with assertions inserted, three were only 7 lines long and the last one 18 lines. But the whole document is 19 typed pages, i.e. about 14 times as long as the raw code. It took me several weeks of hard work to write it, and when it was completed I was grateful for not having been more ambitious as far as size was concerned. It dealt with the design of a recognizer for strings of the syntactic category $<$ sent $>$, originally given by the following syntax:

$$
\begin{aligned}
&<\text{sent}> ::= <\text{exp}> ; \qquad\qquad\qquad\qquad\qquad\qquad\qquad (1)\\
&<\text{exp}> \;::= <\text{term}> \;\big|\; <\text{exp}> + <\text{term}> \;\big|\; <\text{exp}> - <\text{term}>\\
&<\text{term}> ::= <\text{prim}> \;\big|\; <\text{term}> * <\text{prim}>\\
&<\text{prim}> ::= <\text{iden}> \;\big|\; (\; <\text{exp}>)\\
&<\text{iden}> ::= <\text{letter}> \;\big|\; <\text{iden}> <\text{letter}>
\end{aligned}
$$

That was all!

My first experience was that, in order to give a more precise statement about the string of characters that would be read in the case that the input was not an instance of $<$ sent $>$, I needed new syntactic categories, derived from (1) and denoting "begin of...": for each syntactic category $<$ pqr $>$ I needed the syntactic category $<$ bopqr $>$, characterizing all strings that either are a $<$ pqr $>$ or can be extended at the right-hand side so as to become a $<$ pqr $>$ or both.

$$
\begin{aligned}
&<\text{bosent}> ::= <\text{sent}> \;\big|\; <\text{boexp}> \qquad\qquad\qquad\qquad\qquad (2)\\
&<\text{boexp}> \;::= <\text{boterm}> \;\big|\; <\text{exp}> + <\text{boterm}> \;\big|\; <\text{exp}> - <\text{boterm}>\\
&\text{etc.}
\end{aligned}
$$

(In an earlier effort I had also used the notion "proper begin of a $<$ pqr $>$ ", i.e. at the right-hand side extensible so as to become a $<$ pqr $>$ but not a $<$ pqr $>$ by itself. This time I obtained a simpler and more uniform treatment by omitting it and only using "begin of..." as derived syntactic categories.)

The next important step was the decision to denote the fact that the string K belongs to the syntactic category $<$ pqr $>$ by the expression:

pqr(K)

This decision was an immediate invitation to rewrite the syntax as follows:

```
< sent > ::= < exp > < semi >                                    (3)
   < semi > ::= ;
< exp >  ::= < term > | < exp > < adop > < term >
   < adop > ::= + | -
< term > ::= < prim > | < term > < mult > < prim >
   < mult > ::= *
< prim > ::= < iden > | < open > < exp > < close >
< iden > ::= < letter > | < iden > < letter >
   < open > ::= (
   < close > ::= )
```

The invitation, however, was only noticed after I had dealt with the first
line of the syntax, dealing with < sent > ; when dealing with < exp > , it was
the occurrence of both the + and the - that induced the introduction of
< adop > , because without it my formulae became full of insipid duplication. It
was only then that I discovered that the boolean procedure "semi(x)" --only true
if the character x is a semicolon-- and the other boolean procedures that I needed for the classification of single characters were a specific instance of the convention that introduced "pqr(K)" . Finally I realized that the usual BNF , as
used in (2), is an odd mixture in the sense that in the productions the characters
stand for themselves; in (3) this convention is restricted to the indented lines.

A next important decision was to denote for strings (named K, L, ...) and
characters (named x, y, ...) concatenation simply by juxtaposition, e.g. KL , Ky
yLx , etc. Now we could denote the arbitrary nonempty string by yL or Ly and
could derive from our syntax formulae like

$$(exp(L) \text{ and } semi(y)) \Rightarrow sent(Ly)$$

It also enabled me to define the "begin of...":

$$bopqr(K) = (\underline{E} \; L: pqr(KL))$$

I mention the apparently trivial and obvious decision to denote concatenation by
juxtaposition explicitly, because in the beginning my intention to do a really neat
formal job seduced me to introduce an explicit concatenation operator. Its only
result was to make my formulae, although more impressive, unnecessarily unwieldy.

From my earlier effort I copied the convention to express post-conditions in
terms of the string of characters read. With "S" defined as the string of input
characters "read" --or "moved over" or "made invisible"-- by a call of "sentsearch",

and with "x" defined as the currently visible input character, we can now state the desired post-condition for our recognizer "sentsearch":

Rs(S, x, c):   bosent(S) and non bosent(Sx) and c = sent(S)   (4)

The first term expresses that not too much has been read, the second term expresses that S is long enough, and the last term expresses that in the global boolean "c" --short for "correct"-- the success or failure to read a < sent > from the input should be recorded.

In short, we treat S and x as variables (of types "character string" and "character" respectively) that are initialized by a call of sentsearch . I mention this explicitly, because for a while we departed from that convention, and did as if the "input still to come" were defined prior to the call of sentsearch. We tried to derive from our post-condition weakest pre-conditions in terms of the "future" input characters, and the result was a disaster. At some time during that exercise we were even forced to introduce a deconcatenation operator! The trick to regard as "post-defined output" what used to be regarded as "pre-defined input" cannot be recommended warmly enough: it shortened our formulae by a considerable factor and did away with the need for many dummy identifiers.

Another improvement with respect to our earlier effort was a changed interface with respect to the input string. In my earlier trial I had had as a primitive to read the next character

                x:= nextchar

where "nextchar" was a character-valued function with the side-effect of moving the input tape over one place. (If S is the string of characters read, the above assignment to x should be followed implicitly by the "ghost statement" S:= Sx .) Prior to the first x:= nextchar , the value of the variable x was supposed to be undefined. In the new interface, where x is the currently visible character and S the string of characters no longer visible, I chose the primitive "move", semantically equivalent to the concurrent assignment

                S, x := Sx, new character   .

This minor change of interface turned out to be a considerable improvement! In the new interface, the building up of S lags one character behind compared with the old interface. Formula (4) shows how we can now refer --via concatenation-- to two strings, one of which is a character longer than the other. With the old interface we would have needed a notation for a string one character shorter than S , some-

230

thing so painful that in my earlier effort a different specification for sentsearch
was chosen, with the old interface more easily described, but logically less clean
than (4).

I wanted to write a body for sentsearch in terms of a call on expsearch and
the boolean primitive semi(x) which was assumed to be available. I wished to do so
only on account of the syntax for < sent > and discovered that I only could do so
under the assumption --to be verified later when the full syntax was taken into
account-- that

$$sent(L) \Rightarrow \underline{non} \; (\underline{E} \; y: bosent(Ly)) \tag{5}$$

would hold. Confronting this with the specification (4) we conclude that if
sentsearch establishes a final state with c = true , i.e. sent(S) , the second
term --non bosent(Sx)-- is true for all values of x : in other words, postulate
(5) states that the end of an instance of the syntactic category < sent > can be
established "without looking beyond".

We assume the availability of a primitive expsearch . Defining "E" to be the
string of input characters mover over by it, it establishes, analogous to (4):

$$Re(E, x, c): \quad boexp(E) \; \underline{and} \; \underline{non} \; boexp(Ex) \; \underline{and} \; c = exp(E) \tag{6}$$

Called by sentsearch, it implies S:= SE (as "move" implies S:= Sx). A possible
body for sentsearch is now:

    proc sentsearch: {S = empty string}
                    expsearch {Re(S, x, c)};
                    if non c → {Rs(S, x, c)} skip {Rs(S, x, c)}
                    ▯ non semi(x) → {Rs(S, x, false)} c:= false {Rs(S, x, c)}
                    ▯ c and semi(x) → {Rs(Sx, y, c)} move {Rs(S, x, c)}
                    fi {Rs(S, x, c)}
    corp

For its correctness proof I needed three theorems:
Theorem 1.   (Re(L, x, c) and non c) ⇒ Rs(L, x, c)
Theorem 2.   (Re(L, x, c) and non semi(x)) ⇒ Rs(L, x, false)
Theorem 3.   (Re(L, x, c) and c and semi(x)) ⇒ Rs(Lx, y, c)
The proofs of these three theorems and also of

$$boexp(L) \Rightarrow \underline{non} \; sent(L)$$

that I needed in these proofs took more than one-and-a-half page.

In the meantime the first 6 of the 19 pages had been written. The primitive expsearch asked for another three theorems to be proved and was finished 4 pages later; by analogy termsearch took only half a page; the primitive primsearch required another six theorems to be proved and was completed 6 pages later. The remaining two-and-a-half page were needed to prove assumption (5) and the similar

$$(\text{term}(L) \ \underline{and} \ \text{adop}(y)) \Rightarrow \underline{non} \ \text{boterm}(Ly)$$

and
$$(\text{prim}(L) \ \underline{and} \ \text{mult}(y)) \Rightarrow \underline{non} \ \text{boprim}(Ly)$$

and for some closing remarks.

I shall not go with you in any detail through these proofs and programs. I only mention that I had to replace

$$< \text{exp} > ::= < \text{term} > \ | \ < \text{exp} > < \text{adop} > < \text{term} >$$

first by

$$< \text{exp} > ::= \{ \ < \text{term} > < \text{adop} > \ \} \ < \text{term} >$$

in order to open the way for a repetitive construct in the body of expsearch. Thereafter I had to replace it by

$$< \text{exp} > ::= < \text{adder} > < \text{term} >$$
$$< \text{adder} > ::= \{ \ < \text{term} > < \text{adop} > \ \}$$

because I needed the expression "adder(L)" in my proofs and assertions. The syntax for < term > and < prim > were subjected to similar massaging operations.

*   *   *

So much for the description of my experiment. Let me now try to summarize what seem to be the more relevant aspects of the whole exercise.

1)   The routines I designed this time were definitely more beautiful than the ones I had written three years ago. This confirms my experience with the formal treatment of simpler examples, when I usually ended up with more beautiful programs than I had originally in mind.

2)   A slight change in the interface describing the reading of the next input character caused a more serious change in the overall specifications chosen for sentsearch: the formal treatment exposed the original interface as a seed of complexity.

3)   To treat a program absorbing input L formally as a nondeterminstic program assigning, as it were, a "guessed" value to L is a very useful device, so useful, in fact, that all by itself it is probably a sufficient justification for including nondeterminacy in our formal system. (Independently and in another context, also

C.A.R.Hoare was recently led to treat input in this fashion.)

4)   Nearly 11 of the 19 pages don't deal with the programs at all! They are exclusively concerned with exploring the given syntax and proving useful theorems about strings, theorems expressed in terms of predicates derived from the given syntax.

4.1) My earlier treatment of this example took only 7 pages: most of the theorems I proved this time were in the older treatment regarded as "obvious".

4.2) Several patterns of deduction appear in more than one proof; the introduction of a few well-chosen lemmata could probably have condensed somewhat what now took 11 pages.

4.3) The formal treatment of a program requires a formal "theory" about the subject matter of the computations. The development of such a theory may be expected to require the introduction of new concepts that did not occur in the original problem statement.

4.4) In the development of such a theory the choice of notation is crucial. (In this exercise the struggle of developing the theory was mainly the search for an adequate notation; once that had been invented, the development of the theory was fairly straightforward and I don't think that the final document contains more than a single line --at the end, where I was getting tired and lazy-- that could cause a serious reader serious problems.)

5)   There is a wide-spread belief that such formal proofs are incredibly long, tedious to write and boring to read, so long, tedious, and boring as a matter of fact, that we need at least a computer to verify them and perhaps even a computer to generate them. To the idea that proofs are so boring that we cannot rely upon them unless they are checked mechanically I have nearly philosophical objections, for I consider mathematical proofs as a reflection of my understanding and "understanding" is something we cannot delegate, neither to another person, nor to a machine. Because such philosophical objections carry no weight in a scientific discussion, I am happy to be able to report that my experiment completely belied the said wide-spread belief.

Since many years I have found that when I write an essay in which a program is developed, the total length of the essay is a decimal order of magnitude greater than the length of the program in which it culminates. The transition to a highly formal treatment has <u>not</u> changed that ratio significantly: it has only replaced the usual handwaving and mostly verbal arguments by more concise, much more explicit and, therefore, more convincing arguments. The belief that formal proofs are longer than informal arguments is not supported by my experiment.

The belief that the writing and reading of such proofs is tedious and boring

has also certainly not been confirmed: it was an exciting challenge to write it and
those who have seen it have confirmed that it was fascinating to read, because it
all fitted so beautifully --as, of course, in a nice formal proof it should!-- . I
am tending to regard the belief that these formal proofs must be long, tedious and
boring, as a piece of folklore, even as a harmful --because discouraging-- piece of
folklore that we had better try to get rid of. The fact that my formal treatment
was in all respects to be preferred above my former, informal treatment has been
one of the most encouraging experiences from the whole experiment, and I shall not
try to hide the fact that I am getting very, very suspicious of the preachers of the
refuted belief: they are mostly engaged on automatic verification or proving systems.
By preaching that formal proofs are too boring for human beings they are either trying to create a market for their products and a climate favourable for their funding,
or only trying to convince themselves of the significance of their work. The misunderstanding is aggravated by the complicating circumstance that their own activities
seem to support their beliefs: I have seen a number of correctness proofs that have
been produced by (semi-)mechanized systems, and, indeed, these proofs were appalling!

6)   The design consisted of a set of procedures; ignoring the possibility of a recursive call --as would have been the case when the second alternative production
for < prim > had been omitted-- they form a strict calling hierarchy of four layers
deep. It is worth noticing that all through that calling hierarchy the specifications
of the procedures are of an equally simple nature. The fact that, when we go up the
hierarchy, we create in a sense more and more "powerful" machinery is not reflected
in greater complication of the treatment, more elaborate interfaces, or what have
you. This, too, is a very encouraging observation, as it gives us some clue as to
what we might expect when we would undertake a more ambitious experiment with a still
less simple example.

Somewhere in his writings --and I regret having forgotten where-- John von
Neumann draws attention to what seemed to him a contrast. He remarked that for simple
mechanisms it is often easier to describe how they work than what they do, while for
more complicated mechanisms it was usually the other way round. The explanation of
this phenomenon, however, is quite simple: a mechanism derives its usability in a
larger context from the adequacy of its relevant properties and when they are very
complicated, they are certainly not adequate, because then the mechanism is certain
to introduce confusion and complexity into the context in which it is used.

As a result of this observation I feel that there is a reasonable justification
for the expectation that a next more ambitious experiment will just confirm my earlier experiences.

*   *   *

As you will have noticed I have accepted as some sort of Law of Nature that for the kind of programs I talk about, I accept a documentation ten times as long as the raw code, a Law of Nature that relates how we think to the best of our ability when we program to the best of our ability. Those struggling with the maintenance of programs of, say, 100,000 lines of code, must shudder at the thought of a documentation ten times as bulky, but I am not alarmed at all.

My first remark is that for the kind of programs I am talking about, the actual code is apparently a very compact deposit of our intellectual labours. In view of the various --and considerable!-- costs caused by sheer program length, this compactness should be a reason for joy! But then we cannot complain at the same time about the factor ten! You cannot have your cake and eat it....

My second remark to console the man struggling with the 100,000 lines of code is, admittedly, still a conjecture, but a conjecture for which I have not the slightest indication that it might be wrong. The conjecture is that the actual size of 100,000 lines is less dictated by the task he seeks to solve than by the maximum amount of formal text he thinks he can manage. And my conjecture, therefore, is that by applying more formal techniques, rather than change the total amount of 100,000 lines of documentation, he will reduce the length of the program to 10,000 lines, and that he will do so with a much greater chance of getting his program free of bugs.

*   *   *

As a result of this exercise I discovered an omission from all computer science curricula that I have been familiar with: we don't try to teach how to invent notations that are efficient in view of one's manipulative needs. And that is amazing, for it seems much less ambitious than, say, trying to teach explicitly how to think effectively. When teaching standard mathematical subjects, they get acquainted with the corresponding standard notations and these are fairly effective; so they have good examples, but that is all! I think that it could help tremendously if students could be made aware of the consequences of various conventions, consequences such as forced repetition, or all information sinking into the subsubsubscripts, etc.

My last remark is added because you may have noticed quantitative concerns from my side, such as worrying about the length of formulae and proofs. This is partly the result of a small study of elegant solutions. The study is not completed yet, but one observation stands out very clearly: the elegant solutions are short.

Appendix.

By way of illustration I include an excerpt from EWD550 "A more formal treatment of a less simple example." After the establishment of formulae (7) through (11) --as numbered in EWD550!-- , i.e. the choice in the case of (7), (8), and (11), and the derivation in the case of (9) and (10):

Rs(S, x, c):   bosent(S) and non bosent(Sx) and c = sent(S)   (7)

　　　　< sent > ::= < exp > ;   (8)

　　　　< bosent > ::= < sent > | < boexp >   (9)

　　　　boexp(L) ⇒ non sent(L)   (10)

Re(E, x, c):   boexp(E) and non boexp(Ex) and c = exp(E)   (11)

the text continues as follows.

"Designing sentsearch in terms of expsearch means that we would like to have theorems, such that from the truth of a relation of the form Re the truth of relations of the form Rs can be concluded. There are three such theorems.

Theorem 1.   (Re(L, x, c) and non c) ⇒ Rs(L, x, c)

Proof.   Assumed:

0.   Re(L, x, c) and non c

        Derived:

1.   boexp(L)   with (11) from 0

2.   bosent(L)   with (9) from 1

3.   c = exp(L)   with (11) from 0

4.   non c   from 0

5.   non exp(L)   from 3 and 4

6.   non sent(Lx)   with (8) from 5

7.   non boexp(Lx)   with (11) ·from 0

8.   non bosent(Lx)   with (9) from 6 and 7

9.   non sent(L)   with (10) from 1

10.   c = sent(L)   from 4 and 9

11.   Rs(L, x, c)   with (7) from 2, 8, and 10

                                (End of Proof of Theorem 1.)"

(End of Appendix)

CONSTRUCTIVE METHODS

OF PROGRAM DESIGN

M. A. Jackson

Michael Jackson Systems Limited

101 Hamilton Terrace, London NW8

Abstract

Correct programs cannot be obtained by attempts to test or to prove incorrect programs: the correctness of a program should be assured by the
design procedure used to build it.

A suggestion for such a design procedure is presented and discussed.
The procedure has been developed for use in data processing, and can be
effectively taught to most practising programmers. It is based on correspondence between data and program structures, leading to a decomposition of the program into distinct processes. The model of a process
is very simple, permitting use of simple techniques of communication,
activation and suspension. Some wider implications and future possi-
bilities are also mentioned.

1. Introduction

In this paper I would like to present and discuss what I believe to be
a *more constructive method of program design*. The phrase itself is important; I am sure that no-one here will object if I use a LIFO discipline in briefly elucidating its intended meaning.

'Design' is primarily concerned with structure; the designer must say
what parts there are to be and how they are to be arranged. The crucial importance of modular programming and structured programming (even
in their narrowest and crudest manifestations) is that they provide some
definition of what parts are permissible: a module is a separately compiled, parameterised subroutine; a structure component is a sequence, an
iteration or a selection. With such definitions, inadequate though they
may be, we can at least begin to think about design: what modules should
make up that program, and how should they be arranged? should this program be an iteration of selections or a sequence of iterations? Without
such definitions, design is meaningless. At the top level of a problem
there are P^N possible designs, where P is the number of distinct types
of permissible part and N is the number of parts needed to make up the
whole. So, to preserve our sanity, both P and N must be small: modular
programming, using tree or hierarchical structures, offers small values
of N; structured programming offers, additionally, small values of P.

'Program' or, rather, 'programming' I would use in a narrow sense. Modelling the problem is 'analysis'; 'programming' is putting the model on
a computer. Thus, for example, if we are asked to find a prime number
in the range 10^{50} to 10^{60}, we need a number theorist for the analysis;
if we are asked to program discounted cash flow, the analysis calls for
a financial expert. One of the major ills in data processing stems from
uncertainty about this distinction. In mathematical circles the distinction is often ignored altogether, to the detriment, I believe, of our
understanding of programming. Programming is about computer programs,
not about number theory, or financial planning, or production control.

'Method' is defined in the Shorter OED as a 'procedure for attaining an
object'. The crucial word here is 'procedure'. The ultimate method,
and the ultimate is doubtless unattainable, is a procedure embodying a
precise and correct algorithm. To follow the method we need only execute the algorithm faithfully, and we will be led infallibly to the desired result. To the extent that a putative method falls short of this
ideal it is less of a method.

To be 'constructive', a method must itself be decomposed into distinct steps, and correct execution of each step must assure correct execution of the whole method and thus the correctness of its product. The key requirement here is that the correctness of the execution of a step should be largely verifiable without reference to steps not yet executed by the designer. This is the central difficulty in stepwise refinement we can judge the correctness of a refinement step only by reference to what is yet to come, and hence only by exercising a degree of foresight to which few people can lay claim.

Finally, we must recognise that design methods today are intended for use by human beings: in spite of what was said above about constructive methods, we need, now and for some time to come, a substantial ingredient of intuition and subjectivity. So what is presented below does no claim to be fully constructive - merely to be 'more constructive'. The reader must supply the other half of the comparison for himself, measuring the claim against the yardstick of his own favoured methods.

2. Basis of the Method

The basis of the method is described, in some detail, in (1). It is appropriate here only to illustrate it by a family of simple example problems.

Example 1

A cardfile of punched cards is sorted into ascending sequence of values of a key which appears in each card. Within this sequence, the first card for each group of cards with a common key value is a header card, while the others are detail cards. Each detail card carries an integer amount. It is required to produce a report showing the totals of amount for all keys.

Solution 1

The first step in applying the method is to describe the structure of the data. We use a graphic notation to represent the structures as trees:-

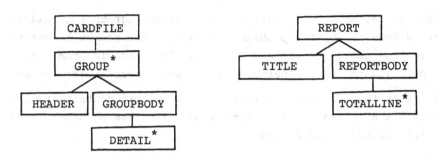

The above representations are equivalent to the following (in BNF with iteration instead of recursion):

$$\langle cardfile \rangle ::= \{\langle group \rangle\}_0^\infty$$
$$\langle group \rangle ::= \langle header \rangle \langle groupbody \rangle$$
$$\langle groupbody \rangle ::= \{\langle detail \rangle\}_0^\infty$$

$$\langle report \rangle ::= \langle title \rangle \langle reportbody \rangle$$
$$\langle reportbody \rangle ::= \{\langle totalline \rangle\}_0^\infty$$

The second step is to compose these data structures into a program structure:-

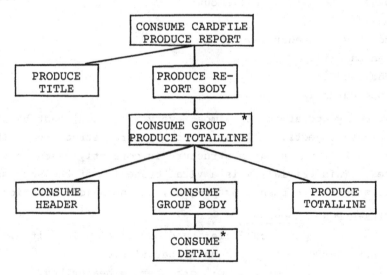

This structure has the following properties:

- It is related quite formally to each of the data structures. We may recover any one data structure from the program structure by first marking the leaves corresponding to leaves of the data structure, and then marking all nodes lying in a path from a marked node to the root.

- The correspondences (cardfile : report) and (group : totalline) are determined by the problem statement. One report is derivable from one cardfile; one totalline is derivable from one group, and the totallines are in the same order as the groups.

- The structure is vacuous, in the sense that it contains no executable statements: it is a program which does nothing; it is a tree without real leaves.

The third step in applying the method is to list the executable operations required and to allocate each to its right place in the program structure. The operations are elementary executable statements of the programming language, possibly after enhancement of the language by a bout of bottom-up design; they are enumerated, essentially, by working back from output to input along the obvious data-flow paths. Assuming a reasonably conventional machine and a line printer (rather than a character printer), we may obtain the list:

1. write title
2. write totalline (groupkey, total)
3. total := total + detail.amount
4. total := 0
5. groupkey := header.key
6. open cardfile
7. read cardfile
8. close cardfile

Note that every operation, or almost every operation, must have operands which are data objects. Allocation to a program structure is therefore a trivial task if the program structure is correctly based on the data structures. This triviality is a vital criterion of the success of the first two steps. The resulting program, in an obvious notation, is:

```
CARDFILE-REPORT  sequence
                 open cardfile; read cardfile; write title;
      REPORT-BODY  iteration until cardfile.eof
                     total := 0; groupkey := header.key;
                     read cardfile;
         GROUP-BODY  iteration until cardfile.eof or
                                        detail.key ≠ groupkey
                       total := total + detail.amount;
                       read cardfile;
         GROUP-BODY  end
                     write totalline (groupkey, total);
```

```
    REPORT-BODY  end
                 close cardfile;
  CARDFILE-REPORT  end
```

Clearly, this program may be transcribed without difficulty into any procedural programming language.

Comment

The solution has proceeded in three steps: first, we defined the data structures; second, we formed them into a program structure; third, we listed and allocated the executable operations. At each step we have criteria for the correctness of the step itself and an implicit check on the correctness of the steps already taken. For example, if at the first step we had wrongly described the structure of cardfile as

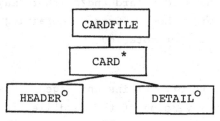

(that is: $\quad$ <cardfile> ::= $\{$<card>$\}_o^\infty$

$\quad\quad\quad$ <card> ::= <header>|<detail>), we should have been able to see at the first step that we had failed to represent everything we knew about the cardfile. If nonetheless we had persisted in error, we would have discovered it at the second step, when we would have been unable to form a program structure in the absence of a cardfile component corresponding to totalline in report.

The design has throughout concentrated on what we may think of as a static rather than a dynamic view of the problem: on maps, not on itineraries, on structures, not on logic flow. The logic flow of the finished program is a by-product of the data structures and the correct allocation of the 'read' operation. There is an obvious connection between what we have done and the design of a very simple syntax analysis phase in a compiler: the grammar of the input file determines the structure of the program which parses it. We may observe that the 'true' grammar of the cardfile is not context-free: within one group, the header and detail cards must all carry the same key value. It is because the explicit grammar cannot show this that we are forced to introduce the variable groupkey to deal with this stipulation.

Note that there is no error-checking. If we wish to check for errors in the input we must elaborate the structure of the input file to accommod-

ate those errors explicitly. By defining a structure for an input file
we define the domain of the program: if we wish to extend the domain, we
must extend the input file structure accordingly. In a practical data
processing system, we would always define the structure of primary input
(such as decks of cards, keyboard messages, etc) to encompass all physically possible files: it would be absurd to construct a program whose
operation is unspecified (and therefore, in principle, unpredictable) in
the event of a card deck being dropped or a wrong key depressed.

Example 2

The cardfile of example 1 is modified so that each card contains a card
type indicator with possible values 'header', 'detail' and other. The
program should take account of possible errors in the composition of a
group: there may be no header card and/or there may be cards other than
detail cards in the group body. Groups containing errors should be listed on an errorlist, but not totalled.

Solution 2

The structure of the report remains unchanged. The structure of the errorlist and of the new version of the cardfile are:

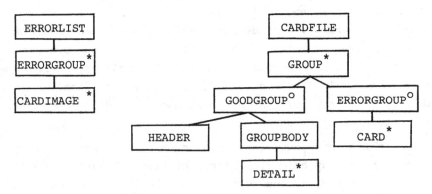

The structure of cardfile demands attention. Firstly, it is ambiguous:
anything which is a goodgroup is also an errorgroup. We are forced into
this ambiguity because it would be intolerably difficult - and quite unnecessary - to spell out all of the ways in which a group may be in error. The ambiguity is simply resolved by the conventions we use: the
parts of a selection are considered to be ordered, and the first applicable part encountered in a left-to-right scan is chosen. So a group can
be parsed as an errorgroup only if it has already been rejected as a
goodgroup. Secondly, a goodgroup cannot be recognised by a left-to-right
parse of the input file with any predetermined degree of lookahead. If
we choose to read ahead R records, we may yet encounter a group contain-

ing an error only in the R+1'th card.

Recognition problems of this kind occur in many guises. Their essence
is that we are forced to a choice during program execution at a time when
we lack the evidence on which the choice must be based. Note that the
difficulty is not structural but is confined to achieving a workable flow
of control. We will call such problems 'backtracking' problems, and tac-
kle them in three stages:-

a Ignore the recognition difficulty, imagining that a friendly
   demon will tell us infallibly which choice to make. In the present problem, he will tell us whether a group is a goodgroup or
   an errorgroup. Complete the design procedure in this blissful
   state of confidence, producing the full program text.

b Replace our belief in the demon's infallibility by a sceptical
   determination to verify each 'landmark' in the data which might
   prove him wrong. Whenever he is proved wrong we will execute a
   'quit' statement which branches to the second part of the selection. These 'quit' statements are introduced into the program
   text created in stage a.

c Modify the program text resulting from stage b to ensure that
   side-effects are repealed where necessary.

The result of stage a, in accordance with the design procedure used for
example 1, is:

```
CFILE-REPT-ERR   sequence
                 open cardfile;  read cardfile;  write title;
      REPORT-BODY  iteration until cardfile.eof
                   groupkey := card.key;
        GROUP-OUTG  select goodgroup
                    total := 0;
                    read cardfile;
          GOOD-GROUP  iteration until cardfile.eof or
                                        detail.key ≠ groupkey
                      total := total + detail.amount;
                      read cardfile;
          GOOD-GROUP  end
                    write totalline (groupkey, total);
        GROUP-OUTG  or errorgroup
          ERROR-GROUP  iteration until cardfile.eof or
                                        card.key ≠ groupkey
                       write errorline (card);
```

```
                        read cardfile;
        ERROR-GROUP   end
      GROUP-OUTG   end
   REPORT-BODY   end
                      close cardfile;
  CFILE-REPT-ERR   end
```

Note that we cannot completely transcribe this program into any programming language, because we cannot code an evaluable expression for the
predicate goodgroup. However, we can readily verify the correctness of
the program (assuming the infallibility of the demon). Indeed, if we
are prepared to exert ourselves to punch an identifying character into
the header card of each goodgroup - thus acting as our own demon - we
can code and run the program as an informal demonstration of its accept-
ability.

We are now ready to proceed to stage b, in which we insert 'quit' statements into the first part of the selection GROUP-OUTG. Also, since quit
statements are not present in a normal selection, we will replace the
words 'select' and 'or' by 'posit' and 'admit' respectively, thus indic-
ating the tentative nature of the initial choice. Clearly, the land-
marks to be checked are the card-type indicators in the header and detail cards. We thus obtain the following program:

```
  CFILE-REPT-ERR   sequence
                    open cardfile; read cardfile; write title;
      REPORT-BODY   iteration until cardfile.eof
                    groupkey := card.key;
        GROUP-OUTG   posit goodgroup
                    total := 0;
                    quit GROUP-OUTG if card.type ≠ header;
                    read cardfile;
          GOOD-GROUP   iteration until cardfile.eof or
                                        card.key ≠ groupkey
                    quit GROUP-OUTG if card.type ≠ detail;
                    total := total + detail.amount;
                    read cardfile;
          GOOD-GROUP   end
                    write totalline (groupkey, total);
        GROUP-OUTG   admit errorgroup
          ERROR-GROUP   iteration until cardfile.eof or
                                        card.key ≠ groupkey;
                    write errorline (card);
```

```
                    read cardfile;
        ERROR-GROUP  end
        GROUP-OUTG  end
    REPORT-BODY  end
                    close cardfile;
 CFILE-REPT-ERR  end
```

The third stage, stage c, deals with the side-effects of partial execution of the first part of the selection. In this trivial example, the
only significant side-effect is the reading of cardfile. In general, it
will be found that the only troublesome side-effects are the reading and
writing of serial files; the best and easiest way to handle them is to
equip ourselves with input and output procedures capable of 'noting' and
'restoring' the state of the file and its associated buffers. Given the
availability of such procedures, stage c can be completed by inserting a
'note' statement immediately following the 'posit' statement and a 'restore' statement immediately following the 'admit'. Sometimes side-effects will demand a more ad hoc treatment: when 'note' and 'restore' are
unavailable there is no alternative to such cumbersome expedients as
explicitly storing each record on disk or in main storage.

Comment

By breaking our treatment of the backtracking difficulty into three distinct stages, we are able to isolate distinct aspects of the problem.
In stage a we ignore the backtracking difficulty entirely, and concentrate our efforts on obtaining a correct solution to the reduced problem.
This solution is carried through the three main design steps, producing
a completely specific program text: we are able to satisfy ourselves of
the correctness of that text before going on to modify it in the second
and third stages. In the second stage we deal only with the recognition
difficulty: the difficulty is one of logic flow, and we handle it, appropriately, by modifying the logic flow of the program with quit statements. Each quit statement says, in effect, 'It is supposed (posited)
that this is a goodgroup; but if, in fact, this card is not what it ought
to be then this is not, after all, a goodgroup'. The required quit
statements can be easily seen from the data structure definition, and
their place is readily found in the program text because the program
structure perfectly matches the data structure. The side-effects arise
to be dealt with in stage 3 because of the quit statements inserted in
stage b: the quit statements are truly 'go to' statements, producing
discontinuities in the context of the computation and hence side-effects.
The side-effects are readily identified from the program text resulting

from stage b.

Note that it would be quite wrong to distort the data structures and the program structure in an attempt to avoid the dreaded four-letter word 'goto'. The data structures shown, and hence the program structure, are self-evidently the correct structures for the problem as stated: they must not be abandoned because of difficulties with the logic flow.

3. Simple Programs and Complex Programs

The design method, as described above, is severely constrained: it applies to a narrow class of serial file-processing programs. We may go further, and say that it defines such a class - the class of 'simple programs'. A 'simple program' has the following attributes:-

- The program has a fixed initial state; nothing is remembered from one execution to the next.

- Program inputs and outputs are serial files, which we may conveniently suppose to be held on magnetic tapes. There may be more than one input and more than one output file.

- Associated with the program is an explicit definition of the structure of each input and output file. These structures are tree structures, defined in the grammar used above. This grammar permits recursion in addition to the features shown above; it is not very different from a grammar of regular expressions.

- The input data structures define the domain of the program, the output data structures its range. Nothing is introduced into the program text which is not associated with the defined data structures.

- The data structures are compatible, in the sense that they can be combined into a program structure in the manner shown above.

- The program structure thus derived from the data structures is sufficient for a workable program. Elementary operations of the program language (possibly supplemented by more powerful or suitable operations resulting from bottom-up design) are allocated to components of the program structure without introducing any further 'program logic'.

A simple program may be designed and constructed with the minimum of difficulty, provided that we adhere rigorously to the design principles adumbrated here and eschew any temptation to pursue efficiency at the cost of distorting the structure. In fact, we should usually discount the benefits of efficiency, reminding ourselves of the mass of error-ridden programs which attest to its dangers.

Evidently, not all programs are simple programs. Sometimes we are presented with the task of constructing a program which operates on direct-access rather than on serial files, or which processes a single record at each execution, starting from a varying internal state. As we shall see later, a simple program may be clothed in various disguises which give it a misleading appearance without affecting its underlying nature. More significantly, we may find that the design procedure suggested cannot be applied to the problem given because the data structures are not compatible: that is, we are unable at the second step of the design procedure to form the program structure from the data structures.

Example 3

The input cardfile of example 1 is presented to the program in the form of a blocked file. Each block of this file contains a card count and a number of card images.

Solution 3

The structure of blockedfile is:

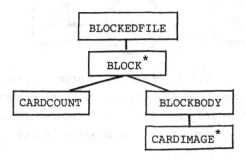

This structure does not, of course, show the arrangement of the cards in groups. It is impossible to show, in a single structure, both the arrangement in groups and the arrangement in blocks. But the structure of the report is still:

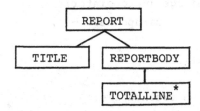

We cannot fit together the structures of report and blockedfile to form

a program structure; nor would we be in better case if we were to ignore
the arrangement in blocks. The essence of our difficulty is this: the
program must contain operations to be executed once per block, and these
must be allocated to a 'process block' component; it must also contain
operations to be executed once per group, and these must be allocated to
a 'process group' component; but it is impossible to form a single program structure containing both a 'process block' and a 'process group'
component. We will call this difficulty a 'structure clash'.

The solution to the structure clash in the present example is obvious:
more so because of the order in which the examples have been taken and
because everyone knows about blocking and deblocking. But the solution
can be derived more formally from the data structures. The clash is of
a type we will call 'boundary clash': the boundaries of the blocks are
not synchronised with the boundaries of the groups. The standard solut
ion for a structure clash is to abandon the attempt to form a single
program structure and instead decompose the problem into two or more
simple programs. For a boundary clash the required decomposition is al
ways of the form:

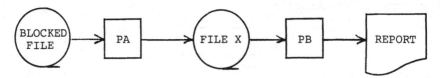

The intermediate file, file X, must be composed of records each of which
is a cardimage, because cardimage is the highest common factor of the
structures blockedfile and cardfile. The program PB is the program pro
duced as a solution to example 1; the program PA is:

```
PA   sequence
         open blockedfile; open fileX; read blockedfile;
PABODY  iteration until blockedfile.eof
             cardpointer := 1;
    PBLOCK  iteration until cardpointer > block.cardcount
             write cardimage (cardpointer);
             cardpointer := cardpointer + 1;
    PBLOCK  end
         read blockedfile;
PABODY  end
         close fileX; close blockedfile;
PA   end
```

The program PB sees file X as having the structure of cardfile in examp

1, while program PA sees its structure as:

Comment

The decomposition into two simple programs achieves a perfect solution.
Only the program PA is cognisant of the arrangement of cardimages in
blocks; only the program PB of their arrangement in groups. The tape
containing file X acts as a cordon sanitaire between the two, ensuring
that no undesired interactions can occur: we need not concern ourselves
at all with such questions as 'what if the header record of a group is
the first cardimage in a block with only one cardimage?', or 'what if a
group has no detail records and its header is the last cardimage in a
block?'; in this respect our design is known to be correct.

There is an obvious inefficiency in our solution. By introducing the intermediate magnetic tape file we have, to a first approximation, doubled
the elapsed time for program execution and increased the program's demand
for backing store devices.

Example 4

The input cardfile of example 1 is incompletely sorted. The cards are
partially ordered so that the header card of each group precedes any detail cards of that group, but no other ordering is imposed. The report
has no title, and the totals may be produced in any order.

Solution 4

The best we can do for the structure of cardfile is:

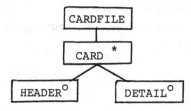

which is clearly incompatible with the structure of the report, since
there is no component of cardfile corresponding to totalline in the report. Once again we have a structure clash, but this time of a different type. The cardfile consists of a number of groupfiles, each one of

which has the form:

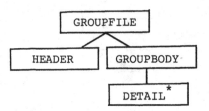

The cardfile is an arbitrary interleaving of these groupfiles. To resolve the clash (an 'interleaving clash') we must resolve cardfile into
its constituent groupfiles:

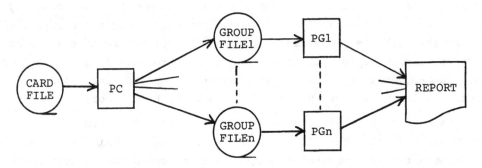

Allowing, for purposes of exposition, that a single report may be produced by the n programs PG1, ... PGn (each contributing one totalline),
we have decomposed the problem into n+1 simple programs; of these, n ar
identical programs processing the n distinct groupfiles groupfile1, ...
groupfilen; while the other, PC, resolves cardfile into its constituent

Two possible versions of PC are:

```
PC1   sequence
          open cardfile; read cardfile;
          open all possible groupfiles;
PC1BODY   iteration until cardfile.eof
              write record to groupfile (record.key);
              read cardfile;
PC1BODY   end
          close all possible groupfiles;
          close cardfile;
PC1   end
```

and

```
PC2   sequence
          open cardfile; read cardfile;
```

```
PC2BODY  iteration until cardfile.eof
 REC-INIT  select new groupfile
              open groupfile (record.key);
  REC-INIT  end
           write record to groupfile (record.key);
           read cardfile;
PC2BODY  end
       close all opened groupfiles;
       close cardfile;
 PC2 end
```

Both PC1 and PC2 present difficulties. In PC1 we must provide a groupfile for every possible key value, whether or not cardfile contains records for that key. Also, the programs PG1, ... PGn must be elaborated
to handle the null groupfile:

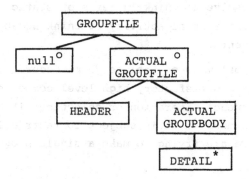

In PC2 we must provide a means of determining whether a groupfile already
exists for a given key value. Note that it would be quite wrong to base
the determination on the fact that a header must be the first record for
a group: such a solution takes impermissible advantage of the structure
of groupfile which, in principle, is unknown in the program PC; we would
then have to make a drastic change to PC if, for example, the header card
were made optional:

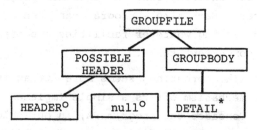

Further, in PC2 we must be able to run through all the actual key values
in order to close all the groupfiles actually opened. This would still

be necessary even if each group had a recognisable trailer record, for reasons similar to those given above concerning the header records.

Comment

The inefficiency of our solution to example 4 far outstrips the inefficiency of our solution to example 3. Indeed, our solution to example 4 is entirely impractical. Practical implementation of the designs will be considered below in the next section. For the moment, we may observe that the use of magnetic tapes for communication between simple programs enforces a very healthy discipline. We are led to use a very simple protocol: every serial file must be opened and closed. The physical medium encourages a complete decoupling of the programs: it is easy to imagine one program being run today, the tapes held overnight in a library, and a subsequent program being run tomorrow; the whole of the communication is visible in the defined structure of the files. Finally, we are strengthened in our resolve to think in terms of static structures, avoiding the notoriously error-prone activity of thinking about dynamic flow and execution-time events.

Taking a more global view of the design procedure, we may say that the simple program is a satisfactory high level component. It is a larger object than a sequence, iteration or selection; it has a more precise definition than a module; it is subject to restrictions which reveal to us clearly when we are trying to make a single program out of what should be two or more.

4. Programs, Procedures and Processes

Although from the design point of view we regard magnetic tapes as the canonical medium of communication between simple programs, they will not usually provide a practical implementation.

An obvious possibility for implementation in some environments is to replace each magnetic tape by a limited number of buffers in main storage with a suitable regime for ensuring that the consumer program does not run ahead of the producer. Each simple program can then be treated as a distinct task or process, using whatever facilities are provided for the management of multiple concurrent tasks.

However, something more like coroutines seems more attractive (2). The standard procedure call mechanism offers a simple implementation of great flexibility and power. Consider the program PA, in our solution to example 3, which writes the intermediate file X. We can readily convert the program into a procedure PAX which has the characteristics of an input procedure for file X. That is, invocations of the procedure PAX will satisfactorily implement the operations 'open file X for reading', 'read file X' and 'close file X after reading'.

We will call this conversion of PA into PAX 'inversion of PA with respect to file X'. (Note that the situation in solution 3 is symmetrical: we could equally well decide to invert PB with respect to file X, obtaining an output procedure for file X.) The mechanics of inversion are a mere matter of generating the appropriate object coding from the text of the simple program: there is no need for any modification to that text. PA and PAX are the same program, not two different programs. Most practising programmers seem to be unaware of this identity of PA and PAX, and even those who are familiar with coroutines often program as if they supposed that PA and PAX were distinct things. This is partly due to the baleful influence of the stack as a storage allocation device: we cannot jump out of an inner block of PAX, return to the invoking procedure, and subsequently resume where we left off when we are next invoked. So we must either modify our compiler or modify our coding style, adopting the use of labels and go to statements as a standard in place of the now conventional compound statement of structured programming. It is common to find PAX, or an analogous program, designed as a selection or case statement: the mistake is on all fours with that of the kindergarten child who has been led to believe that the question 'what is 5 multiplied by 3?' is quite different from the question 'what is 3 multiplied by 5?'. At a stroke the poor child has doubled the difficulty of learning the multiplication tables.

The procedure PAX is, of course, a variable state procedure. The value of its state is held in a 'state vector' (or activation record), of which a vital part is the text pointer; the values of special significance are those associated with the suspension of PAX for operations on file X - open, write and close. The state vector is an 'own variable' par excellence, and should be clearly seen as such.

The minimum interface needed between PB and PAX is two parameters: a record of file X, and an additional bit to indicate whether the record is or is not the eof marker. This minimum interface suffices for example 3: there is no need for PB to pass an operation code to PAX (open read or close). It is important to understand that this minimum interface will not suffice for the general case. It is sufficient for example 3 only because the operation code is implicit in the ordering of operations. From the point of view of PAX, the first invocation must be 'open', and subsequent invocations must be 'read' until PAX has returned the eof mar-

ker to PB, after which the final invocation must be 'close'. This feli-
citous harmony is destroyed if, for example, PB is permitted to stop
reading and close file X before reaching the eof marker. In such a case
the interface must be elaborated with an operation code. Worse, the seq
uence of values of this operation code now constitutes a file in its own
right: the solution becomes:

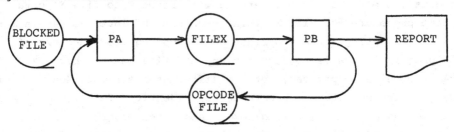

The design of PA is, potentially, considerably more complicated. The
benefit we will obtain from treating this complication conscientiously i
well worth the price: by making explicit the structure of the opcode fil
we define the problem exactly and simplify its solution. Failure to recognise the existence of the opcode file, or, just as culpable, failure
to make its structure explicit, lies at the root of the errors and ob-
scurities for which manufacturers' input-output software is deservedly
infamous.

In solution 4 we created an intolerable multiplicity of files - group-
filel, ... groupfilen. We can rid ourselves of these by inverting the
programs PG1, ... PGn with respect to their respective groupfiles: that
is, we convert each of the programs PGi to an output procedure PGFi,
which can be invoked by PC to execute operations on groupfilei. But we
still have an intolerable multiplicity of output procedures, so a further step is required. The procedures are identical except for their
names and the current values of their state vectors. So we separate out
the pure procedure part - PGF - of which we need keep only one copy, and
the named state vectors SVPGF1, ... SVPGFn. We must now provide a mechanism for storing and retrieving these state vectors and for associating
the appropriate state vector with each invocation of PGF; many mechanism
are possible, from a fully-fledged direct-access file with serial read
facilities to a simple arrangement of the state vectors in an array in
main storage.

5. Design and Implementation

The model of a simple program and the decomposition of a problem into
simple programs provides some unity of viewpoint. In particular, we may

be able to see what is common to programs with widely different implementations. Some illustrations follow.

a A conversational program is a simple program of the form:

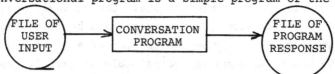

The user provides a serial input file of messages, ordered in time; the conversation program produces a serial file of responses. Inversion of the program with respect to the user input file gives an output procedure 'dispose of one message in a conversation'. The state vector of the inverted program must be preserved for the duration of the conversation: IBM's IMS provides the SPA (Scratchpad Area) for precisely this purpose. The conversation program must, of course, be designed and written as a single program: implementation restrictions may dictate segmentation of the object code.

b A 'sort-exit' allows the user of a generalised sorting program to introduce his own procedure at the point where each record is about to be written to the final output file. An interface is provided which permits 'insertion' and 'deletion' of records as well as 'updating'.

We should view the sort-exit procedure as a simple program:

To fit it in with the sorting program we must invert it with respect to both the sortedfile and the finaloutput. The interface must provide an implementation of the basic operations: open sortedfile for reading; read sortedfile (distinguishing the eof marker); close sortedfile after reading; open finaloutput for writing; write finaloutput record; close finaloutput file after writing (including writing the eof marker).

Such concepts as 'insertion' and 'deletion' of records are pointless: at best, they serve the cause of efficiency, traducing clarity; at worst, they create difficulty and confusion where none need exist.

c Our solution to example 1 can be seen as an optimisation of the solution to the more general example 4. By sorting the

cardfile we ensure that the groups do not overlap in time: the
state vectors of the inverted programs PGF1, ... PGFn can
therefore share a single area in main storage. The state vector consists only of the variable total; the variable groupkey
is the name of the currently active group and hence of the
current state vector. Because the records of a group are contiguous, the end of a group is recognisable at cardfile.eof or
at the start of another group. The individual groupfile may
therefore be closed, and the totalline written, at the earli-
est possible moment.

We may, perhaps, generalise so far as to say that an identifier is stored by a program only in order to give a unique name
to the state vector of some process.

d   A data processing system may be viewed as consisting of many
simple programs, one for each independent entity in the real
world model. By arranging the entities in sets we arrange the
corresponding simple programs in equivalence classes. The
'master record' corresponding to an entity is the state vector
of the simple program modelling that entity.

The serial files of the system are files of transactions ordered in time: some are primary transactions, communicating
with the real world, some are secondary, passing between simple programs of the system. In general, the real world must
be modelled as a network of entities or of entity sets; the
data processing system is therefore a network of simple programs and transaction files.

Implementation of the system demands decisions in two major
areas. First a scheduling algorithm must be decided; second,
the representation and handling of state vectors. The extreme
cases of the first are 'real-time' and 'serial batch'. In a
pure 'real-time' system every primary transaction is dealt
with as soon as it arrives, followed immediately by all of the
secondary and consequent transactions, until the system as a
whole becomes quiet. In a pure 'serial batch' system, each
class (identifier set) of primary transactions is accumulated
for a period (usually a day, week or month). Each simple program of that class is then activated (if there is a transaction
present for it), giving rise to secondary transactions of various classes. These are then treated similarly, and so on until no more transactions remain to be processed.

Choosing a good implementation for a data processing system is difficult, because the network is usually large and many possible choices present themselves. This difficulty is compounded by the long-term nature of the simple programs: a typical entity, and hence a typical program, has a lifetime measured in years or even decades. During such a lifetime the system will inevitably undergo change: in effect, the programs are being rewritten while they are in course of execution.

e An interrupt handler is a program which processes a serial file of interrupts, ordered in time:

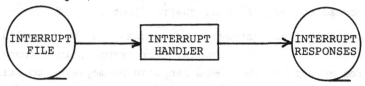

Inversion of the interrupt handler with respect to the interrupt file gives the required procedure 'dispose of one interrupt'. In general, the interrupt file will be composed of interleaved files for individual processes, devices, etc. Implementation is further complicated by the special nature of the invocation mechanism, by the fact that the records of the interrupt file are distributed in main storage, special registers and other places, and by the essentially recursive structure of the main interrupt file (unless the interrupt handler is permitted to mask off secondary interrupts).

f An input-output procedure (what IBM literature calls an 'access method') is a simple program which processes an input file of access requests and produces an output file of access responses. An access request consists of an operation code and, sometimes, a data record; an access response consists of a result code and, sometimes, a data record. For example, a direct-access method has the form:

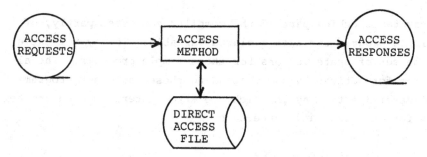

By inverting this simple program with respect to both the file
of access requests and the file of access responses we obtain
the desired procedure. This double inversion is always possible without difficulty, because each request must produce a response and that response must be calculable before the next request is presented.

The chief crime of access method designers is to conceal from
their customers (and, doubtless, from themselves) the structure
of the file of access requests. The user of the method is thus
unable to determine what sequences of operations are permitted
by the access method, and what their effect will be.

g   Some aspects of a context-sensitive grammar may be regarded as
    interleaved context-free grammars. For example, in a grossly
    simplified version of the COBOL language we may wish to stipu-
    late that any variable may appear as an operand of a MOVE state-
    ment, while only a variable declared as numeric may appear as
    an operand of an arithmetic (ADD, SUBTRACT, MULTIPLY or DIVIDE)
    statement. We may represent this stipulation as follows:

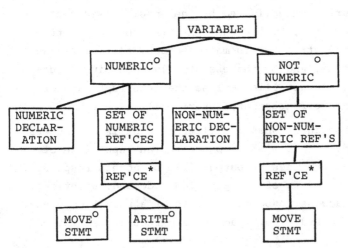

The syntax-checking part of the compiler consists, partly, of
a simple program for each declared variable. The symbol table
is the set of state vectors for these simple programs. The algorithm for activating and suspending these and other programs
will determine the way in which one error interacts with another
both for diagnosis and correction.

6. A Modest Proposal

It is one thing to propose a model to illuminate what has already been done, to clarify the sources of existing success or failure. It is quite another to show that the model is of practical value, and that it leads to the construction of acceptable programs. An excessive zeal in decomposition produces cumbersome interfaces and pointlessly redundant code. The "Shanley Principle" in civil engineering (3) requires that several functions be implemented in a single part; this is necessary for economy both in manufacturing and in operating the products of engineering design. It appears that a design approach which depends on decomposition runs counter to this principle: its main impetus is the separation of functions for implementation in distinct parts of the program.

But programs do not have the intractable nature of the physical objects which civil, mechanical or electrical engineers produce. They can be manipulated and transformed (for example, by compilers) in ways which preserve their vital qualities of correctness and modifiability while improving their efficiency both generally and in the specialised environment of a prticular machine. The extent to which a program can be manipulated and transformed is critically affected by two factors: the variety of forms it can take, and the semantic clarity of the text. Programs written using today's conventional techniques score poorly on both factors. There is a distressingly large variety of forms, and intelligibility is compromised or even destroyed by the introduction of implementation-orientated features. The justification for these techniques is, of course, efficiency. But in pursuing efficiency in this way we become caught in a vicious circle: because our languages are rich the compilers cannot understand, and hence cannot optimise, our programs; so we need rich languages to allow us to obtain the efficiency which the compilers do not offer.

Decomposition into simple programs, as discussed above, seems to offer some hope of separating the considerations of correctness and modifiability from the considerations of efficiency. Ultimately, the objective is that the first should become largely trivial and the second largely automatic.

The first phase of design would produce the following documents:-

- a definition of each serial file structure for each simple program (including files of operation codes!);

- the text of each simple program;

- a statement of the communication between simple programs, perhaps in the form of identities such as

$$\text{output } (p_i, f_r) \equiv \text{input } (p_j, f_s).$$

It may then be possible to carry out some automatic checking of self-consistency in the design - for instance, to check that the inputs to a program are within its domain. We may observe, incidentally, that the 'inner' feature of Simula 67 (4) is a way of enforcing consistency of a file of operation codes between the consumer and producer processes in a very limited case. More ambitiously, it may be possible, if file-handling protocol is exactly observed, and read and write operations are allocated with a scrupulous regard to principle, to check the correctness of the simple programs in relation to the defined data structures.

In the second phase of design, the designer would specify, in greater or lesser detail:-

- the synchronisation of the simple programs;

- the handling of state vectors;

- the dissection and recombining of programs and state vectors to reduce interface overheads.

Synchronisation is already loosely constrained by the statements of program communication made in the first phase: the consumer can never run ahead of the producer. Within this constraint the designer may choose to impose additional constraints at compile time and/or at execution time. The weakest local constraint is to provide unlimited dynamic buffering at execution time, the consumer being allowed to lag behind the producer by anything from a single record to the whole file, depending on resource allocation elsewhere in the system. The strongest local constraints are use of coroutines or program inversion (enforcing a single record lag) and use of a physical magnetic tape (enforcing a whole file lag).

Dissection and recombining of programs becomes possible with coroutines or program inversion; its purpose is to reduce interface overheads by moving code between the invoking and invoked programs, thus avoiding some of the time and space costs of procedure calls and also, under certain circumstances, avoiding replication of program structure and hence of coding for sequencing control. It depends on being able to associate code in one program with code in another through the medium of the communicating data structure.

A trivial illustration is provided by solution 3, in which we chose to invert PA with respect to file X, giving an input procedure PAX for the file of cardimages. We may decide that the procedure call overhead is intolerable, and that we wish to dissect PAX and combine it with PB. This is achieved by taking the invocations of PAX in PB (that is, the statements 'open fileX', 'read fileX' and 'close fileX') and replacing those invocations by the code which PAX would execute in response to them. For example, in response to 'open fileX', PAX would execute the code 'open blockedfile'; therefore the 'open fileX' statement in PB can be replaced by the statement 'open blockedfile'.

A more substantial illustration is provided by the common practice of designers of 'real-time' data processing systems. Suppose that a primary transaction for a product gives rise to a secondary transaction for each open order item for that product, and that each of those in turn gives rise to a transaction for the open order of which it is a part, which then gives rise to a transaction for the customer who placed the order. Instead of having separate simple programs for the product, order item, order and customer, the designer will usually specify a 'transaction processing module': this consists of coding from each of those simple programs, the coding being that required to handle the relevant primary or secondary transaction.

Some interesting program transformations of a possibly relevant kind are discussed in a paper by Burstall and Darlington (5). I cannot end this paper better than by quoting from them:

> "The overall aim of our investigation has been to help people to
> write correct programs which are easy to alter. To produce such
> programs it seems advisable to adopt a lucid, mathematical and
> abstract programming style. If one takes this really seriously,
> attempting to free one's mind from considerations of computational
> efficiency, there may be a heavy penalty in program running time;
> in practice it is often necessary to adopt a more intricate ver-
> sion of the program, sacrificing comprehensibility for speed.
> The question then arises as to how a lucid program can be trans-
> formed into a more intricate but efficient one in a systematic
> way, or indeed in a way which could be mechanised.

> " ... We are interested in starting with programs having an ex-
> tremely simple structure and only later introducing the complic-
> ations which we usually take for granted even in high level lang-
> uage programs. These complications arise by introducing useful
> interactions between what were originally separate parts of the
> program, benefiting by what might be called 'economies of inter-
> action'."

References

(1) Principles of Program Design; M A Jackson; Academic Press 1975.

(2) Hierarchical Program Structures; O-J Dahl; in Structured Programming; Academic Press 1972.

(3) Structured Programming with go to Statements; Donald E Knuth; in ACM Computing Surveys Vol 6 No 4 December 1974.

(4) A Structural Approach to Protection; C A R Hoare; 1975.

(5) Some Transformations for Developing Recursive Programs; R M Burstall & John Darlington; in Proceedings of 1975 Conference on Reliable Software; Sigplan Notices Vol 10 No 6 June 1975.

TEAM ORGANISATION IN INTEGRATED ON-LINE COMPUTER PROJECTS

P. Hammersley

Director of Computer Unit

Addenbrooke's Hospital

Hills Road, Cambridge CB2 2QQ, UK

1. INTRODUCTION

For most of the 1960's the development of computer systems for business purposes was centred on those systems which could be implemented in terms of a single batch program, or a 'suite' of such programs, processing sequential magnetic tape files with input from a card reader and output to one or more line printers.   The programs usually were written in COBOL and most often were concerned with financial applications. The organisation of the computer department necessary to sustain this type of development has been described fully.   An excellent summary appeared in Coates (1974). In general, systems design, programming, and operations formed three distinct sections, each operating with a strictly hierarchical management structure.

The 1970's saw, however, a rapid expansion in the number and type of on-line systems. The need for computers to be used in promoting change in the decision making processes (Hardcastle, 1971), a requirement that information should be made available at least as quickly as it was before computer systems became commonplace, a requirement by users to control the input to and output from the systems which supported them, and a desire to exploit the communication properties of on-line systems in order to eliminate errors, losses, and delays, all contributed their part to that expansion.

From the point of view of team organisation there were many different types of on-line system.   Many were concerned with small dedicated computers, undertaking some form of machine control, in which a single program coped with a limited set of processes.   Others, particularly those using remote job entry terminals, displayed no different characteristics to the batch processing systems which they displaced.   A third group had the characteristics of both of the two former; terminals were used for capturing data on-line during the day, with the data being written to file and accessed only in the evening.   Then it was used as a serial file forming the input to a batch 'suite'.   Among the remaining systems there was one special type, about which this paper is concerned, in which the computer system covered many different aspects of an organisation and in which terminals attached to the system could input, access, or demand processing of any item of data supplied by any other terminal. For the purposes of this paper such a system is referred to as an Integrated Information and Communication System (IICS).

Among those organisations which have seen the need for an IICS have been hospitals. In England a number of hospitals have been able to establish an IICS through the direct support of the Department of Health and Social Security.   One of them has been Addenbrooke's Hospital, Cambridge, where a team has been working on such a system since

1969. Addenbrooke's is a long established teaching hospital which has recently moved into new buildings on the outskirts of the city. From the outset of planning the new buildings the IICS was seen as the only satisfactory method of overcoming the management and communication problems which were likely to arise when the buildings were commissioned (Hammersley, 1972).

A special characteristic of the development at Addenbrooke's was a restriction on the amount of finance available, leading to a relatively small team of systems and programming staff, fourteen in all. On the other hand the task was complex. Users would have available approximately one hundred and fifty different possible operations, many of which would interact directly with others, these operations accessing a database with one hundred and ten record types exhibiting approximately one hundred set relationships. It was felt that in order to complete the project in the time and with the resources available a new method of team organisation and planning strategy was needed. This paper describes the type of organisation chosen, the problems which it has thrown up, and the ways in which those problems were tackled. It attempts to assess whether or not the particular organisation chosen has achieved the results which were expected of it.

2. THE REASONS FOR CHOOSING A NEW STRUCTURE

Early in the life of the project certain characteristics of an IICS were observed which indicated a different approach from that adopted previously. These were:

1. An on-line transaction between a user and the computer consisted of a set of inputs and responses, each covering a few items of information. Therefore the whole development had to be seen as a chain of equivalent tasks and not as a hierarchy of different ones.

2. Because much of the processing organisation was carried out by software packages the amount of code generated for each user operation was relatively small. This is shown clearly in the diagram of store utilisation given in Fig. 1. In the Xerox TP package, used to implement the system at Addenbrooke's, it was assumed that the user provided code would be written in COBOL. These two criteria indicated that the programming operation would occupy a smaller place relatively than had been the case before.

3. The success of an on-line system depended on the computer being able to respond to prompts in a time acceptable to the user. This required the systems designer to be fully aware of all aspects of the techniques used by the software packages to control the on-line operation.

4. The possible interaction of any one part of the total system with any other meant that any one user operation could generate effects elsewhere in the system. Hence each designer had to be fully aware of the operation of the total system and not the one application on which he was working.

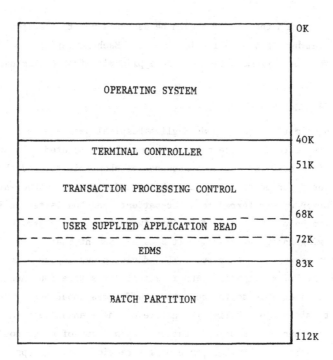

Fig. 1   Layout of core storage showing relative
occupancy of user supplied program.

5. The involvement of users who had not themselves taken any part in the decision to proceed with a computer system, who were suspicious, and who were "naive" in the sense that they were unaware of the potential of computer systems, yet who would be operating the terminals on their own behalf, led to a situation where systems specifications would be changing continuously, right up to the time of implementation.   This meant that there was a need for the systems designer to be aware of the total implications of an application so that changes could be effected quickly and painlessly.

6. A total IICS was too large for any one individual to be able to see the scope for improvements and extensions.   Each individual had to be in a position to feed new ideas into the development.

Against these requirements had to be set also the question of motivation, the element necessary to produce a complex system with the minimum of effort.   Many programming departments have regarded programmers as coding clerks and have suffered from the consequences of a feeling by staff that they are not involved.   It was essential to ensure that this situation did not arise.

The twin considerations of the nature of an on-line system, with its emphasis on the need for effective communication, and the need for considerable motivation for staff led to the conclusion that staff should be assigned not to a systems team nor to a programming team but to an applications team. Each member of the project would be responsible for the implementation of one application from preliminary study to final cutover.

3. THE INITIAL TEAM STRUCTURE

The provision of patient care in an English hospital was seen as falling into two clear divisions, care for those patients who could be treated in a short space of time, say half-an-hour, or during a sequence of short visits, and those who needed to be treated over a period of a few days whilst under constant observation in the hospital. The former were referred to as outpatients and the latter as inpatients. The transactions to be provided also fell into two groups, those serving outpatient areas and those serving inpatient areas. It became apparent that a division of available staff into two teams was necessary. This division was imposed also by the geography of the hospital. The outpatient and inpatient areas were four hundred metres apart and the offices available to the computer staffs were separated by the same distance. Within each team's responsibility the nature of the transactions to be provided could be divided into four groups of applications, each group of which could be implemented as a complete entity, although because of interactions some groups would need to be introduced before others. Within each team one systems analyst was allocated to each of the four groups of applications.

The requirement for speedy implementation implied a requirement for as rigid a system of project control as could be achieved consistent with providing motivation. Initially this was provided by allocating to each team two senior designers each of whom was responsible for the control of two of the applications. Early in the life of the project it was not clear what form of software system would need to be developed for the project nor what form the central data-bank, to which all the applications would interface, would take. Two members of the design staff were allocated to considering respectively the software needs and the database needs of the project. Each senior designer, and each software expert, reported to the Chief Systems Designer. The structure of the team was then that of Fig. 2.

4. DEVELOPMENTS OF THE TEAM STRUCTURE

The team structure described in Section 3 was created to achieve two results, to eliminate the user-designer and designer-programmer communication barriers which occur normally and to provide motivation. It proved satisfactory so long as the primary task was systems analysis or the broad outline of the systems design. Once detailed design work began then a number of holes began to appear. Among problems were:

1. Design staff tended to work in isolation, the provision of two senior designers per team merely aggravating the problem rather than easing it. This led to duplication of effort in many cases and problems of interfacing being "put off" and eventually

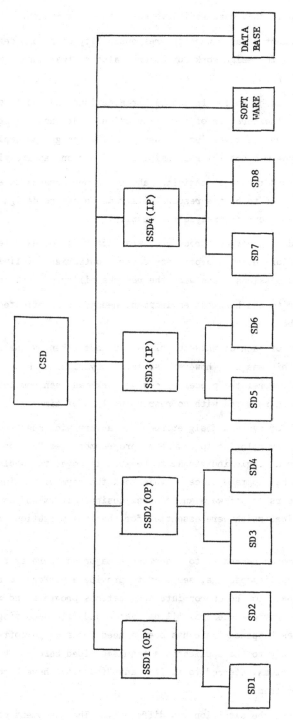

Fig. 2   Original team structure

forgotten altogether, until they were rediscovered at the last minute.

2. Many areas of development clearly were the responsibility of no one designer. Such areas were not restricted to design work but covered also software and administrative tasks. Some examples were:

(a) Many transactions could be called from other transactions and had to store (and restore) information for the duration of the transaction. At the end they had to know where to return and what information to supply. The design and implementation of interfaces of this type was not the responsibility of any cne application.

(b) Each transaction needed to store statistics about its performance to allow tuning to take place. It appeared to be the responsibility of no-one to design the form of storage or provide the programs to analyse the results.

(c) Aspects of systems design spread across many transactions, for example the provision of a standard form for letters to patients covered outpatients (clinic appointments) and inpatients (admissions), and were the responsibility of more than one team.

(d) Physical alterations to the hospital environment needed to be effected before the computer systems could be implemented.

In practice the solution of each of these problems was undertaken by the first systems designer to meet it. This was not, however, satisfactory since in many cases problems were highlighted only after related pieces of design work had been completed. That design work then had to be repeated with corresponding loss of time.

3. The newly defined job of systems designer required a very wide spectrum of skills, varying from industrial psychologist to low level programmer (see Section 5). In practice it was rare for a single individual to be able to cover the whole spectrum and some specialisation had to take place. This took the form of two individuals being allocated as advisors on software and central design matters and as writers of those machine code routines which were essential for the implementation of the applications.

In many IICS's it has proved necessary to undertake a major software exercise, firstly to provide a terminal handling package, secondly to provide a package to route the messages from the terminals to the appropriate applications programs and to return the replies, and thirdly to provide a central filing system and file accessing method (see Fig. 1). Where this has happened there has been a need for a large software team structured in a similar way to the applications team described here. Where such a team has existed the problems referred to in 2(a) and 2(b) above have become the responsibility of the software team.

At Addenbrooke's, however, the situation was different. The equipment chosen for the project, a Xerox Sigma 6 computer, already had available transaction processing software (Xerox TP) and a database management system (EDMS) based on the CODASYL proposals

Hence there was no need for a large team.   Yet there was a need **to** interface to the suppliers, Rank Xerox Data Systems, and to provide general advice to the applications teams.   The designer allocated to the study of software was suitable for the role of liaison-advising but was not sufficiently senior to take over the design functions required by 2(a) and 2(b).   Similarly there was a need for a database structure to be designed, again covering all applications and again requiring a designer with some degree of seniority.   The responsibilities of the database designer would be those described in Palmer (1975).

The problems outlined at the beginning of this section were problems not of organisation but of communication.   Nevertheless the organisation had to be one which supported, and not opposed, the communication mechanism.

The problems of gaps in the organisation were covered in three ways:

1. By changing the role of the second senior designer in each team to that of an advisor on low-level programming and software.

2. By creating senior posts covering software design and implementation and database design and implementation.

3. By creating a post of administrator with responsibility for those areas of systems design which were concerned with the overall interface to the hospital at large, for example physical alterations and standard stationery.

The team structure now became that shown in Fig 3.

The problems of communication across applications could have been solved by the introduction of hierarchical management, already in being because of the need for project control.   It was felt that this would reduce the motivation factor and would not be entirely effective.   Instead a series of "think tank" sessions was introduced.   Each team had its own session once per week.   A combined session of senior designers with the chief systems designer was held every two weeks.   Early in the project meetings of the whole project team were held regularly, at least once per month, but these were found to be more disruptive than helpful, largely because different team members would interpret discussions in different ways and further meetings of the type described already would need to be held in order to resolve the differences.   This system was backed up by an extensive standards manual covering every aspect of the project from administration to operations.

5.   STAFFING POLICY AND RECRUITMENT

The skills required of any one systems designer in the organisation described above were extensive.   They covered:

1. Operational Research - required both in the study of the uses to which the computer should be put and in the design of the on-line system itself (Martin, 1967).

2. Industrial Psychology - on-line systems introduced the idea of direct man-machine

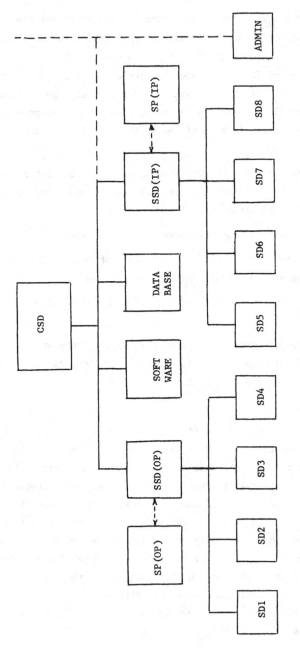

Fig. 3 First development of team structure

interaction (Martin, 1973). It was essnetial that the problems of the naive user in this respect (Eason, 1976) were understood if the implementation was to succeed.

3. Systems Analysis - the conventional systems analysis techniques were still needed.

4. Transaction Processing Software Design - the interactions between applications could be provided only in the context of facilities which were available in, or could be added to, the existing TP software.

5. Database Design - because of response time considerations the suitability of a particular implementation could be determined only in the context of how the database management system handled the data references. As many of the accesses were through chains and not direct this was highly significant.

6. Programming - all members of the team were required to program in COBOL and FORT-RAN. Machine code programming was not essential but was encouraged. Later in the project the provision of an APL database interface required an extension of expertise.

7. Knowledge of Developments - the short implementation timescale required that the latest techniques of program development (where relevant) should be employed. The concepts of structured programming were introduced from the outset, on-line program development was introduced as soon as facilities became available.

Was it possible to engage staff to work on this basis?

Fortunately, the salaries which could be offered, the environment of the project within the hospital, and the nature of the computing activity were all aspects which made working with the team attractive. The problem was to ensure that recruitment strategies were directed towards those individuals whose pyschological needs for job satisfaction (Mumford, 1972) met most closely what the project had to offer. A number of different recruitment strategies were applied, for example:

1. To advertise specifying qualifications and experience in the broad sense, say a degree plus some on-line experience.

2. To advertise specifying only a restricted experience, say three years COBOL programming.

3. To recruit directly from university, through official contacts and personal visits, and provide training.

4. To recruit from within the hospital service and provide training.

From the returns obtained by evaluating these strategies a clear profile emerged of the type of individual likely to be at home within the structure. He would be a graduate in either a scientific discipline or one with a logical content (e.g. music or philosophy). He would have had some computer training, either as part of his university course or subsequently, and he would have had some experience of the environment, in this case the hospital environment, either directly or through appropriate M.Sc courses. Alternatively it was found that computer professionals who had spent some time working with computer consultants or computer science students recruited directly from university were quick to adapt to the type of work. There were two groups who clearly did not fit the psychological role demanded by the organisation, hardware and software "boffins" and the large class of COBOL, PL/1, BAL, etc. programmers who had developed within the conventional analyst/programmer environment.

In almost all cases a large amount of training had to be given, particularly in the fields of the role of the systems designer in a commercial organisation and in the nature of transaction processing and database design. In all planning it was assumed that training would take up the first six months of the time of any new member of staff. A feature of motivation is continuous career development. To this end a large and comprehensive library was provided and staff were encouraged to read and to discuss the relevance of what they had read to the aims and conduct of the project. It was important that staff should not be allowed to drift into the domain of ignorance discovered by Parkin (1975). In addition, to emphasize their involvement in their own career progress they were encouraged to publish any results which they derived which were not affected by considerations of medical confidentiality. This policy was deliberate and in direct contradiction to that employed in conventional DP installations (Fisher, 1974). A full knowledge of what had gone before and an insight into the theoretical background of what they were doing was considered essential if systems designers were to plan their work according to known and successful concept

6. THE ROLE OF THE CHIEF PROGRAMMER

In the structure defined above there appears to be no one who has the direct responsibility for defining programming standards, defining programming timetables, and monitoring that both the standards and the timetables were being kept. In the conventional installation this would be the role of the chief programmer.

Where the development of an IICS has included a large software exercise the role of the chief programmer has become that of a chief software designer, with responsibility for application program standards and timetables passing to the senior programmers in the application teams. At Addenbrooke's there was no major software exercise and hence no need for a chief software designer. In practice the planning of timescales and the monitoring of progress and standards was taken up naturally by the senior designers in each team. The outstanding task was the establishment of standards. Many of these were defined through the manufacturer supplied software and needed only to be communicated. The project standards documentation system referred to earlier was adequate to cope with this. The remainder were concerned with problems which arose within teams but applied across teams. Here a definitive solution was required. This problem alone did not justify the appointment of a chief programmer and was solved by further sub-team meetings, this time between the senior programmers and senior software and database designers and the chief systems designer, taking place monthly.

An obvious conclusion is that in a team developing an IICS there is no role for a chief programmer. Not only is this the case but the creation of such a post is likely to create problems because of the significant overlap of duties between the chief programmer and the chief systems designer. It has been noted that in those organisations developing IICS's, where a chief programmer has been appointed and his changed role has not been clearly defined, then this has led to a noticeable strain.

7. THE CHIEF PROGRAMMER TEAM CONCEPT

One obvious problem of the application orientated structure was that individual computer staffs did not work at the same rate, nor did each group of applications involve the same amount of work. Although applications could not be implemented at the same time the rate of individual progress was not known before work began on an application and the affect of unforseen problems on different applications could not be predicted. This problem of differing rates of progress had led, in a different context, to the formation of the Chief Programmer Team concept (Baker,1972). It is interesting to note how a similar concept developed at the Addenbrooke's project. Addenbrooke's had an additional problem. Staffing levels were fixed and loss of production caused by staff leaving could be made up only by employing programmers on a fixed term basis.

If one application slipped badly it was likely that another, later in the implementation schedule, would be ahead. The designer who was ahead could move over to assist the designer attempting to catch up and could most readily assist by taking over the testing and training function. The freelance programmer also could be assigned to assist with the application and was usually found to be most useful in the area of programming incidental background jobs, for example the printing of back-up versions of directories overnight. The administrator already was responsible for the general aspects of documentation and hospital interfacing. Hence a team consisting of chief programmer, back-up programmer, librarian, and secretary had been formed by accident.

From this result it seems likely that the optimum organisation for the development of a large IICS is a set of chief programmer teams each allocated to an application. Support for such a conclusion was given by the team implementing the LACES project.

8. THE PROGRAMMER-OPERATOR RELATIONSHIP

In batch processing installations the relationship between operators and programmers usually is one of segregation. The computer room is the shrine of the operators into which the programmer must not stray. An operator may not comment on a program, he may only run it on demand, according to the instructions supplied, and return the output promptly.

In on-line installations such an arrangement is not practicable. Whilst systems are under test, or when a software fault arises during live running, programmers must have access to the computer. If a fault occurs then operators must be involved. They are first in the firing line for the wrath of the users and they are the first level for attempting to effect a recovery. A further problem is that when the on-line service is live, and invariably taking over the whole of the computer, there is little for the operators to do.

One solution is to have two computers. At Addenbrooke's this solution is not possible due to insufficient total load on the computer. Hence there is a need for an alternative. The on-line network is live from 0800 to 1800 and during this time no system testing other than the final parallel run can proceed. In the evening there is a competing demand for resources from the operators running the background batch work and the programmers wishing to do systems testing.

At the time of writing the problem has been identified but no firm solution reached. Clearly, however, any solution must involve some form of overlap between the duties of operators and programmers. It will be interesting to see the affect of any solution on the team structure defined above. Previously operations had employed a hierarchical management structure, reporting to the project director and independent of that designed for the applications teams.

9. CONCLUSIONS

When the Addenbrooke's IICS project was established a positive attempt was made to create a team structure through which the problems of communication would be removed and motivation increased, leading to higher productivity.

A measure of the success of communication is the extent to which the system created meets the real needs of the user and does not prove ineffective due to poor systems design. Against this measure it is possible to claim a fair degree of success. The principal users are enthusiastic, there have been no complaints of misinterpretation and only one case has come to light where the techniques for man-machine interfacing have fallen short.

Measures of the degree of productivity achieved are the speed at which "fully tested" systems are produced and the number of errors found in the final product. The actual rate of production achieved for the first group of applications was 35,000 lines of code (mixed COBOL, FORTRAN, and machine code) from eight man years of effort, including all systems analysis and design. It was not possible, however, to relate this to any other achievement for two reasons. Firstly the project was subjected to many delays from outside over which it had no control. Secondly, the use of high level languages, the use of structured programming techniques, and the availability of on-line program development facilities all contributed to improving productivity. The part played by any one of these factors could not be identified. To date sixty three errors have been found in the initial applications. None of these has been sufficiently serious to require the on-line system to be withdrawn while repair was effected, even for seconds. Measured against these criteria of productivity it is believed that the performance of the team rates quite high.

One major defect of the application orientated structure is clear. It is very vulnerable to staff leaving and it makes it difficult for staff to move between applications. It encourages staff to become inward looking and to be resistant to criticism from others. On the other hand the structure does generate motivation and job satisfaction. The average length of stay within the project is over three and a half years, which again compares favourably with similar installations.

10. REFERENCES

BAKER, F.T. (1972). Chief programmer team management of production programming. IBM Systems Journal, Vol. 11, No. 1, pp. 56-73.

COATES, H.N. (1974). Management in the computer business. The Computer Journal, Vol. 17, No. 3, pp. 279-282.

EASON, K.D. (1976). Understanding the naive computer user. The Computer Journal, Vol. 19, No. 1, pp. 3-7.

FISHER, G.A. (1974). Letter to the editor. The Computer Journal, Vol. 17, No. 1, p.95.

HAMMERSELY, P. (1972). Principles of control in patient administration. Proceedings of the Toulouse Conference 'Journees d'Informatique Medicale', IRIA, Vol. 1, pp 319-335.

HARDCASTLE, A.R.K. (1971). Management implications of DP systems. The Computer Bulletin, Vol. 15, No. 2, pp. 60-62.

MARTIN, J. (1967). Design of real-time computer systems, Prentice-Hall.

MARTIN, J. (1973). Design of man-computer dialogues, Prentice-Hall.

MUMFORD, E. (1972). Job satisfaction, Longman.

PALMER, I. (1973). Database management, SCICON.

PARKIN, A. (1975). Professional programmers - do they read? Computer Bulletin, Series 2, No. 4, p. 13.

A CASE STUDY OF STRUCTURED PROGRAMMING WITH CORRECTNESS PROOFS

J.D. Ichbiah, J.C. Heliard

Compagnie Internationale pour l'Informatique, Louveciennes, FRANCE

1. INTRODUCTION : STATIC PROGRAMMING

One of the starting points of Structured Programming is the recognition of the fact that our mind is "rather geared to master static relations" than dynamic, time evolving relations {1, 2}.

A well-structured program is thus a program which is understandable in a static fashion. It must be possible to qualify each point of such a program by a set of properties, called invariants, which are satisfied whenever this point is reached, and for arbitrary executions of the program.

The main justification for the simplicity of the control structures used in structured programming (sequences of statements, if and case statements, simple loops, subprograms) is precisely that they simplify the deduction of the properties satisfied at a given program point from those satisfied at preceding points.

Similarly, the systematic use of typed data contributes to the static character of structured programs. Thus the declaration

$$x : (green | orange | red) ;$$

introduces an invariant relation for all the life-time of the variable x, that is, the value of x is either "green" or "orange" or "red", all other values being excluded.

This same character of static programming is also found in program verification theory {3, 4, 8}. In order to explicit this static character let us review the principles of these verifications.

To verify a program Q with respect to a precondition P and a resulting condition R is to prove that if P holds before execution of Q then the condition R will hold after execution of Q. We write this P{Q}R in Hoare's notation.

The verification of a program which is a sequence of statements {Q1 ; Q2} may be sub-divided into a sequence of verifications. Thus, in order to prove P{Q1 ; Q2}R it suffices to prove that P{Q1}R1 and R1{Q2}R. In other words, it must be shown that the condition satisfied after execution of Q1 is the precondition for the execution of Q2 to produce R.

This work has been supported by Iria-Sesori.

Similarly, the verification of a conditional statement may be broken down into elementary verifications. Thus in order to show that P{IF B THEN Q1 ; ELSE Q2 ; END}R we must show that P AND B {Q1} R and also that P AND NOT B {Q2} R.

The verification of a loop P {UNTIL B LOOP Q ; REPEAT} R necessitates the identification of a condition I which is implied by P and which is such that I AND B implies R. Furthermore, I must satisfy I AND NOT B {Q} I. In other words, I must be invariant through the execution of the loop.

To summarize, the verification of a program reduces to that of a set of elementary conditions which do not depend on specific executions of the program. As in structured programming, all dynamic aspects have been abstracted from the verification.

Nevertheless a major difficulty remains which is the determination of loop invariants. In general, this requires a deep understanding of the programs considered. Consequently, a posteriori certification appears impractical for programs written initially without any intent of proof. Even if it demonstrates the feasibility of this approach for programs of up to a few hundred lines, the work done by London and his followers {6} does not enable one to conclude that the approach can be generalized economically.

Hoare {5}, was the first to propose the integration of verifications in the construction process of structured programs. The previous discussion, which has brought out the common static character of both structured programming and program verifications, shows that this is a very natural idea. Indeed it has been followed by several authors {7, 9, 10, 11}.

We have experimented with this approach during the construction of a program of more than 2000 lines, written in LIS {12} and treating a non-trivial problem.

As an example, the proof performed for one of the sub-programs of this program is given in detail in the second part of this paper. It should be noted that this is the proof of a sub-program dealing with structured data and pointers.

Finally we conclude by a global appraisal of this experiment of structured programming with informal program proofs.

2. EXAMPLE : SORTING A LINEAR LIST

The example described hereafter involves linear lists of qualified elements. The problem is to write a program which reorders the elements of a list in such a way that elements having the same qualification appear consecutively in the final list. As an additional requirement, the order in which elements of a same qualification appear may not be modified.

On the average, the lists considered are rather short (say ten elements) but much longer lists will also occur. Qualifications are analogous to names ; there is an infinite number of possible qualifications. In most cases there will be very few element having the same qualification, if any.

Clearly, a classical sorting algorithm could be used for the problem considered. However, the short length of the lists does not justify the use of sophisticated algorithms. In addition, the need to decode and encode the list information in a form acceptable for a given sorting routine would offsett the advantage of having an already written algorithm. Hence a sorting algorithm working directly on the list structure will be developed. The emphasis will be on correctness, not on time considerations.

The precondition P is expressed in the form "F-L is a list". It means that :

	(a) F designates the first element
	(b) L designates the last element
P :	(c) For each element X,
"F-L	X.QUAL designates the qualification of X
is a	X.SUC designates the successor of X
list"	(d) L.SUC = NIL
	(e) The elements of the list are
	F, F.SUC, F.SUC.SUC, ..., L

Note that the "successor" relation (direct or indirect) is an order relation on the elements of the linear list. By convention we will write A <= B to indicate that B designates either a successor of A or the same element as A.

With this notation, the condition R to be satisfied at the end of the program is :

	(1) F-L is a list
	(2) If A and B satisfy F <= A <= B <= L and
	if A.QUAL = B.QUAL then
R	(a) A <= B was also true initially
	(b) For each element X such that A <= X <= B,
	we have A.QUAL = X.QUAL = B.QUAL

The precondition P and the resulting condition R form the specification of our program at level zero. Proceeding top-down, we will successively introduce program specifications at lower levels.

The proof issued at a given level may require that a condition be satisfied by a lower level. Such conditions will be indicated by a vertical bar in the left margin.

LEVEL 1

The principle of an iterative solution may be derived from the statement of R. To that end we introduce an intermediate element G subject to a condition (the G invariant) similar to R :

I(G)

> If A and B satisfy F <= A <= B <= G and
> if A.QUAL = B.QUAL then
> (a) A <= B was also true initially
> (b) for each element X such that A <= X <= B,
>   we have A.QUAL = X.QUAL = B.QUAL

Hence the first statement of the algorithm will be :

ALGORITHM A1

```
        G := F ;
        UNTIL G = L LOOP
            "advance G while maintaining I(G)" ;
        REPEAT ;
```

PROOF 1

The condition I(G) is satisfied after the assignment "G := F". In addition, I(G) implies R at the end of the loop since G = L.

The program is hence correct provided that the loop terminates.

Note This formulation takes care of the cases

F = L = NIL   (no element)

F = L ≠ NIL   (a unique element)

LEVEL 2   "Advance G while maintaining I(G)"

In order to advance G we are looking for elements having the same qualification as G among its successors. If the immediate successor of G is a synonym, G is made to de-signate this successor, otherwise it is convenient to define FA, the first antonym of G :

I(FA)	(a) FA is the successor of G (FA = G.SUC)
	(b) FA is an antonym of G (FA.QUAL $\neq$ G.QUAL)

Once FA is located, me may remove the synonyms of G which are successors of FA and start another iteration with the successor of G (i.e. FA).

ALGORITHM A2

```
        IF G.QUAL ≠ G.SUC.QUAL THEN
            FA := G.SUC ;
            "Remove synonyms of G which are successors of FA" ;
        END ;
        G := G.SUC ;
```

PROOF 2

. Within the loop G $\neq$ L implies G.SUC $\neq$ NIL. Hence G.SUC.QUAL has a meaning.

. If G.QUAL = G.SUC.QUAL, the invariant I(G) remains satisfied after the assignment G := G.SUC

If G.QUAL $\neq$ G.SUC.QUAL then for A2 to satisfy I(G) after the assignment G := G.SUC it suffices that the execution of "Remove ... FA" leave no synonym of G beyond FA and maintain I(G) and I(FA).

. The loop A1 terminates because of the assignment G := G.SUC (assuming also that ele-ments of the sublist F-G are never added to the sublist G-L).

LEVEL 3 "Remove synonyms of G which are successors of FA"

We are looking for the synonyms of G which are between FA and L. To that end we introduce a cursor C defined as follows :

	(a) C is an antonym of G (C.QUAL $\neq$ G.QUAL)
I(C)	
	(b) Every element X such that FA <= X <= C is an antonym of G (X.QUAL $\neq$ G.QUAL)

ALGORITHM A3

        C := FA ;

        UNTIL C = L LOOP

            "Treat the successor of C" ;

            REPEAT ;

PROOF 3

The invariant I(C) is satisfied after the initialization C := FA.

At the end of the loop C = L implies that all synonyms of G have been removed from FA-L provided that "Treat the successor of C" maintain I(C) and also I(G) and I(FA). In addition, termination of the loop A3 must be demonstrated.

LEVEL 4   "Treat the successor of C"

If the successor of C is not a synonym of G we simply let C progress down the linear list and designate this successor. Otherwise let us denote the successor of G by SG (Synonym of G).

We now have to extract the element designated by SG from the sublist C-L and to insert it between G and FA. Then SG may be taken as the new G.

ALGORITHM A4

```
        IF G.QUAL ≠ C.SUC.QUAL THEN
            C := C.SUC ;
        ELSE
            SG := C.SUC ;
            "Insert SG between G and FA" ;
            G := SG ;
        END ;
```

PROOF 4

. C ≠ L within the loop A3 implies C.SUC ≠ NIL. Hence C.SUC.QUAL has a meaning.

. If G.QUAL ≠ C.SUC.QUAL, the assignment C := C.SUC maintains I(C). Otherwise the insertion of an element between G and FA also maintains I(C).

. I(FA) remains satisfied after the assignment G := SG since SG.QUAL = G.QUAL and since SG.SUC = FA will be true after execution of "Insert SG between G and FA".

. Let A designate an element such that A <= G and such that for each X satisfying A <= X <= SG we have A.QUAL = X.QUAL = G.QUAL. Since SG.QUAL = G.QUAL the condition (b) of I(G) is still satisfied after the assignment G := SG. In addition we have G<SG before as well as after the assignment. Hence the invariant I(G) is maintained

. For each iteration of A3 either C progresses by one element or an element is removed from the sublist C-L. Hence the loop A3 terminates.

. This proof assumes that "Insert SG between G and FA" does not violate the nature of the list F-L and maintains I(C).

LEVEL 5   "Insert SG between G and FA"

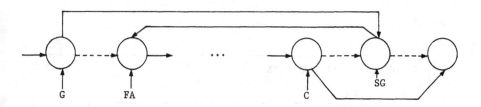

The above diagram illustrates the transformation. Note that it is the first operation encountered so far which modifies the order of elements of the list F-L. Hence
we must check that after the insertion, F-L is still a list satisfying the conditions
P. In particular L must still designate the last element. Precautions are hence required in the case SG = L.

ALGORITHM A5

```
        IF SG = L THEN
            L := C ;
        END ;
        C.SUC  := SG.SUC ;
        SG.SUC := FA ;
        G.SUC  := SG ;
```


PROOF 5

. If SG = L then the assignments L := C and C.SUC := SG.SUC imply that L.SUC = NIL

. A5 only modifies the successor fields of the elements C, SG, G and each of these
  elements is provided with a new successor. Hence each element has a successor in the
  resulting list F-G, SG, FA-C-L. It is clear also that no loop has been created.

. I(C) is maintained since the sublist FA-C is not modified and since C and G still
  designate the same elements as before.

FINAL ALGORITHM

```
(1)      G := F ;

(2)      UNTIL G = L LOOP

(3)          IF G.QUAL ≠ G.SUC.QUAL THEN

(4)              FA := G.SUC ;

(5)              C  := FA ;

(6)              UNTIL  C = L LOOP

(7)                  IF G.QUAL ≠ C.SUC.QUAL THEN

(8)                      C := C.SUC ;

(9)                  ELSE

(10)                     SG := C.SUC ;

(11)                     IF SG = L THEN

(12)                         L := C ;

(13)                     END ;

(14)                     C.SUC   := SG.SUC ;

(15)                     SG.SUC := FA ;

(16)                     G.SUC   := SG ;

(17)                     G := SG ;

(18)                 END ;

(19)             REPEAT ;

(20)         END ;

(21)         G := G.SUC ;

(22)     REPEAT ;
```

Insert SG between G and FA

Treat the successor of C

Remove synonyms of G which are successors of FA

Advance G while maintaining I(G)

3. CONCLUSIONS ON THE USE OF THIS METHODOLOGY IN AN EXPERIMENT

The example described above is part of a program of more than 2000 lines which deals with rather complex data structures. This program computes the displacements of the attributes of plex declarations in the LIS language. Given the descriptive facilities offered in LIS, this is a combinatorial problem analogous to a "knap-sack" problem and complicated by alignment requirements. The approach used is of heuristic nature. It delivers a "good" solution without any claim to optimality.

The program itself is not a "toy" program working in isolation. Much to the contrary it is integrated in a 25000 lines compiler. Its main interface with the latter is the dictionary of symbols, hence a complex data structure containing pointers. To summarize, this experiment dealt with a real program developed in a usual industrial context.

It is worth mentioning that when the work started we had no well defined idea of the algorithm to be used. The formulation of the solution and the program writing were both developed in parallel in a top-down structured approach. This means that several alternatives were initiated and then later rejected. As lower level refinements were produced, our intuition became more precise and we often knew enough to reject solutions which had appeared desirable at higher levels. The final 2000 lines are in fact what remains of more that the double of this number of lines written through several attempts.

In spite of the structured approach and of the use of informal proofs about twenty errors were found during program testing. The most frequent error could indeed have been avoided by a more careful approach. It was the omission of incrementations of cursors in loops. We had so much concentrated our attention on maintaining loop invariants that we had neglected to prove loop termination.

Two more serious errors were found corresponding to algorithm misconceptions. They required the rewriting of a hundred lines.

On the whole however, the error rate found in this programs is much smaller than for other parts of the compiler which we had judged to be simpler and for which this meticulous approach had not been used as systematically.

The whole work, designing, writing and testing, represented an effort of four manmonths. In terms of productivity we must then conclude to the success of this practical experiment of structured programming with informal program proofs, expecially if we consider the complexity of the problem solved.

Although the construction of program proofs seems to proceed very slowly during the procedure by procedure writing of the program, it appears that the reduction in testing time is big enough to justify the approach on the whole.

REFERENCES

1.   Dijkstra, E.W., "Goto statement considered harmful",
    CACM, Vol. II (March 1968) pp 147-148.

2.   Dijkstra, E.W., "Notes on structure programming",
    in Structured Programming, pp 1-82, Academic Press, London (1972).

3.   Floyd, R.W., "Assigning meanings to programs",
    Proc. Am Math. Soc. Symp in Applied Math. 19 (1967) pp 19-31.

4.   Hoare, C.A.R., "An axiomatic basis for computer programming",
    CACM, Vol. 12 (October 1969) pp 576-583.

5.   Hoare, C.A.R., "Proof of a program : FIND",
    CACM, Vol. 14 (January 1971) pp 39-45.

6.   Good, D.I., London, R.L., "Computer Interval Arithmetic : definition and
    proof of correct implementation",
    JACM, Vol. 17,4 (October 1970) pp 603-612.

7.   Wirth, N., "Systematic Programming : An Introduction",
    Prentice Hall, Englewood Cliffs, N.J., (1973).

8.   Manna, Z., "Mathematical Theory of Computation",
    Mc Graw Hill, (1974).

9.   Robinson, L., Levitt, K.N., "Proof techniques for hierarchically structured
    programs",
    Stanford Research Institute, SRI technical report, (January 1975).

10.   Infante, R., Montanari, U., "Proving Structured programs correct, level by
    level",
    Proc. Int. Conf. on Reliable Software, (April 1975) pp 427-436.

11.   Mills, H.D., "How to write correct programs and know it",
    Proc. Int. Conf. on Reliable Software, (April 1975) pp 363-370.

12.   Ichbiah, J.D., Rissen, J.P., Heliard, J.C., Cousot, P., "The system imple-
    mentation language LIS",
    CII technical report 4549 E/EN (December 1974).

PROGRAM OPTIMIZATION USING INVARIANTS

by

Shmuel Katz

IBM Israel Scientific Center
Technion City, Haifa, Israel

ABSTRACT

Optimizing a computer program is defined as improving the execution time without disturbing the correctness. We show how to use invariants generated from the program to change the statements in and around the program's loops. This approach is shown to systematize existing optimization methods, and to sometimes allow stronger optimizations than are possible under the standard transformation approach.

1. INTRODUCTION

For many years compilers have contained sections which are supposed to "optimize" the code produced from computer programs. As has been often noted, this term is a misnomer because a really "optimal" solution to the "optimization" problem would involve throwing away the original program and producing in its place the best possible program to perform the desired task.

In view of the present state of program synthesis, we adopt a more standard (and considerably less ambitious) definition as the goal of optimization. Optimization is intended to improve the execution time of a given program by changing or moving some of the statements, without disturbing the correctness of the program. The control structure of the original program usually will be left intact, and the same crucial relationships will be maintained among the variables, but the computations and tests will be altered in order to reduce the time required for computation.

A wide variety of techniques are presently grouped under the term optimization. Among these are various machine-dependent operations (including register allocation) which use special characteristics of a given computer and are best applied to machine code. We concentrate on the other large class of techniques, namely, various program transformations which are independent of the machine code, and are typically applied to an intermediate-level program (similar in complexity to a flowchart language), before actual machine code is generated.

In this paper, a method is presented for performing optimizations of the above type with the aid of a proof of correctness of the program. That is, in addition to the program, the user has provided (i) an input specification, defining the acceptable input values which the program is intended to treat, and (ii) an output specification defining the desired relationship between the input and the output. Then, automatically or by hand, intermediate 'invariant assertions' have been attached to prechosen points in the program. These assertions allow proving the correctness of the program w.r.t. its specification. Note that by 'correctness' we mean that for every legal input the program will terminate, and the output will satisfy the output specification (this is often called total correctness).

An invariant assertion (or invariant* for short) at a point A is any claim about the variables which is always true when the control of the program reaches point A. The following section contains the definitions needed to give a precise criterion for proving an assertion to be an invariant.

A situation in which we would like to perform optimization of a program and also have available the program specification and a proof of correctness, including the invariants used in that proof, could arise from at least two sources:

(i) The program may have been developed in a top-down manner by stepwise refinement using structured programming techniques (see, e.g., Wirth [1973]). We assume a stage at which a complete but unoptimized program has been obtained, and that at each stage the correctness has been proven by demonstrating the needed invariants. In this case the invariants are available, even though they may not be organized in the manner described in this paper. Moreover, the final optimization stage can be done at least semi-automatically, even though earlier stages of the refinement do not seem to be as amenable to automatization.

(ii) The program (either developed by stepwise refinements, or in any more haphazard manner) may have undergone logical analysis, preferably automatically, so that the invariants have been extracted from the program independently of the output specification. Elements of such a system exist, and several such systems are proposed or under construction (e.g., Cheatham & Wegbreit [1972], Katz & Manna [1976]). If the program is incorrect, a logical analysis system would be used to prove this, and to help diagnose and correct the errors. If it is correct, partial correctness and termination would be proven for the given specification, also using the invariants. Once the program has been proven, a logical analysis system would pass to an optimizer, with the invariants already organized as indicated in the following section.

In either of the above cases, the time-consuming and difficult task of finding the proper invariants and the proof would be done primarily for other reasons, and not merely for optimization. Thus, it is worthwhile to take advantage of the added information which is available "free of charge", as an aid in optimization. In Section some definitions and facts about invariants are presented, and their organization for the purpose of optimization is described. Section 3 examines some specific optimizations

---

* Note that we use the word 'invariant' in the sense common to program verification and not as sometimes used in articles on optimization, where an 'invariant expression' means an expression containing only variables unchanged in the loop.

which are facilitated by using invariants. In the conclusion (Section 4), the techniques described below are compared with the usual optimizations found in compilers, and with related work on transformations which preserve correctness.

2. INVARIANTS AND THEIR ORGANIZATION FOR OPTIMIZATION

First some definitions and facts related to invariants are briefly summarized. The presentation follows Katz [1976].

For convenience of explanation, blocked programs are assumed (although this is not really necessary to the ideas). That is, the programs treated are divisible into (possibly nested) "blocks" in such a way that every block has at most one top-level loop (in addition to possible lower-level loops which are already contained in inner blocks). The blocks considered have one entrance and may have many exits. Algorithms for identifying such blocks can be found in Allen [1971]. Every "structured program" e.g., program without goto statements (see Wirth [1973]) can be decomposed into such blocks.

The block structure allows treating the program first by considering inner blocks (ignoring momentarily that they are included in outer blocks), and working outwards. Thus for each block its top-level loop can be analyzed using information obtained from the inner blocks.

The top-level loop of a block can contain several branches, but all paths around the loop must have at least one common point. For each loop, one such point is chosen as the cutpoint of the loop.

Counters attached to each block containing a loop are an essential tool in our techniques. Since each loop has a unique cutpoint, a counter is associated with the cutpoint of the loop. The counter is initialized before entering the block so that its value is zero upon first reaching the cutpoint, and is incremented by one exactly once somewhere along the loop before returning to the cutpoint. In the continuation, a local initialization of each counter is assumed, immediately before the entrance to its block. Experience has shown that this is generally the most convenient choice.

The counters play a crucial role both for generating invariants and for proving termination. They are used to denote relations among the number of times various paths have been executed, and also to help express the values assumed by the program variables. Thus $y_i(n)$ denotes the value of y_i the $(n+1)$-th time the cutpoint is reached since the most recent entrance to the block. It should be noted that it is unnecessary to add the counters physically to the body of the program. Their location can merely be indicated, since their behavior is already fixed.

It is also sometimes convenient to add auxiliary cutpoints at the entrance and exit of a block. In addition, a special cutpoint is added on each arc immediately preceding a HALT statement. Such cutpoints will be called halt-points of the program.

In the following definitions, $\bar{x}$ denotes the input values, and $\bar{y}$ the values of the program variables at the cutpoint being considered.

A predicate $q_i(\bar{x},\bar{y})$ is said to be an <u>invariant assertion</u> (or invariant for short) at cutpoint i w.r.t. $\phi(\bar{x})$ if for every input $\bar{a}$ such that $\phi(\bar{a})$ is true, whenever we reach point i with $\bar{y}=\bar{b}$, then $q_i(\bar{a},\bar{b})$ is true. An invariant at i is thus some assertion about the variables which is true for the current values of the variables each time i is reached during execution.

For a path λ from cutpoint i to cutpoint j, we define $R_\lambda(\bar{x},\bar{y})$ as the condition for the path λ to be traversed, and $r_\lambda(\bar{x},\bar{y})$ as the transformation in the $\bar{y}$ values which occurs on path λ. A set S of cutpoints of a program P is said to be <u>complete</u> if for each cutpoint i in S all the cutpoints on any path from START to i are also in S.

We now state a sufficient condition (proven in Manna [1969]) for showing that assertions at a complete set of cutpoints are actually invariants.

<u>Lemma A.</u> <u>Let</u> S <u>be a complete set of cutpoints of a program</u> P. <u>Assertions</u> $\{q_i(\bar{x},\bar{y}) \mid i \in S\}$ <u>will be a set of invariants for</u> P <u>w.r.t.</u> ϕ <u>if</u>

(a) <u>For every path</u> λ <u>from the START statement to a cutpoint</u> j <u>(which does not contain any other cutpoint)</u>

$$\forall x [\phi(\bar{x}) \wedge R_\lambda(\bar{x}) \supset q_j(\bar{x}, r_\lambda(\bar{x}))],$$

and (b) <u>For every path</u> λ <u>from a cutpoint</u> i <u>to a cutpoint</u> j <u>(which does not contain any other cutpoint)</u>

$$\forall \bar{x} \forall \bar{y} [q_i(\bar{x},\bar{y}) \wedge R_\lambda(\bar{x},\bar{y}) \supset q_j(\bar{x}, r_\lambda(\bar{x},\bar{y}))].$$

As noted in the Introduction, invariants can either be provided by the user, or be generated directly from the program. Among the main methods for this generation are the solution of difference equations which express the change in the variables for one pass around inner loops. These can be obtained from the path functions $r_\lambda(\bar{x},\bar{y})$. Another technique is to examine what was established by the tests made as the paths are followed. This is in the path condition $R_\lambda(\bar{x},\bar{y})$. By their construction, the results of these techniques must be invariants, and they are therefore termed 'algorithmic' methods.

Another approach seeks to "guess" invariants by using heuristics to identify like or desireable candidates. These could be based on the desired specification, on existing invariants, or on various indications in the program. Any candidates so generated must be checked using the above Lemma.

The final result of the above processes should be conjunctions of invariants at each cutpoint (and including the output specifications at the HALT-points) which satisfy the Lemma. The detailed justification of the use of these invariants to prove partial correctness, termination, or incorrectness is beyond the scope of this paper. A deeper look into the invariant-generating techniques, and proving properties of programs with invariants, can be found in, e.g., Elspas [1974], Katz & Manna [1973, 1976], Wegbreit [1974].

In order to effectively use the invariants and the proof of a program for optimization, we need to record the source of each invariant, i.e., precisely how (and which) program statements and/or other invariants were used in its derivation and/or proof.

This can be done in a table which notes for each invariant (on the one hand) the other invariants and the statements on the path(s) from previous cutpoints which are used in its derivation or proof, as well as recording the specific technique used. On the other hand, the uses of that invariant for proving other invariants must also be noted. The invariants can either be organized in separate tables for each cutpoint, or one large table where each invariant is also associated with the cutpoint at which it is true. By convention, the order of the statements on the path is indicated by their order from left to right in the table.

For simple programs with only one or two loops, the table may be represented pictorially as a directed acyclic graph having the immediate sources as the fathers of each invariant. At the bottom of the graph is the specification, proven from the invariants. Since we talk about the 'ancestors' and 'sons', using terminology similar to trees, we call this graphic representation an invariant tree.

In the continuation, for clarity we refer to various operations on this tree, but it should be clear that the tabular representation is the one which actually would be used in an implementation. Once the program has been proven correct and the tree has been generated, the invariants used in the correctness proof are marked. The basic optimization procedure will then be to 'cut' the tree at invariants which we will decide are essential, and try to compute these invariants - or other invariants with an equivalent effect - in a more efficient way. Then any ancestor statement not used in either the new derivation, or in the derivation of another invariant, can be removed from both the tree and the program. The precise methods used to obtain the invariant in a new way are described in the following section.

This cutting of the tree will in effect define a level of optimization. The nearer the cut is to the leaves of the tree (i.e., to the program statements) the more local the optimization, while the nearer the cut is to the roots of the tree (i.e., the vital invariants for proving the specification), the more global the optimization. It is usually best to directly find the invariants closest to the roots for which we can optimize.

Before describing the optimizations considered, a simple example is given to demonstrate the table, the tree representation, and the levels. For the moment, the full justification of the optimizations performed is not given.

Example 1. From the Fortran statements (obviously a segment of a program)

$$K = 0$$
$$D\emptyset \quad 3 \quad I \quad = \quad 1,1000$$
$$3 \quad K \quad = \quad L+1+I+K$$
$$PRINT \quad K$$

we might obtain the intermediate segment shown in Figure 1A. In Figure 1B, we show the invariant tree at A for this segment (in solid lines), generated by using only algorithmic techniques.

For this tree, no other cutpoints inside the loop except A are used. The dotted lines indicate the invariant tree at C after the loop. In Figure 1C, the table representation is given if two cutpoints were chosen inside the loop, one after the assignment to T, and one at A, before the test. In this case the tree would be harder to draw, but conceptually there is no change. The numbers to the left of the statements and invariants are identifiers which clearly would be replaced by pointers.

In the remainder of this example, the tree of Figure 1B is used. By 'cutting' this tree at various levels we obtain differing strengths of optimizations. Considering the line denoted in Figure 1B as Level 1, we would like to compute the invariant at A S=L+1+I, in a different way. This can be done trivially by inserting S ← L+1+I, just before A. All the statements above the invariant which are not used in other invariants may now be removed (in this example T ← L+1 and S ← T+I).

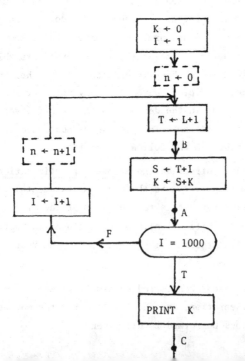

Figure 1A.

Simple intermediate program.

293

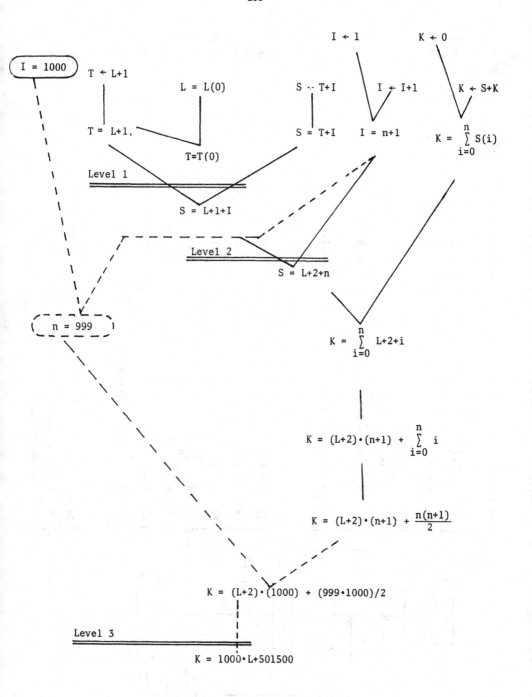

Figure 1B   The invariant tree at A and at C.

Figure 1C. The table for cutpoints A,B and C.

	Invariants	Sources	Initial y	Uses
10	$T = L+1$	4		17
11	$I = n+1$	19,8	2	19
12	$K = \sum_{i=1}^{n-1} S(i)$	20	1	20
13	$n = 0 \vee S = L+I$	21,8	3	
14	$n = 0 \vee S = L+1+n$	22,11	3	
17	$T = L+1$	10		21
18	$S = T+I$	5		21
19	$I = n+1$	11		22,24
20	$K = \sum_{i=0}^{n} S(i)$	12,6		23
21	$S = L+1+I$	17,18		22,13
22	$S = L+2+n$	19,21		23,14
23	$K = \sum_{i=1}^{n} L+2+i = (L+2)(n+1) + \frac{n(n+1)}{2}$	22,20		25
24	$n = 999$	7,19		
25	$K = (L+2)(1000) + 999 \cdot 1000/2$	23,24		25
26	$K = 1000 \cdot L+501500$	25		26

294

If level 2 is instead considered, we would like to compute S=L+n+2 differently. However, since this invariant implies that S is linear in the counter n, and L is unchanged in the loop, this could be achieved by initializing S to L+2 before entering the loop, and then increasing S by 1 at each iteration, just as n is increased. Most of the old statements above the invariant S=L+n+2 can then be removed. The resulting program is shown in Figure 1.D, and the new invariant tree in Figure 1E.

Finally, if we optimize at level 3, we see that K = 1000 · L + 501500 is obtained by the simple assignment statement K ← 1000 · L + 501500, and that the entire loop is then extraneous. This assignment could lead to overflow, and involves one multiplication. However, the overflow would occur anyway in the original loop if it would occur here, and one multiplication seems better than a few thousand additions and 1000 tests.

Note that in this example the various levels of optimization could either have been treated consecutively or independently, and that it is most worthwhile to start at level 3, since then the other levels need not be considered at all.

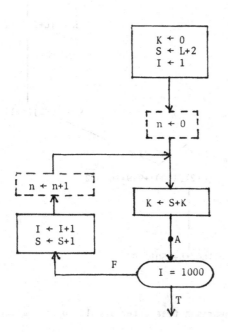

Figure 1D.   Program after Level 2 optimization

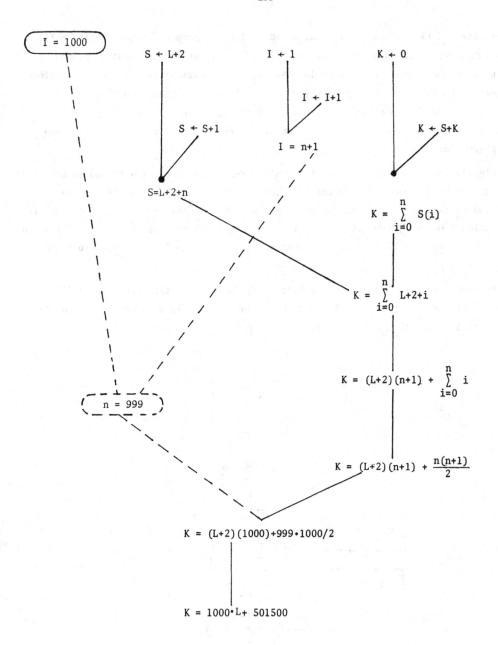

Figure 1E. Invariant tree after level 2 optimization

3. TYPICAL OPTIMIZATIONS USING INVARIANTS

Most of this section demonstrates that several well-known optimizations used in compilers can be easily applied using the information already in the invariants, rather then the various information-gathering algorithms generally employed. At the end of the section optimizations stronger than those possible in standard compilers are described. Note that the optimizations described are not language-dependent.

The basic tool for improving programs using the invariant tree will be eliminating redundant or 'dead' (unused) statements. Simply, any statement not an ancestor of any marked invariant in the invariant tree can immediately be removed from both the tree and the program, since it has no effect on the correctness of the program.

Of course, in a program written with any care at all, there should not be any such extraneous statements in the original tree. However, after a cut has been made, and new statements inserted as the ancestors of an invariant (using the following optimizations), the old immediate ancestors are no longer needed for that invariant, and the relevant links are removed from the tree. If the statements which were ancestors are thereby no longer needed for any invariant involved in the correctness proof, (i.e., are "dead"), they can be removed. Since statements will only be removed when they become "dead", we have a double-check on the legality of other optimizations (which may seem to preserve correctness, but in unusual situations might not). In the continuation this tool will be called the elimination criterion.

Note that a regular optimizer will often eliminate statements which have become syntactically dead (e.g., they cannot be reached in any way). Here statements can be removed which are logically redundant or because of logical relations will not be reached, even if syntactically they appear to be necessary.

The optimizations described below will all use an identical replacement procedure. They all discover potential optimizations to compute, say, a variable y in a new way based on an invariant p (involving y) which is true at the cutpoint of the loop in question.

Then the new generated statements are inserted in the tree as p's ancestors, and the old fathers are disconnnected from p. If the elimination criterion can then be used to remove the old ancestor statements, the particular optimization is complete. If not, some of the ancestor statements are still needed for another invariant, say q, involved in the correctness proof. In this case, we try to derive q in a new way, based on p and/or other invariants, perhaps adding new statements, so that the old ancestors of p are not used. If this cannot be done, we must insert a new variable name, say t, in place of v in the original ancestor statements of p, and also replace v by t in q (and the other remaining derived invariants). Generally, the old statements can be in themselves optimized.

Intuitively, the relatively rare cases where a new variable is added occur when a variable fulfills two or more roles in the loop (e.g., is similar to a counter at one point in the loop, but is a constant at another point in the loop). In fact, it is generally good programming practice to delegate the roles of a variable to different variables, which can then be optimized separately.

Now some optimizations which lend themselves to the procedure described are examined in more detail. The common compiler optimizations described below loosely follow Allen [1969].

(a) Constant propagation involves replacing a variable by its constant value, and performing at compile time operations with constants. This optimization arises naturally from the invariant tree, since such substitutions occur during the search for simpler invariants. Consider an expression in an invariant with a constant c which was derived by using an invariant v=c. The expression can usually be derived directly by substituting the constant c for the variable v in the other invariants or statements used to derive the expression. Then the modified invariants can be "pushed" back up the tree, until the relevant ancestor statements have been modified. The link from v=c is then removed, and the elimination criterion may be relevant. Similarly, algebraic simplification is employed to replace by its value an expression involving constants, and this too can be pushed back up to the relevant statement.

Example:

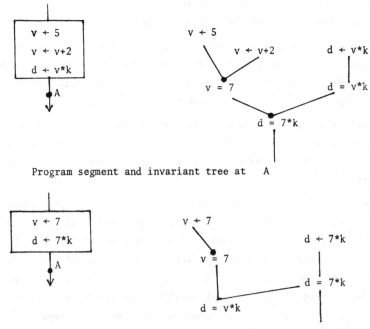

Program segment and invariant tree at A

Program segment and invariant tree at A after constant propagation.

If only d=7*k is used in the proof of correctness, d = v*k and v=7 are extraneous invariants, and they and their ancestor v←7 may be removed.

This type of optimization can also be used for an invariant of the form $v=$ if... then c_1 else c_2 arising from branching tests around the loop. No matter which statements are originally used to compute c_i, it can be obtained alternatively by inserting $v \leftarrow c_i$ on the segment of the loop which is reached if the condition for v to be equal to c_i is true, and by using the replacement procedure with the old ancestors.

(b) <u>Moving statements outside of loops</u> is probably one of the most beneficial optimizations. We call a variable v <u>constant w.r.t. the loop</u> if an invariant $v=v(0)$ is true at the cutpoint of the loop. Recall that $v(0)$ denotes the value of v the first time the <u>cutpoint</u> is reached (and <u>not</u> necessarily the value at the entrance to the loop). Thus $v = v(0)$ is an invariant if at the cutpoint, v is always equal to its value the first time the cutpoint is reached. The change in v along the paths from an entrance of the loop to the cutpoint can be computed as the path functions of that path. If this change is denoted as $entr(v)$, we can add $v \leftarrow entr(v)$ before that entrance to the loop (or add nothing if the value is not changed between the entrance and the cutpoint). The replacement procedure will then be followed. Note that if the old assignments to v cannot be removed, v must be renamed in them to avoid interference with the new way of computing the invariant $v=v(0)$.

Once such an invariant $v=v(0)$ has been found, other appearances of v in invariants can be inspected to discover <u>expressions</u> which are constant with respect to the loop. For such an expression a new variable t can be defined, equal to the expression, and since $t=t(0)$, its calculation can be removed from the loop.

<u>Example:</u> If we have the segment

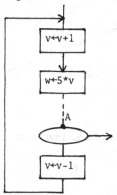

where v and w appear only as indicated and are used only at A, then $v=v(0)$ at A and, $entr(v)$ is $v+1$. Moreover, $w=5*v$ at A, i.e., $w=5*v(0)=w(0)$. Thus we may add $v \leftarrow v+1$ and $w \leftarrow 5*v$ before the loop and remove the original statements (again using the replacement procedure), obtaining

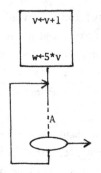

(c) <u>Reduction in strength</u> involves computing variables by using weaker operators in place of stronger one, e.g., addition in place of multiplication.

The conditions for applying this optimization are particularly easy to identify by using invariants. Any invariant which connects a variable linearly to the loop counter, e.g., $v = c_1 \cdot n + c_2$, can be computed by initializing to c_2 and then incrementing v by c_1, i.e., inserting $v \leftarrow v + c_1$ to the loop (of course, the previous statements used to compute v must be removed or changed using the replacement procedure). In Example such an optimization was performed. More generally, if we have a difference equation $v = c_o + \underline{if} \ \ldots .. \ \underline{then} \ \ c_1 \cdot n \ \underline{else} \ c_2 \cdot n$ then, as in constant propagation, we can initialize to c_o and increment v by c_i on the segment reached if the i-th condition ($i \geq 1$) is true.

Example :

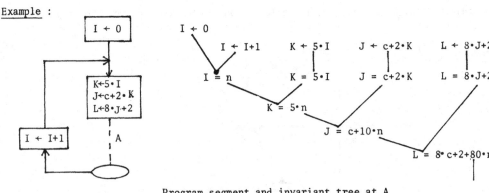

Program segment and invariant tree at A

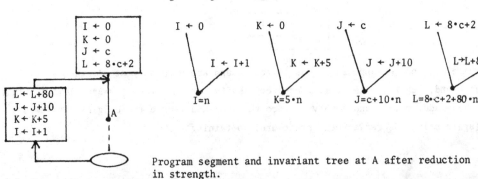

Program segment and invariant tree at A after reduction in strength.

Clearly, if, for example, only the invariant involving L were needed in the proof, the invariants and statements with I, K, and J would be removed.

Other reductions in strength, such as multiplication in place of raising to a power, are also easy to identify, and thus it does not cost much to check for even these more unusual cases (which are sometimes ignored in compilers). For example, an invariant $v = c_1 \cdot c_2^n$, for c_1, c_2 constants w.r.t. the loop, can be computed by initializing to $v \leftarrow c_1$ and inserting $v \leftarrow c_2 \cdot v$ in the loop, in place of any other computations of v.

(d) <u>Replacing test statements by equivalent tests</u> which use different variables is a common optimization. In this way, we can sometimes remove computations used only to allow making the original tests. In order to do this, we can inspect whether the invariants from the test, and the invariant which becomes true upon exit from the block, could be obtained by testing other variables. In particular, if an invariant involving a variable linear in the counter is used <u>only</u> to allow a test of the counter, there may be other variables also linear in the counter, which could be used instead.

<u>Example 1</u> (continued)

From the invariant tree of Figure 1E it is clear that the test I=1000 and the invariant I=n+1 mean that we are testing whether n=999. Since after doing Level 2 optimization, I=n+1 is used <u>only</u> in this test, we check whether another variable could be used instead, and see that S=L+2+n. Thus n=999 is equivalent to S-(L+2)=999, i.e. to S=L+1001. We may test S=L+1001, and remove the iteration of I, which is now unnecessary (see Figure 1F).

Since L=L(0), L+1001 can be identified as a constant expression, using optimization (b), and be replaced by t, with an invariant t=L+1001 at A and at C, having as its ancestor the assignment t←L+1001 before the loop.

(e) <u>Common subexpression elimination</u> involves introducing new temporary variables which are equal in value to subexpressions which appear in several statements (or several times in one statement). In our framework, common subexpressions in <u>invariants</u> are eliminated even if the statements used to derive the invariants including the common subexpression do not look similar. Using the invariants at the cutpoints also avoids the problem of a special algorithm to guarantee that statements which appear to have identical subexpressions, actually do not (because some of the variables involved were changed between the statements containing the subexpressions). The information from pattern matching which identifies common subexpressions would be available from the invariant-generating process, since during that process an attempt is made to combine algebraically invariants into new invariants by eliminating such expressions.

The temporary variable is computed before the point where the subexpression is first used, and replaces all uses of the subexpression. The computation of the temporary variable can then sometimes be further optimized using (a) - (d).

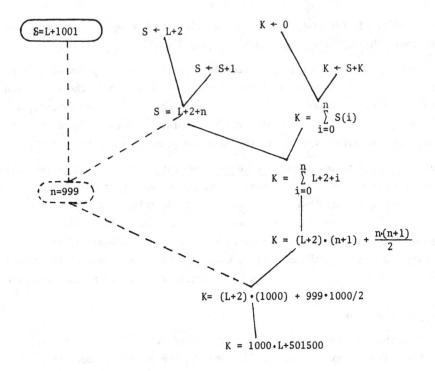

$S = L+1001$

$S \leftarrow L+2$

$K \leftarrow 0$

$S \leftarrow S+1$

$K \leftarrow S+K$

$S = L+2+n$

$K = \sum_{i=0}^{n} S(i)$

$n = 999$

$K = \sum_{i=0}^{n} L+2+i$

$K = (L+2) \cdot (n+1) + \frac{n \cdot (n+1)}{2}$

$K = (L+2) \cdot (1000) + 999 \cdot 1000/2$

$K = 1000 \cdot L + 501500$

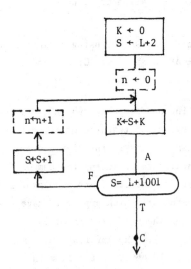

Figure 1F. The invariant tree and program after test replacement

Example:

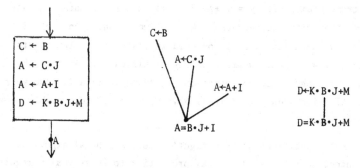

Program segment and invariant tree at A before
subexpression elimination

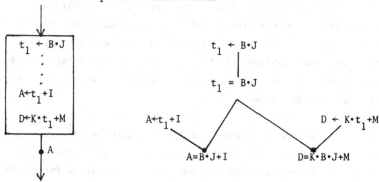

Program segment and invariant tree at A after
eliminating B·J

So far we have discussed how some well-known compiler optimization techniques can be applied by using invariants. However, it is sometimes possible to perform optimizations which are impossible unless the program specification and its proof are available. This occurs in three situations :

(1) The output specification is "loose" i.e. could be satisfied by many values. The original (correct) program will compute one of these values. However, it may be possible to compute another of these acceptable values more efficiently. The danger of such optimizations is, of course, that the programmer really wanted the value computed by the original program, but gave too vague a specification. Thus this class of optimizations should only be done under some sort of 'approval' from the user. Such situations can arise in numerical algorithms where the result need only be within some specified range (say, within ε of an actual root), or in a sorting algorithm, where the final order of equally valued elements is unimportant.

(2) An essential invariant q at some level is recognized as being too strong for the output specification. That is, a weaker (more general) invariant q' of the same form as the original q suffices to establish the needed invariants at a lower level. The weaker q' can then be substituted for q, and the ancestors modified accordingly.

As an extreme example if $y = (r+z)/2 \land r<z$ are invariants, but only $r \leq y < z$ is really needed to prove correctness, then any more convenient relation which fulfills the needed inequalities could be used in place of the invariants. One possible such invariant, $r = y \land r<z$, would probably significantly simplify the ancestor statements. Although these optimizations could theoretically involve radically changing the algorithm, only relatively obvious cases could probably be recognized automatically.

(3) The input specification is 'tight', i.e., a general algorithm is used with inputs guaranteed to fulfill additional properties to those really required by the algorithm. This is a common situation, and often allows optimizations. For example, a program for matrix manipulation might have special tests and treatment for empty matrices, or matrices of one element, while if the input specification guarantees that $m \geq 2$ and $n \geq 2$ for an $m \times n$ matrix, the special sections and the tests can be removed. In general, such optimizations will be done automatically using the elimination criterion, since the statements will be seen to be unnecessary to prove the essential invariants, and will be removed.

Example 2.   In this example a simple nested-loop program is considered. More than one cutpoint is usually required in order to prove correctness of programs with nested loops. In effect, at each cutpoint an entire table of invariants is built up, with interconnections among the entries in each table.

In this situation optimization should be done first on innermost blocks considered as separate entities. Only then should the resultant outer loops be treated. It is often convenient to add cutpoints at the entrances and exits of inner blocks, in order to 'isolate' the block from the remainder of the outer loop.

The program in Figure 2A is an intermediate version with the invariant table of the Pascal program

```
begin    for  i:=1 to n do
             begin  sum:=0;
                 for j:=1 to i do  sum:=sum+a[j] ;
                 b[i]:=sum
             end
     end
```

The input specification is $n \geq 1 \land n \in \{integers\}$ and a and b are vectors of integers. The program is intended to compute in b the 'partial sums' of a, i.e.

$$\forall i (1 \leq i \leq n \supset b[i] = \sum_{j=1}^{i} a[j])$$

The optimization demonstrated on this program illustrates the importance of which proof is used to show correctness. Moving from one proof to another is one of the more difficult tasks which we would like an optimizer based on invariants to attempt.

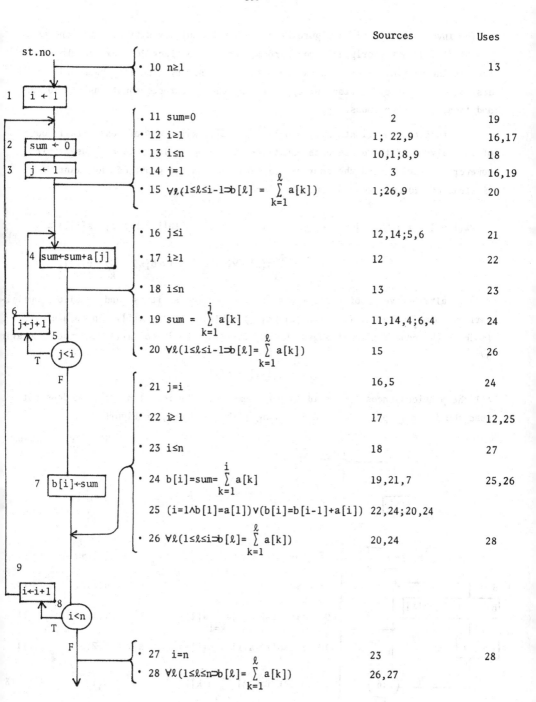

st.no.		Sources	Uses
	10 $n \geq 1$		13
1 — $i \leftarrow 1$			
	11 sum=0	2	19
	12 $i \geq 1$	1; 22,9	16,17
2 — sum $\leftarrow 0$	13 $i \leq n$	10,1;8,9	18
3 — $j \leftarrow 1$	14 $j=1$	3	16,19
	15 $\forall \ell (1 \leq \ell \leq i-1 \supset b[\ell] = \sum_{k=1}^{\ell} a[k])$	1;26,9	20
	16 $j \leq i$	12,14;5,6	21
4 — sum$\leftarrow$sum+a[j]	17 $i \geq 1$	12	22
	18 $i \leq n$	13	23
6 — $j \leftarrow j+1$	19 sum $= \sum_{k=1}^{j} a[k]$	11,14,4;6,4	24
5 — $j<i$	20 $\forall \ell (1 \leq \ell \leq i-1 \supset b[\ell] = \sum_{k=1}^{\ell} a[k])$	15	26
	21 $j=i$	16,5	24
	22 $i \geq 1$	17	12,25
	23 $i \leq n$	18	27
7 — b[i]$\leftarrow$sum	24 $b[i]=$sum$= \sum_{k=1}^{i} a[k]$	19,21,7	25,26
	25 $(i=1 \wedge b[1]=a[1]) \vee (b[i]=b[i-1]+a[i])$	22,24;20,24	
	26 $\forall \ell (1 \leq \ell \leq i \supset b[\ell] = \sum_{k=1}^{\ell} a[k])$	20,24	28
9 — $i \leftarrow i+1$			
8 — $i<n$	27 $i=n$	23	28
	28 $\forall \ell (1 \leq \ell \leq n \supset b[\ell] = \sum_{k=1}^{\ell} a[k])$	26,27	

Figure 2A. Partial sums program and invariant table.

The invariants listed in Figure 2A are not particularly difficult to generate. The ones used in the original proof are marked with a black dot next to the number identifying the invariant, and can be obtained either by 'pulling backwards' the desired output specification, or by analyzing the difference equations of the inner, and then, the outer loops.

Note that the invariant $b[i] = b[i-1] + a[i]$, which more or less 'falls out' of an analysis of the difference equations of the outer loop, is not used. If, however, we substituted the sources 20 and 25 in the proof of invariant 26, (instead of 20 and 24 directly) we would have

$$\forall \ell (1 \leq \ell \leq i-1 \supset b[\ell] = \sum_{k=1}^{\ell} a[k]) \wedge ((i=1 \wedge b[1]=a[1]) \vee (b[i] = b[i-1] + a[i])) \supset$$
$$b[i] = \sum_{k=1}^{i} a[k] \wedge \forall \ell (1 \leq \ell \leq i \supset b[\ell] = \sum_{k=1}^{\ell} a[k]).$$

This alternative proof still works for the program as it is, and it allows optimization. Simply enough, $(i = 1 \wedge b[1] = a[1]) \vee (b[i] = b[i-1] + a[i])$ can be achieved (much as in reduction in strength) by initializing $b[1]$ to $a[1]$, and then iterating by

$$b[i] \leftarrow b[i-1] + a[i] \quad .$$

All the previous ancestors could then be removed. The resulting program does not need the inner loop at all, and is shown, with its proof, in Figure 2B.

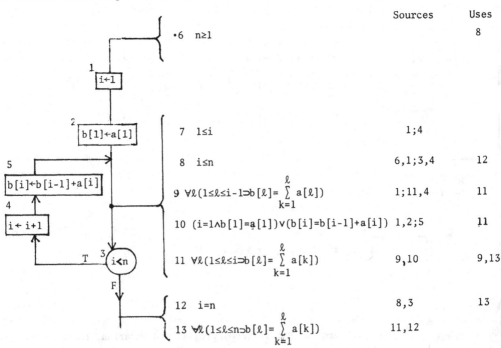

	Sources	Uses
•6 $n \geq 1$		8
7 $1 \leq i$	1;4	
8 $i \leq n$	6,1;3,4	12
9 $\forall \ell (1 \leq \ell \leq i-1 \supset b[\ell] = \sum_{k=1}^{\ell} a[\ell])$	1;11,4	11
10 $(i=1 \wedge b[1]=a[1]) \vee (b[i]=b[i-1]+a[i])$	1,2;5	11
11 $\forall \ell (1 \leq \ell \leq i \supset b[\ell] = \sum_{k=1}^{\ell} a[k])$	9,10	9,13
12 $i=n$	8,3	13
13 $\forall \ell (1 \leq \ell \leq n \supset b[\ell] = \sum_{k=1}^{\ell} a[k])$	11,12	

2B. Optimized partial sums program with invariant table.

4. CONCLUSION

The present paper attempts to link two worlds: on the one hand, program verification and proofs of equivalence between programs, and on the other hand, practical considerations of optimizing compilers.

In the context of program verification, Gerhart [1975] has expounded the idea of proving systematically that various transformations preserve correctness. Other work in this area has been largely devoted to converting recursive programs to more efficient iterative ones (see Darlington and Burstall [1973], Burstall and Darlington [1975], Knuth [1974]). Thses works do not primarily use the existing proof and invariants to determine the form the transformation will take. That is, the analysis of the program in order to decide whether a certain optimization is applicable is done elsewhere, and the invariants (or some other proof construct) are used only to check that the transformation preserves correctness. The statements which are to be replaced, for example, are not determined by the existing proof, as is done here.

It should be noted that, as is shown in Example 2, an alternative correctness proof of a given program might have a different set of essential invariants, and therefore lead to an different optimization. In some sense, the proof which leads to the greatest gains in execution time will be the most elegant, because the minimum needed information is used at each stage, and extraneous computation is thereby clearly identified. Even a less than optimal proof should at least allow the optimizations done in standard compilers.

The technique presented here can also be modified to provide formal justification of general transformations by proving that any invariants at cutpoints of a given schema will be preserved in another given schema, if the invariants and statements satisfy the conditions for applying the transformation.

In the context of the 'real' world, the natural question which arises is: "what is gained by basing optimization on invariants,when compilers have been optimizing for years without generating any invariants?"

A few answers to this question are:

1. Invariants systematize the established techniques because the correctness criterion is clear. "Overzealous" optimizations, which can introduce errors, for example, by moving code out of its context, are easier to avoid since we know exactly what must be maintained, and are able to always check whether we are really maintaining it.

As noted by Allen and Cocke [1972], the assurances that a given transformation does not disturb the correctness of the original program are presently built into the algorithm implementing the transformation, and are an ad hoc collection of considerations. Implementors of optimizations have occasionally overlooked problematic situations, and 'illegal' optimizations have resulted.

2.   Even when it is clear which transformations are legal, information must be
gathered from the program in order to ascertain whether the conditions exist which
allow applying a transformation. For example, certain transformations require
identifying the "induction variables", i.e., those variables incremented by a constant value at each iteration. It is also valuable to discover variables which are
constant (unchanged) in a loop. There are separate algorithms to find each of these
and many other characteristics, and the algorithms are often guaranteed to find
only relatively obvious cases of whichever characteristic is being considered.
Using invariants can make the information-gathering process easier and more uniform.

3.   Finally, as noted in the previous section, the availability of a correctness
proof and the organization based on invariants sometimes allows more radical optimizations than are possible using 'blind' transformations. In particular, the optimization can be tailor-made for the information revealed by the proof.

Of course, it should be recalled that in a logical analysis system the invariants
would be available anyway because of their other applications, and so the considerabl
price of their generation would not be 'charged' to any possible optimizations.

To date, the optimization technique suggested here has not been implemented. It
is hoped (and planned) that this will be rectified as part of logical analysis system
being developed. Until then, the technique is still applicable for hand changes to
programs, and as a justification of the transformations method.

REFERENCES:

Allen [1969]   Allen F.E.: Program Optimization, Annual Review in Automatic
                 Programming, Vol. 5, Permagon, Elmsford, N.Y., 1969.

Allen [1971]   Allen F.E.: A basis for program optimization. Proc. IFIP 1971,
                 Vol. 1, Ljubljana, Yugoslavia (August 1971).

Allen & Cocke   Allen F.E. and Cocke J.: A Catalogue of optimizing transfor-
    [1972]   mations in Design and Optimization of Compilers (R. Rustin, ed.),
                 Prentice Hall, 1972, pp.1-30.

Burstall &   Burstall R., and Darlington J.: Some transformations for
Darlington   developing recursive programs. Proc. International Conference
    [1975]   on Reliable Software, Los Angeles, April 1975.

Cheatham &   Cheatham, T.E. and Wegbreit B.: A laboratory for the study of
Wegbreit   automating programming. Spring Joint Computer Conference, 1972,
    [1972]   pp. 11-20.

Darlington &   Burstall, R. and Darlington, J.: A system for the automatically
Burstall   improves programs. Proc. 3rd Intl. Conf. on Artificial Intelligence.
    [1973]   Stanford, 1973, pp. 479-485.

Elspas [1974]   Elspas, B.: The semiautomatic generation of inductive assertions
                 for proving program correctness. Research report, SRI, Memlo Park,
                 Calif. (July 1974).

Gerhart [1975]   Gerhart, S.: Correctness-Preserving program transformations,
                 Proc. 2nd ACM Symposium on Principles of Programming Languages,
                 Palo Alto, January 1975, pp. 54-65.

Katz   [1976]   Katz, S.: Logical analysis and invariants of programs, Ph.D. thesis
                 Weizmann Institute of Science, Rechovot, Israel, to appear, 1976

Katz & Manna   Katz, S. and Manna Z.: A Heuristic approach to program verifica-
    [1973]   tion. Proc. 3rd Intl. Conf. on Artificial Intelligence, Stanford,
                 1973, pp. 500-512.

Katz & Manna   Katz, S. and Manna Z.: Logical analysis of programs, CACM, to
    [1976]   appear, 1976

Knuth [1974]   Knuth, D.: Structured Programming with GØTØ statements, ACM
                 Computing Surveys, Vol. 6, No.4, December 1974.

Manna [1969]   Manna, Z.: The correctness of programs, J. Computer and System
                 Science, 3, 2, May 1969, pp. 119-127.

Wegbreit [1974] Wegbreit, B.: The synthesis of loop predicates. CACM 17, 2
                 (February 1974), pp. 102-112.

Wirth [1973]   Wirth, N.: Systematic Programming, Prentice-Hall, 1973.

THE GEM COBOL MONITOR SYSTEM

Antonio Salvadori
Computing and Information Science
University of Guelph
Guelph, Ontario
CANADA N1G 2W1

INTRODUCTION

During the past five years an increasing number of people have been
searching for an answer to the question: How do people write, debug
and optimise a computer program? Several authors have written numerous
papers in the "considered harmful" series not really knowing if what
they were admonishing against was actually taking place in the real
world environment. Only recently have Knuth and several other
authors [1-4] tried to shed some light on this fascinating problem.

It was during the course of a discussion with Professor Uzgalis of
UCLA that the present system was begun. All studies had confined
themselves to studying how students in a University environment
solving university type problems behaved. This seemed unsatisfactory
to me since such a population would necessarily consist of amateurs
and not professionals, hence, I set out to develop a system which
could be used by professionals. The language that I chose to monitor
was COBOL which is the most common language used in the data processing
industry. This system is now being used in several environments. The
analysis from the data collected is presently in press.[5]

GEM STRUCTURE

GEM, a synonym for Guelph Efficiency Monitor, is a preprocessor system
which can analyse a COBOL program at any development or running stage.
The system has been developed to provide all levels of management with
a tool for improving the total efficiency of COBOL programs. It may
be used during the development of new programs to monitor their performance or used to optimise the run time of existing programs.

There are four procedures to the system providing the following facilities:

GEM1.   STATIC PROFILE.   Summarises all COBOL constructs coded in the identification, environment, data and procedure divisions.

GEM2.   DIAGNOSTIC PATTERNS.   Summarises the COBOL diagnostics generated during program development and keeps a date account of the number of times a program is run.

GEM3.   DYNAMIC FREQUENCY PROFILE.   Identifies and calculates the frequency of verb and code segment usage in the procedure division at run time as the program is processing test or live data.

GEM4.   DYNAMIC TIME PROFILE.   Accounts for the C.P.U. time spent in segments of Procedure Division code as the program executes.

One or more of the four modules may be used to:

. Identify which parts of operating programs are frequently used, so that the code may be optimised.

. Check whether certain parts of a program have never been tested on test data or used in live data.

. Accurately describe programs operating on live data for the selection of a benchmarking suite.

. Provide information for the programming training staff on the common errors made during program development, including the use of non-ANSI COBOL verbs.

. Provide the CODASYL committee or anyone interested in language design and implementation with statistics regards language usage.

GEM source code is available in either ANSI COBOL or PL/I.   Both systems have been thoroughly tested on a variety of programs in different environments.   GEM is currently proving itself to be a useful tool to both programmers and managers.

GEM 1 MODULE

The system diagram for the GEM1 procedure is shown in Figure 1. As

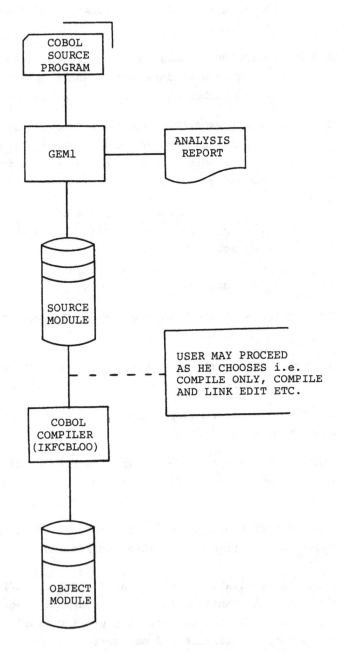

COBOL
SOURCE
PROGRAM

GEM1

ANALYSIS
REPORT

SOURCE
MODULE

USER MAY PROCEED
AS HE CHOOSES i.e.
COMPILE ONLY, COMPILE
AND LINK EDIT ETC.

COBOL
COMPILER
(IKFCBLOO)

OBJECT
MODULE

Figure 1. System Diagram for the GEM1 module.

input, the system only requires the user's COBOL source program. GEM1 scans the source code for the relevant statistical information and then submits the unaltered code for processing according to the user's wishes. The code may be compiled and executed in a normal way.

The statistics gathered and printed consist of:

. a COBOL clause and verb count.

. a percentage breakdown of PROCEDURE DIVISION verbs used.

. the number of source records, number of comment cards, indications of non-ANSI standard verbs, etc.

Part of a typical report from GEM1 is shown in Figure 2. This report

COBOL STATIC STATISTICS

USER ID : XXXXXXXX   PROGRAM ID : XXXXXXXX

PROCEDURE DIVISION

	ACCEPT	0	PERFORM	0
	ADD	1	* PROCESS	0
	ALTER	0	READ	1
	CALL	0	RECEIVE	0
	CANCEL	0	RELEASE	0
	CLOSE	1	RETURN	0
	COMPUTE	2	REWRITE	0
	COPY	0	SEARCH	0
	DECLARATIVES	0	* SEEK	0
	DELETE	0	SEND	0
	DISABLE	0	SET	0
	DISPLAY	0	SORT	0
	DIVIDE	0	START	0
	ENABLE	0	STOP (*GOBACK)	1
*	EXAMINE	0	STRING	0
	EXIT	0	SUBTRACT	0
	GENERATE	0	SUPPRESS	0
	GO TO	2	* SUSPEND	0
*	HOLD	0	TERMINATE	0
	IF	1	UNSTRING	0
	INITIATE	0	USE	0
*	INITIALIZE	0	WRITE	5
	INSPECT	0	+	1
	MERGE	0	-	1
	MOVE	13	/	0
	MULTIPLY	0	*	4
*	NOTE	0	**	0
	OPEN	2		

Figure 2. Part of the report produced by GEM1.

should prove useful for benchmarking, COBOL programmer training, ANSI or in-house standards and various language developers.

GEM 2 MODULE

GEM 2 was motivated by a desire to understand how programs are written and develop from the initial stages to the production phase. A record is kept of each run of the program together with any observable errors which can be automatically gathered. The system diagram for the procedure is shown in Figure 3.

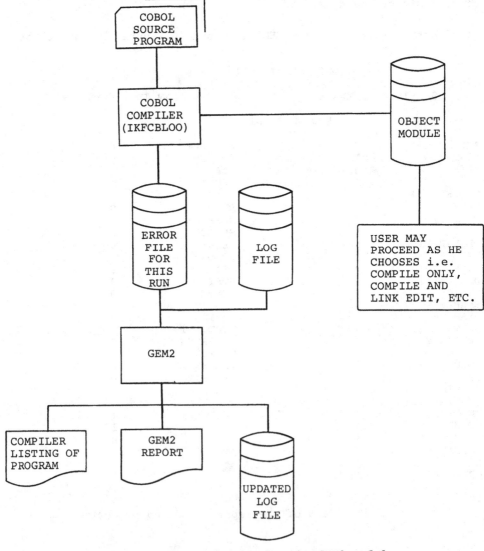

Figure 3. System diagram for the GEM2 module.

The output from the various levels is scanned for diagnostics and the history record is updated with the new information. These diagnostics are recognised by the manufacturer generated codes. No distinction is made between such codes and user produced results, should the user produce these codes as part of his normal output.

The report generated by GEM2 is shown in Figure 4. Since a record is

```
                    COBOL ERROR STATISTICS

USER ID : XXXXXX           PROGRAM ID : SOCRUPD          DATE : 10/02/75

                              RUN NUMBER
ERROR     1   2   3   4   5   6   7   8   9   10  11  12  13  14  15  16   TOTAL
MESSAGE
1087W     2   2   0   2   2   1   0   0   4   2   1   2   2   1   0   0    21
1004E     1   0   1   1   1   0   0   0   0   1   1   1   1   0   0   0     8
3001E     7   7   7   0   0   0   0   0   2   2   1   7   0   0   0   0    33
1081W     3   3   1   1   0   0   0   0   1   0   0   3   0   0   0   0    12
1080W     3   0   0   0   0   0   0   0   1   0   0   3   0   0   0   0     7
1117E     0   1   0   0   0   0   0   0   0   0   0   0   0   0   0   0     1
1128W     0   3   0   0   0   0   0   0   0   0   0   0   0   0   0   0     3
1078W     0   0   2   0   0   0   0   0   0   0   0   0   0   0   0   0     2
1042E     0   0   0   1   0   0   0   0   0   0   0   0   0   0   0   0     1
1003W     0   0   0   0   0   1   0   0   0   0   0   0   0   0   0   0     1
1016E     0   0   0   0   0   0   0   0   1   0   0   0   0   0   0   0     1

TOTAL    16  16  11   5   3   2   0   0   9   5   3  16   3   1   0   0

    TOTAL ERRORS FOR SOCRUPD IS 90


  START DATE : MON   09/22/75
                              NUMBER OF RUNS

                           1   2   3   4   5   6
                   DAY
                         -----------------------------
               MON   1   |*******
               TUE   2   |****
               WED   3   |************
               THR   4   |*******
               FRI   5   |
               SAT   6   |****************
               SUN   7   |
               MON   8   |
               TUE   9   |
               WED  10   |
               THR  11   |*******
               FRI  12   |*******

                    TOTAL JOBS = 0016
```

Figure 4.   Part of the GEM2 report.

kept of the frequency distribution of errors this information should help a programmer diagnose his deficiencies with respect to COBOL and thereby remedy these. Further, when figures are kept on a more global scale true language deficiencies and troublesome points are found which can be remedied in future development and new language design. Supervisors and management should also find the development time information useful for it allows them to assess programming and debugging time accurately and therefore plan later projects more accurately and efficiently. A programmer efficiency index has also been proposed by the author based on this type of information.[6]

GEM 3 MODULE

The PROCEDURE DIVISION of a COBOL programme is divided into paragraphs and sections. Execution of statements within a paragraph is sequential unless a branching statement is encountered in which case, execution resumes at the beginning of the new paragraph to which branching has occurred. If we therefore wish to monitor the execution of statements, it is obvious that the paragraph level subdivision is too coarse and

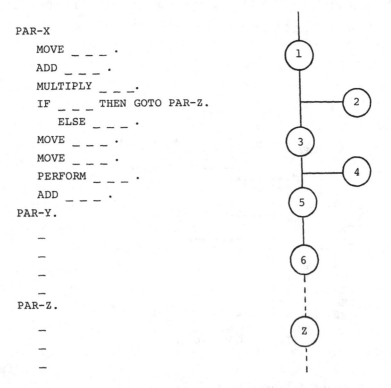

Figure 5.   Subdividing a program into basic blocks.

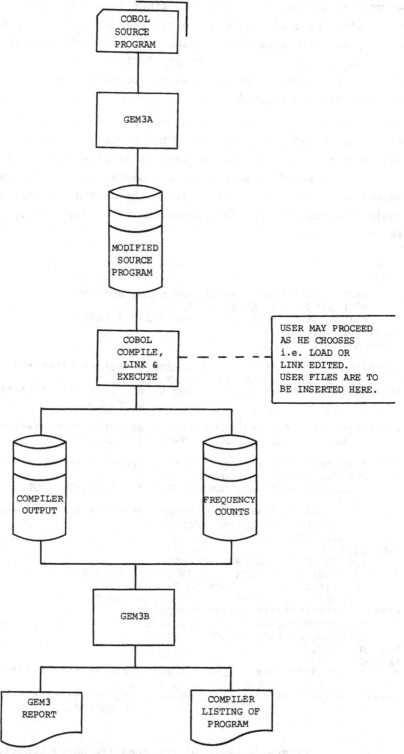

Figure 6. The system diagram for the GEM3 module.

we must subdivide paragraphs into finer segments. Hence we define a
basic block as a linear sequence of program instructions having one
entry point (the first instruction executed) and one exit point (the
last instruction executed). Figure 5 illustrates how a program can be
divided into basic blocks. These may be represented as the nodes of
the control flow graph.[7]

GEM3 is divided into two parts as shown in the system diagram in
Figure 6. GEM3A subdivides the COBOL PROCEDURE DIVISION into segments
and inserts monitoring code to keep track of execution time frequency
counts. The modified source is then passed to the compiler, linkage
editor or loader and executed giving the user his normal output.
GEM3B then performs an analysis of the results and produces the reports
shown in Figure 7.

```
                                                          FREQUENCY

      WRITE HEADING-LINE AFTER ADVANCING NEW-PAGE
      MOVE LINE-2 TO HEADER-LINE.
      WRITE HEADING-LINE AFTER ADVANCING 2 LINES.
*BEGIN DYNAMIC
 READ-A-CARD.

********************* BLOCK NUMBER 00001*******************    17
      READ EMPLOYEE-FILE RECORD; AT END
********************* BLOCK NUMBER 00002*******************     1
                             GO TO EOJ.

********************* BLOCK NUMBER 00003*******************    16
      IF NO-OF-HOURS IS GREATER THAN 40 THEN

********************* BLOCK NUMBER 00004*******************     1
      COMPUTE GROSS-PAY ROUNDED =
        HOURLY-RATE * 40 + HOURLY-RATE * 2 * (NO-OF-HOURS - 40)
      ELSE
********************* BLOCK NUMBER 00005*******************    15
          COMPUTE GROSS-PAY ROUNDED =
      HOURLY-RATE * NO-OF-HOURS.
*END DYNAMIC
      ADD GROSS-PAY TO GROSS-COUNT.
      IF COUNT-A > 4 THEN PERFORM PARA-1 THRU PAR1-EXIT.
      IF HOURLY-RATE > 3 THEN GO TO PARA-1
        ELSE GO TO PARA-1, PARA-2 DEPENDING ON THE-FLAG
**************************** COMMENT
      MOVE NO-OF-HOURS TO NO-OF-HOURS.
      MOVE HOURLY-RATE TO HOURLY-RATE.
*BEGIN DYNAMIC
PARA-1.
********************* BLOCK NUMBER 00006*****************    16
          ADD 1 TO COUNT-A ON SIZE ERROR
********************* BLOCK NUMBER 00007*****************    NOT
                        GO TO EOJ.                       TESTED
```

Figure 7. Part of the GEM3 frequency report.

These reports show, among other items, the frequency of execution of each segment of code. The user may use this information in essentially two ways. Firstly, in a debugging or testing environment, he may isolate the areas of code which have never been tested. He may consequently draw up test data to exercise these parts. Second, he may isolate frequently executed parts of code and see if some optimisation can take place. In several cases it was found that by looking at GEM3 results programs could be made up to 20% more efficient by removing certain pieces of code that had become obsolete and by optimising some crucial tests.

The greatest use of GEM3 is at the programmer level. He may directly benefit from its use. However, GEM3 can also be used for very accurate benchmarking purposes.

GEM4 MODULE

This module performs a task similar to GEM3 except that instead of frequency counts CPU timings are given for each section. The inserted code is a call to an assembler routine which disables the input/output interrupts and records the time from the absolute time of day clock of the machine. As a result of this, a specific assembler routine has to be written for the host machine or at best for a line of machines. Professor Gordon at the University of Guelph is presently writing a suite of assembler routines which will allow GEM4 to run on a variety of machines.

In my preliminary study of GEM4 it appears that little or no extra information can be gathered from using GEM4 over GEM3 since the timing is of necessity only marginally accurate due to the routines overhead and also because of the side effects, such as, taking over control of the machine which is undesirable.

SYSTEM OVERHEAD

GEM requires 80k bytes of main memory to execute. Source statements are scanned at the approximate rate of 0.5 seconds per 100 statements on an IBM 370/155 running under MVT.

CASE STUDY

Since the information gathered by GEM is of necessity of a confidential nature, the results must therefore be lumped together to preserve anonimity.

In the study presented here a random sample of novice and experienced programmers were analyzed. Fifty-six programs which they had written were divided into two classes. The first class consisted to programs of an editing nature, i.e. where input data was edited for correctness and an updating file prepared. The second class consisted of programs of an analysis nature, i.e. programs in which data was analysed and reports issued. Figure 9 shows the results of applying GEM2 as the programs were being developed and figure 10 shows the dynamic frequency counts of the verbs used for both groups.

Description of Diagnostic	Percentage of Total
Identifier has not been declared	16.48
Ambiguous reference to identifier	5.76
Undefined procedure or paragraph name	2.44
Warning - this statement cannot be reached	2.24
Paragraph has no statements	2.07
Invalid record name in WRITE statement	1.94
Illegal use of ELSE or OTHERWISE	1.48
Invalid file name in OPEN statement	1.12
Illegal operand in PERFORM statement	0.84
Constant or variable required AFTER advancing	0.68
Variable has too many subscripts	0.51
Procedure or paragraph name already defined	0.36
Variable has too few subscripts	0.29
Residual (other miscellaneous errors)	0.20

Figure 9. The error statistics gathered in the case study for the PROCEDURE DIVISION.

DISCUSSION

As the results show, GEM has proved itself very useful in getting a better understanding of the error-proneness of COBOL. This information has been very useful to the subsequent teaching of the language since students can now be forewarned about the various pitfalls. The language features used by programmers have allowed us to understand the manner in which programs are written. Programmers are greatly influenced by their immediate environment. They tend to write programs using similar language features to those of their colleagues at whatever installation they are at. They tend to follow installation

VERB	EDIT PROGRAM %		ANALYSIS PROGRAM %	
	a	b	a	b
MOVE	26.2	26.2	49.1	42.0
IF	24.7	24.6	16.1	19.4
GOTO	15.0	4.4	10.8	2.3
PERFORM	13.8	15.2	5.6	12.0
ADD	8.1	7.0	3.4	4.0
WRITE	6.5	5.4	10.4	13.4
SET	2.2	7.0	0	0
READ	1.0	2.9	1.2	1.2
EXIT	0.7	2.0	0.4	1.6
OPEN	0.7	0.9	1.1	1.7
CLOSE	0.5	0.6	1.0	1.2
STOP	0.4	2.6	0.8	1.2
SUBTRACT	0.2	0	0.2	0
SEARCH	0.1	1.2	0	0

a: notices   b: professionals

Figure 10.   The verb usage statistics in the case study.

guidelines closely but not necessarily correctly. For example, at
one installation where programmers were supposed to write structured
programs without ever using the GO TO statement, it was found that
indeed they never used the GO TO statement but were using the PERFORM
verb just like the GO TO.

Not enough feedback has yet been received on the use of GEM3 and GEM4
to analyse the results in detail. In a few live test cases some
significant improvements were obtained. So far programmers are
finding it very useful in program testing and in improving the
reliability of a program. However nothing can as yet be said about
general code optimisation.

ACKNOWLEDGEMENTS

The author wishes to thank Professors C.K. Capstick and J.D. Gordon
for their participation in this work, Peter McMullen for diligently
translating his thoughts into code, the University of Guelph and the
Department of Supply and Services of the Canadian Government for
providing financial assistance.

REFERENCES

1. Knuth, D.E.: An Empirical Study of FORTRAN Programs.
    Software - Practice and Experience, 1, 105-133(1971).

2. Uzgalis, R., Simon, G., Speckart, W.: Compiler Measures in the
    Perspective of Program Development, a comparison of the IBM
    PL/I F-Level Compiler with Cornell's PL/C in a Student Environment.
    Proc. Sixth Hawaii International Conference on System Science,
    104-107(1973).

3. Litecky, C.R., Davies, G.B.: A Study of errors, Error-Proneness,
    and Error Diagnosis in COBOL. CACM, 19, 1, 33-37(1976).

4. Endres, A.: An Analysis of Errors and Their Causes in System
    Programs, International Conference on Reliable Software, Los
    Angeles, 327-336(1975).

5. Gordon, J.D., Capstick, C.K., Salvadori, A.: An Empirical Study
    of COBOL Programmers, in press INFOR(1976).

6. Salvadori, A., Gordon, J.D., Capstick, C.K.: A System for Evalu-
    ating Programmer Performance, Proc. Thirteenth Annual Conference
    on Computer Personnel Research, Toronto, 100-113(1975).

7. Allen, F.E., Cocke, J.: A Program Data Flow Analysis Procedure.
    CACM, 19, 3, 137-147(1976).

A New Series

Texts and Monographs in Computer Science

Editors:
F. L. Bauer, Munich,
and D. Gries, Ithaca, N. Y.

This series will consist of high quality, definitive texts, both at the undergraduate level and graduate level, and monographs of interest to researchers in computer science. The undergraduate texts will serve as guides to further study in all the basic areas of computer science; the graduate texts and monographs will thoroughly investigate advanced topics and lead the reader to the frontiers of computer science research.

H. W. Gschwind, E. J. McCluskey

Design of Digital Computers
An Introduction

2nd edition 1975
375 figures. IX, 548 pages.
ISBN 3-540-06915-1

Contents: Number System and Number Representations. Boolean Algebras.
Integrated Circuit Gates. Storage Elements. Computer Circuits. The Basic Organization of Digital Computers. The Functional Units of Digital Computers. Unorthodox Concepts. Miscellaneous Engineering and Design Considerations.

The Origins of Digital Computers Selected Papers
Edited by B. Randell

2nd edition 1975
120 figures. XVI, 464 pages
ISBN 3-540-07114-8

Contents: Analytical Engines. Tabulating Machines.
Zuse and Schreyer. Aiken and IBM. Bell Telephone Laboratories. The Advent of Electronic Computers. Stored Program Electronic Computers.

This series aims to report new developments in computer science research and teaching – quickly, informally and at a high level. The type of material considered for publication includes:

1. Preliminary drafts of original papers and monographs

2. Lectures on a new field, or presenting a new angle on a classical field

3. Seminar work-outs

4. Reports of meetings, provided they are

   a) of exceptional interest and

   b) devoted to a single topic.

Texts which are out of print but still in demand may also be considered if they fall within these categories.

The timeliness of a manuscript is more important than its form, which may be unfinished or tentative. Thus, in some instances, proofs may be merely outlined and results presented which have been or will later be published elsewhere. If possible, a subject index should be included. Publication of Lecture Notes is intended as a service to the international computer science community, in that a commercial publisher, Springer-Verlag, can offer a wider distribution to documents which would otherwise have a restricted readership. Once published and copyrighted, they can be documented in the scientific literature.

Manuscripts

Manuscripts should comprise not less than 100 pages.

They are reproduced by a photographic process and therefore must be typed with extreme care. Symbols not on the typewriter should be inserted by hand in indelible black ink. Corrections to the typescript should be made by pasting the amended text over the old one, or by obliterating errors with white correcting fluid. Authors receive 75 free copies and are free to use the material in other publications. The typescript is reduced slightly in size during reproduction; best results will not be obtained unless the text on any one page is kept within the overall limit of 18 x 26.5 cm (7 x 10½ inches). The publisher will be pleased to supply on request special stationery with the typing area outlined.

Manuscripts in English, German or French should be sent to Prof. G. Goos, Institut für Informatik, Universität Karlsruhe, Zirkel 2, 7500 Karlsruhe/Germany, Prof. J. Hartmanis, Cornell University, Dept. of Coputer-Science, Ithaca, NY/USA 14850, or directly to Springer-Verlag Heidelberg.

Springer-Verlag, Heidelberger Platz 3, D-1000 Berlin 33

Springer-Verlag, Neuenheimer Landstraße 28–30, D-6900 Heidelberg 1

Springer-Verlag, 175 Fifth Avenue, New York, NY 10010/USA

ISBN 3-540-07804-5
ISBN 0-387-07804-5